The Christian Religion
and Human Progress

Being the Spring Lectures at the School of Religion
Athens, Greece
Together with a Selection from
The Published and Unpublished Addresses of

EDWARD INCREASE BOSWORTH

Edited, with an Introductory Note, by
ERNEST PYE

A COMPANION VOLUME TO

THE BIOGRAPHY OF A MIND

BOSWORTH OF OBERLIN

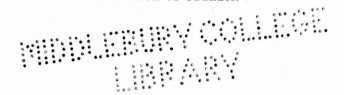
THE BOSWORTH MEMORIAL COMMITTEE
OF THE
BOARD OF SPONSORS
NEW YORK

PRINTED IN THE UNITED STATES OF AMERICA
AT THE LAKESIDE PRESS, R. R. DONNELLEY & SONS COMPANY
CHICAGO, ILLINOIS, AND CRAWFORDSVILLE, INDIANA

Preview

INTRODUCTORY NOTE

Fundamental Religious Ideas That Should Become
Commonplaces of Thought

Page ix

SECTION I

The Christian Religion and Human Progress

Page 1

SECTION II

Studies

Page 93

SECTION III

Interpretative Addresses

Page 207

v

CONTENTS

PAGE

Introductory Note ix

Section I

THE CHRISTIAN RELIGION
AND HUMAN PROGRESS

Address

I. Definition of Terms 3

II. The Christian Idea of God and Human Progress . 13

III. The Christian Idea of Suffering and
Human Progress 23

IV. Christian Prayer as a Force in Human Progress . 31

V. The Christian Way of Living and Human
Progress 41

VI. The Christian Way of Living and Human
Progress, Cont'd 53

VII. The Contribution of Jesus' Personality to
Human Progress 61

VIII. The Relation of Jesus' Death to Human Progress . 71

IX. The Christian Idea of Life After Death and
Human Progress 81

Section II

STUDIES

X. The Story of Paul's Life 95

XI. Paul the Founder and His Foundation . . . 107

XII. The Search for a Religion 123

XIII. The Central Idea in the Christian Religion . . 133

ADDRESS   PAGE

  XIV. The Period of Doubt Among the Friends of Jesus .   151

   XV. Faith   171

  XVI. The New Testament Conception of the Disciple
and his Money   187

 XVII. Conduct and Destiny   199

SECTION III

INTERPRETATIVE ADDRESSES

 XVIII. The Fine Art of Getting on With Men .   .   .   209

  XIX. The Discovery of God   229

   XX. The Eternal Yet Changing Gospel   .   .   241

  XXI. The Gospel of Forgiveness   .   .   .   251

 XXII. Can Prayer Accomplish Anything Apart from the
Man Who Prays: Its Practical Consideration .   267

XXIII. Can Prayer Accomplish Anything Apart from the
Man Who Prays: Its Philosophical Approach .   277

 XXIV. The Meaning of Life   291

  XXV. Vital Elements in the Development of Personal
Power   303

 XXVI. The Daily Practice of Immortality and Its
Influence on Character   315

Index   325

INTRODUCTORY NOTE

IN the pages of this volume Bosworth himself speaks. The addresses cover a wide range in time. They culminate in the remarkable series of nine lectures which he delivered as *The 1927 Spring Lectures* at the School of Religion at Athens and which, though wholly unguessed as he left us in Greece to return to the United States, closed his public work as Teacher and Lecturer. The general subject of those Lectures is made the title of this book.

That title bears thinking about. The Christian religion is imbued with Purpose; also, it is instinctive in human nature to seek progress; and the responsibility, above all other responsibilities laid upon men, is to bring their varying progress into identity with Divine Purpose. This forms the undergirding argument which threads Doctor Bosworth's addresses into unity.

A glance at the *Contents* will show that the book falls into certain large divisions. The addresses focus on five fundamental religious ideas, fresh from his pen and concerning which he felt so strongly should "become commonplaces of thought." I am setting these down on the following page, just as they appear on a sheet from his files.

Much in the introductory remarks to Volume I, *The Biography of a Mind,* applies here and need not be repeated.

If something from his strong mind and heart shall be reproduced afresh in his present readers, even as it was in those who listened to his original message, the good and the true within us will, I am sure, thereby become yet more permanently established.

E. P.

Winter Park, Florida
March 1, 1948.

FUNDAMENTAL RELIGIOUS IDEAS

That Should Become Commonplaces of Thought

1. *God,* a living force, a vast good will working out a vast good purpose in all the universe, and especially in the lives of individual human beings and their developing civilization on this planet.

2. *Men,* a human race, being urged on by the will of God to work together with him and with each other to develop a world civilization characterized in all its peoples and institutions by growing knowledge, power, honesty and friendliness.

3. *Jesus Christ,* a personality in which the life of God has so lifted itself up as to make him the immortal Leader of the race in its development of a wise, powerful, honest and friendly world.

4. *The Church,* as Jesus' way of living, a variety of organizations whose business it is to recruit, train and continually inspire men, women and children to work together with the will of God under the leadership of Jesus Christ for a wise, honest and friendly world.

5. An idea of *life after death* that will make a powerful appeal to men to do and be their best here and now. Life after death, a situation in which honest and friendly workers in all the various occupations of men before death will be provided with larger powers and opportunities to work on the unfinished universe of God, and in which the persistently dishonest and unfriendly will necessarily experience growing weakness, idleness, and consequent pain.

E. I. B.

ACKNOWLEDGMENT

Quoted materials appear here and there in the following Lectures and Addresses as they were originally written by Dean Bosworth. For the most part, acknowledgment of permission to quote appears either in footnotes in this volume or in the list printed in Vol. I. Diligent search, however, through Dr. Bosworth's files, also in libraries, and through the New York Times Book Review service has failed to disclose the source of some of the quoted material. Generous acknowledgment is here made to each such author, publication and publisher, though as yet unknown to me, of the courtesy of allowing the quotations to stand in the text as constructed by Dr. Bosworth.

SECTION I

The Christian Religion and Human Progress

The brief day to day walk to his lecture room took him past an open vista looking off to the eastward. In the distance stood the Parthenon crowning the Acropolis in blue April haze, as it has these twenty-three Centuries and more. In this setting he addressed us.

These Lectures do not discuss the pros and cons of the question: Is progress possible? In this presentation Bosworth assumes that it is. Whether the discerning reader will deem this an unwarranted assumption will depend largely upon the extent to which he discovers within the thought content of the Lectures that inclusive grasp of Reality which ultimately furnishes the justification of any assumption.

Even on more restricted grounds, we find one of the penetrating writers of the day recognizing the fact of progress, but also recognizing that there has been far too easy an optimism associated therewith.

"All political and economic achievements must be informed by a religion and a culture, which know that history is a realm of infinite possibilities and that each new level of maturity places new responsibilities upon us. But it must also be understood that all historic achievements are limited and precarious; that human egoism, individual and collective, can be transmuted and sublimated on many new levels, but that it cannot be eliminated from history. . . Human existence is precarious and will remain so to the end of history. Human achievement contains a tragic element of frustration and corruption and will contain it to the end of history. There is an ultimate answer to these tragic aspects of human existence, but that answer can be known only to those who have stopped looking for some easy escape from tragedy."

—Reinhold Niebuhr, in *Fortune Magazine*
July, 1942.

DEFINITION OF TERMS

Lecture I

DEFINITION OF TERMS

THE great facts behind the words "Religion," "Christian" and "Human Progress" are too vast for precise definition. Yet it is necessary to describe in general what will be meant by them in these lectures.

I

What do we mean by "religion"? Religion includes three human activities:

1. Men reaching out in various ways to a superior invisible Power conceived to be near by and able to give intelligent help;
2. Men seeming to themselves to find this Power;
3. Men attempting to organize life according to the supposed desire of this superior Power.

Involved in all this religious activity is an intellectual element, an exercise of the reasoning faculty. The world is intellectually conceived and the superior Power is for certain reasons located somewhere in this world. A certain organizing of life is supposed to be desired by the superior Power for good reasons. The experience of finding the Power is explained in a certain way that seems reasonable. Certain intellectual theories about the nature of the superior Power and the experience that he produces grow up. Religion is both art and theory. Professor Alfred North Whitehead in his book, *Religion in the Making* says that "religion is the art and the theory of the internal life of man, so far as it depends on the man himself and on what is permanent in the nature of things."

The experience and the theory by which the experience is explained both *grow*. Every living thing grows, that is, becomes more or less. Even the most obdurate theories in the history of human thought change, at least a little, in spite of themselves.

5

Earlier forms of religious experience and theory in later periods of their growth may seem crude and may sometimes be called superstition. Modern religions are not discredited because they began in what are now called superstitions. All modern science began in what we now call superstition but it is not discredited by such an origin.

II

What do we mean by the Christian Religion?

The Christian religion is the religion which Jesus Christ experienced and proposed to lead all men into. Our chief sources of information regarding the religion of Jesus Christ are the early Christian writings that constitute the New Testament. These writings all agree that Jesus had a religious experience. They make it evident that he conceived of a superior invisible Power called God, the Heavenly Father, near by and able to give intelligent help; that he reached out to this superior Power and felt sure that he found it; that he proposed to make the life of the world accord with the desire of this Power. We shall have occasion later to discuss the nature of the religious experience of Jesus; how he reached out to God; what he found God to be; what he found God wanting the life of man to be.

Jesus proposed to share his religious experience with all men. In consequence Christianity, the Christian religion, has become a recognized fact in the life of the world.

In considering the Christian religion as it appears in the life of man it is necessary to distinguish between Christian experience and the interpretation of this experience called Christian theology. This distinction is well illustrated in a letter written by a Marsovan student in war time to his college president.

"My dear Teacher, I have forgotten nearly all the Biblical and Philosophical theories and various views of Theology and the Science of Homiletics, etc., which I learned in the college and seminary before the war. I am very happy, however, to let you know that one thing I have not lost, that is the Christian life, the Christian experience. One thing is deepened in me day after day under shells, bombs and bullets, and that is the Christian Faith."

Both Christian experience and Christian theology *develop*. In our dealings with the unseen force, electricity, we have had a rapidly developing experience. We have more and more *felt* it in many ways. Out of this growing experience have arisen various theories regarding the nature of electricity by which we have tried to explain our growing experience. The history of our growing experience with electrical force records many theories once held and afterward abandoned. In something the same way men, following the leadership of Jesus Christ, have had a growing Christian experience with God. They have felt God in new and various ways. Jesus is reported in one of the New Testament writings to have predicted this growing experience. He said "I have many things to say unto you but ye cannot bear them now." As Christian experience has grown so also the theological theories by which we try to explain Christian experience have changed. In the history of growing Christian experience some of these theories have been abandoned. These abandoned theories, whether in the case of electrical experience or Christian experience, are not to be despised. They were useful in their time. They constituted forward steps in the advancing experience of mankind.

III

What do we mean by "Human Progress"?

We evidently mean an advance toward better living. But what kind of living is "better living"? What constitutes one kind of living "better" than another? Better living is living that brings an organism on toward what its nature indicates it ought to become. But how do we find out what the nature of any organism indicates that it ought to become? We find this out by seeing what the organism does with deepening content and joy. Professor Bergson of the College de France has expressed this clearly:

Philosophers who have speculated on the meaning of life and on the destiny of man have failed to take sufficient notice of an indication which nature itself has given us. Nature warns us by a clear sign that our destination is attained. That sign is joy. I mean joy, not pleasure.[1]

It was this great truth that Jesus expressed in simpler language when he promised that those who would walk his way would find "rest" for their souls.

[1]Bergson, *Mind Energy,* Macmillan 1921 ed., p. 23.

But we must push our inquiry still further along this line. How do we find out what human beings, either singly or in the great human group, can do with deepening contentment and joy? We find this out by examining the nature of man and the nature of his environment. Man is evidently made for action in an environment. What he can do is determined by what he is and where he is.

What is man?

He is a being able to make certain great affirmations. He is able to say "I am," "I was," "I, who today am, was yesterday." He can say "I know"; "I can"; "I ought"; "I will"; "I can understand a joke and laugh"; "I can feel pain of body or mind, and may even shed tears"; "I can feel beauty, the beauty of the sunset flowing in radiant color across the Salamis waters into my soul as I stand on the Parthenon steps." He can say "I want something to do." This deep instinct for creative action expresses itself in the little child's repeated appeal, "Tell me something to do," and in the old man's story, told to all who will listen, of what he used to be able to do. This strange human being says, "I want not to be long alone; I want a mate; I want others with whom to laugh and cry and work." This deep desire appears in the little child's dread of being alone and the prisoner's dread of confinement in the solitary cell. The man says, "I am becoming." The mystery of growth is in his consciousness; he is told that he was once a formless embryo; he remembers that he was a child, a young man, a man in middle life and now he knows that he is old and his powers are failing. He is able to say, "I can infer." He has a marvelous capacity for inference. It enables him to tell what the stars are made of, how far away they are, where they will be a million years in the future. He counts the annular rings of growth in the stumps of great trees in California, notes their varying width and infers what the weather in the Roman campagna was at a definite time more than two thousand years ago. He looks at the parasites in certain frogs and infers that South America and Australia were once continuous land. By his power of inference he discovers the evolutionary process and sets himself to the high task of tracing the growth of all things. Such and much more is man.

Where is man?

He is in the midst of the mystery of time, something of which no beginning or ending can be conceived. He is in the midst of the mystery of space, which also has no limit. Solar systems extend in apparently unlimited series, and the atomic protons and electrons resolve, it may be, into ever new minutiae. He is in the midst of unceasing motion. The planets swing ceaselessly and silently along their orbits; the electrons revolve with incredible speed about the protons. He is in the midst of the mysterious stream of life. Life in all its forms is appearing in birth and disappearing in death age after age. He is in the midst of a universal becoming. Nothing is steadily the same. The universe is changing. He is more and more sure that he is in the midst of some one Force in all things. He expresses this assurance in his theory of the universality of law. He finds that the vast planets and the minute electrons move alike in mathematically calculable orbits. One force is in both. There is the science of atomic astronomy. He finds himself in the midst of some force favorable to the transmission of thought and feeling. Man's environment lends itself to the transmission of thought and feeling through speech, through the telegraph, through the telephone, through the wireless and perhaps through telepathic action.

Such and much more is man; such and much more is his environment. Evidently some big thing is going on. We see only into the edges of it. We cannot escape from it. We do not want to escape from it. We wish to penetrate further into it. We already have some sense of being at home in it. We are where we belong. We mean to find out how such beings as we are can live in such an environment in such a way as to find deepening contentment and joy.

IV

From this survey of man and his environment can we now form an idea of the lines of life along which man must act in order to reach this deep and lasting joy which is the sign of progress for himself and his human group?

It is clear that he must *know* more. He must follow the deep instinct that drives him to the exploration of his world. He must find out the reasons for things. He must discover how everything came to be as it is.

He must also develop *power*. He must control all the forces of nature. Scientific discoveries and inventions must proceed to an indefinite enlargement of man's power.

He must be able to *work with others in a friendly way,* that is, for the good of the group. He must develop his deep desire for society, his joy in the life of the group.

This is all summed up in the statement that he must learn to *create with and for his group* whatever the group needs. The deepest instinct of his nature is to create. This is the essence of sexual desire, of the building instinct, of the desire for beauty. It leads him to create what is necessary for defense and for ease of operation. He is born to be a creator. As he becomes a more and more effective creator of things good for himself and his group he experiences more and more the deepening joy and contentment that are the sure signs of progress. It is this idea that Bergson has gone on to express so clearly:

He who is sure, absolutely sure, of having produced a work which will endure and live, cares no more for praise and feels above glory, because he is a creator, because he knows it, because the joy he feels is the joy of a god.[2]

V

The Problem in Main Outline

We have described in general what we mean by religion, by the Christian religion, and by human progress. Our problem is this: Can we find in Christian experience and in a reasonable interpretation of this experience, that is, in the Christian religion, anything that incites to human progress? Can we discover and interpret the religious experience that Jesus had and proposed to share with all men in such a way as to find in it an incentive to human progress?

We recognize at once that certain theological interpretations of Christian experience, once useful, outlasted their usefulness and became hindrances to progress. They were explanations of Christian experience in terms of the thought world that existed when they were made. Life progressed beyond this thought world and a new thought world necessarily came into existence. The earlier

[2]Bergson, *ibid.,* p. 24.

theological explanations did not fit the new thought world. But they had sometimes come to seem sacred and authoritative and so they opposed the progressive movement of humanity in its new world of thought and life. For instance, a great advance in life and thought began when Copernicus proposed the theory that the earth revolves on its axis and travels around the sun. The universe at once was seen to be more vast than men had supposed. The way was opened for the discovery of a vaster God in the vaster universe, and religious experience with the vaster God had a chance to assume larger dimensions. But this new theory seemed contrary to certain ancient theological theories about the Bible, and so Christian theology was for a time opposed to human progress. John Calvin read in the ninety-third Psalm, "The world also is established that it cannot be moved," and he said "Who will venture to place the authority of Copernicus above that of the Holy Spirit?" Martin Luther said:

"People give ear to an upstart astrologer who strove to show that the earth revolves and not the heavens, the firmament, the sun and the moon. . . . This fool wishes to reverse the entire science of astronomy; but sacred scripture tells that Joshua commanded the sun to stand still and not the earth."

We recognize that we are not bound to obsolete or obsolescent theological explanations of Christian experience. Can our age make a new interpretation of Christian experience in the terms of a new thought world? Can we discover and so interpret the religious experience of Jesus and his disciples as to find in it something that will urge men on to produce a civilization that will yield the deepening joy and contentment characteristic of true progress?

THE CHRISTIAN IDEA OF GOD
AND HUMAN PROGRESS

Lecture II

THE CHRISTIAN IDEA OF GOD
AND HUMAN PROGRESS

WHAT do we mean by God?
   If we are right in thinking of the Christian religion as the religion which Jesus possessed and proposed to share with all men, the question becomes this: What did Jesus mean by God? What and where was God in the experience of Jesus?

I

Jesus did not argue about the existence of God. He simply tells in his teaching what he found God to be and what men must do to find God for themselves. Mr. Edison does not argue about the existence of electricity. He simply takes an inquirer into his laboratory and shows him how to find and feel electricity.

In general, to Jesus, God was a *life,* vast and strong, close up and active, working always for good with human life. Jesus directly felt this life. As he walked through the fields to and from his work he felt the life of God in the rain that wet him to the skin. God was making his rain fall on the fields of good Ben Abraham that lay on one side of the path and also upon those of bad Ben Judas that lay on the other side. The rain was God's rain and God made it fall on the fields of the righteous and the unrighteous. He felt God's life in the color and fragrance of flowers. When he faced the sick in compassion he felt God's healing life flowing out through him into them. When he faced penitent men and women he felt God's welcoming love flowing heartily out through him into their repentant hearts. He felt God's life flowing out through him in friendly conversation and laughter as he sat with the publican's wife and children and neighbors about the publican's hospitable table. He felt the laughter of the life of God within himself.

All this means that to Jesus God was a *loving* life. What do we mean by love? Loving a person means wanting him; wanting to be with him; wanting him to become the utmost he is capable of being; wanting to help him be his best and utmost; wanting to see him get on well in all his ways. We read in the words attributed to Jesus that God loves the world. This means that he wants to see the world get on well in all its ways—in business, industry, politics, diplomacy, art, learning, and universal friendliness.

Jesus most frequently spoke of God's life as *will*. "I came to do the will of God," he said of himself; "Whoever shall do the will of God is my brother and my sister and my mother." What do we mean by *will*? We know in a way what our own wills are. A person's will is the set of his personality toward a goal. It is the pull of a personality upon a situation to change it. A man brings his will to bear on his business and changes it from a small beginning to a large development. A mother and father bring their wills to bear on a home, and children grow up who go out from under the power of these loving wills to carry the blessing of the home far and wide.

Jesus seems to have thought of the living, loving will of God as a Force vast and strong, close up and active, urging all things on toward a good goal. It was a Force vast enough to fill all the immeasurable spaces between the stars; a Force strong enough to keep the planets moving in their orbits and to keep fierce fires burning in a million million suns. It is a Force close up, vitalizing every atom of our bodies; active in the inconceivably swift movement of the electrons within the atom. It is a loving Force always wanting us for some good thing.

Such a Force Jesus often called "the Heavenly Father," probably because such a Force, like a father, is the source of our being, has authority over us and provides for our welfare.

II

Can we moderns follow Jesus in his great idea of God? Can we think of the Vast Life that we know to be all about us in atom and planet as Intelligent Good Will? We are certain of the existence of some Vast Force outside ourselves. We count upon it in every act of every waking moment of our lives. But have we a right to think of it as Intelligent Good Will? Have we a right to find our clue as to its nature in that form of Being which seems to be its highest and clearest expression, namely, men of good will able to bring good things to pass? Human good will, the good will of Jesus and of men who follow him, is the highest phenomenon we distinctly know. Such wills act as causes. They cause certain things to be by their power to manipulate natural forces, and to bring motions to bear upon their fellow men. They perform scientific experiments and in this way cause the occurrence of certain chemical and physical results. They purposely treat each other in certain ways that cause certain results in human behavior. Can we let this great and admitted fact of the causative human will furnish us a clue that shall lead us on to a better and truer understanding of the Vast Life all about us?

It requires no more credulity to think of this Vast Force as intelligent causative good will than to think of it as anything else. Its vastness is overwhelming and hard to conceive, but we add nothing to this difficulty by conceiving it to be Intelligent Good Will. This planet is but a speck of dust in the vast universe. It seems conceited to suppose that all the intelligent good will in the universe is confined to us humans on this speck of dust. As we have noted before, the Vast Force in the midst of which we live is of such a nature as to facilitate the transmission of thought and feeling between humans. It requires no more credulity to think that its vastness includes thought and feeling of its own than to suppose that it does not.

To think of the Vast Life as including intelligent good will is sometimes said to be an anthropomorphic idea; that is, to be conceiving of God as a man. This is not so. God is not conceived as an infinitely enlarged human being. A human personality may be thought of as embryonic, as rudimentary personality. The embryo is often very unlike the highly developed organism. The vast life of God may be thought of as including in highly developed form, thought and feeling and will that exist in rudimentary form in embryonic human personality. Man may serve as a suggestion of God.

If we do not think of the Vast Force as good will, we seem necessitated to take a mechanistic view of the universe, that is, to think of the activities of the Vast Force as machine like. But this certainly is anthropomorphic. The idea of a machine is derived from something man has made. Man makes machines and mechanisms. It is just as anthropomorphic to get our idea of the universe from something man has made as to get it from what man himself is. This point has recently been brought out with great clearness by Burton H. Streeter in his book *Reality*.

We may then think of God as Conscious Intelligent Good Will without doing violence to any observed phenomena. We may think of the universe as charged with thought and feeling. We may think of ourselves as living in the midst of a Vast Good Will. What will is made of, either God's will or man's will, makes very little practical difference. Our chief interest is in the operations of will. We know that will is a force that operates intelligently on situations to change them.

III

Since, then, the will of God is working on the human situation to change it, what is the goal toward which he is urging all human life?

We look for the answer to this question in two places. We look first to the experience of Jesus. He profoundly felt God. What did he feel God doing? The answer is fourfold. He felt God urging men on toward *knowledge*. He urged his disciples to be wise— to be "wise as serpents;" to be keen observers understanding "the signs of the times." He felt God urging men on toward *power*. The man who should touch the vital force of God in "faith," that is in cooperative effort, would find all things becoming possible. He would move mountains. He would in the future do mightier works than the works of Jesus. Jesus felt God urging men on toward *honesty*, toward utter sincerity. They were first of all to "repent," that is, to make an honest confession of the facts, no matter how dark those facts might be. They were to be so utterly sincere that no oath would ever be able to strengthen their simple "yes" and "no." He felt the will of God urging men on toward *friendliness*. They were to love all the people in the neighborhood. This, he said, was what God had always been urging through law and prophets.

This same goal of the will of God appears when we look to the second source of information, the evolving life of man. In the long evolution of the life of man the will of God has evidently been urging man upward. There has been a deep trend toward *knowledge*. The cave man knew but little and fought with the beasts for a chance to live. We know much about the forces of nature. We have even learned how to trace the evolution of life from small beginnings to its present development. There has been a deepening trend toward *power*. We are mastering nature. We know how to sail under the surface of the sea out of reach of storms that rage upon its surface. We have power to fly in a few hours across the ocean without stopping to rest. Sir Oliver Lodge has recently spoken hopefully about man's prospective control of the weather, of rainfall and wind.[1] There has been a deep trend toward reliability, toward *honesty*. The situations are multiplying in which men must, and with safety do, rely upon each other. Every hour of the day we assume that men are truthful, that liars are the exception. We travel over the earth, do business in banks and stores, make social engagements with the confident expectation that we shall find men in the main reliable. The cave man was obliged to assume that all men were untrustworthy. But honesty has been increasing and lying has been decreasing since the cave man's day. There has been evolving a deep trend toward *friendly cooperation*. All the great enterprises that are being established demand and receive it. Men more and more cooperate, in scientific societies, in trades unions, in political parties, in alignments of nations.

That is, the vast good goal toward which the will of God is urging life forward, as it appears in the fragment of God's total purpose that is being wrought out on and around this little earth, is to establish a race of men wise, powerful, honest and friendly. The will of God has been urging the life of man on, notwithstanding his fortuitous and studied waywardness, toward an ideal civilization. An ideal civilization is one in which men work together with such intelligence and good will as to secure a full healthy development of body and spirit among all classes of society. It is

---

[1]In delivering the lecture, Doctor Bosworth here remarked: "But none of us would particularly wish to be on the Weather Program Committee!"

a civilization in which all men, all laws, customs and institutions shall express wisdom, power, sincerity, friendliness; in which all the latent powers of personality shall be developed and all the forces in man's environment shall be discovered and utilized.

When such a race has been developed what will be done with it? What will happen next? All we seem able to say is that it will be turned loose in the unfinished universe of God to work for the completion of the universe in ways that we cannot now predict.

IV

How has the will of God been working toward this goal? It has been working through an evolutionary process. We know that God works now through such a process. The phenomenon of growth is on every side. Every one of us was once a formless embryo weighing less than an ounce, indistinguishable from the embryo of lower animals. Because God is so working now on every side we naturally assume that he has worked so in the past. In the slow evolutionary process God was expressing his desire for men. He was patiently loving men into existence. We do not feel disgraced by the supposition that we have come out of lower animal life by such a process.

We do not have occasion in this connection to discuss the different theories of evolution and the convincing evidence that evolution by some method has surely taken place.

Is God himself evolving? The idea that he is assumes two forms. The first is that man on earth represents the highest stage that the life of God has reached. Man is God as far as God has yet become. When man becomes more, God will be more. This is an unsatisfactory idea for two reasons. It fails to provide a vast unifying force operating through the universe. When life on the earth had developed to the fish stage then God must have been in the fish stage. But when life on this earth was in the fish stage, planets were evolving and solar systems were forming. A God in the fish stage would not have been equal to such operations.

Furthermore such a theory does not meet the deep demand of man's nature for a superior Power. Humanity as a whole is not sufficiently superior to man as an individual to satisfy the unquenchable religious desire of his nature. He needs something more than the crowds of people who throng the city streets.

The other form assumed by the idea of an evolving God admits that God is a superior Being but considers him nevertheless to be evolving along the lines of his superiority. Such a theory does away with the intolerable monotony that would seem necessarily to characterize a changeless existence. But on the other hand, if God is always becoming greater, how small was he once? We simply have to confess that the human mind in its present stage of development cannot think fruitfully about the problem of beginnings and ultimate developments.

V

What incentive to human progress is afforded by the Christian idea of God as we have conceived it?

We have thought of progress as such extension of knowledge, power, reliability and co-operative creative good will as shall produce deep and lasting joy in the souls of men. This idea of God stimulates progress because it sees, and endeavors directly to feel, in God a vast good will urging men on into larger knowledge, power, reliability and co-operative creative good will.

Does the evolutionary idea involved in this conception of God lessen human initiative and responsibility? Will men relax effort and rest lazily back upon it? No, because the idea lays new responsibility on men. Men are called upon to use the evolutionary process in creating. It appeals to their deep creative instinct. It is a new tool put into their hands, and men love to use a new tool. They see in it a way to create new forms of animal and vegetable life and to determine future social conditions. In the discovery of the evolutionary theory God has led men into the outer edges of his own creative activity. Henceforth they will work more contentedly and joyfully with God in the further shaping of his universe. The Christian idea of God becomes the fundamental and everlasting incentive to human progress. Even the present darkness of the world makes a powerful appeal to man to use his new tool, to work with God through a better understanding of the evolutionary way.

THE CHRISTIAN IDEA OF SUFFERING
AND HUMAN PROGRESS

THE CHRISTIAN IDEA OF SUFFERING AND HUMAN PROGRESS

I

THE PROBLEM

THE widespread and many-sided fact of suffering seems opposed to the Christian idea of God and his relation to human progress. The presence of suffering is everywhere. It affects all ages. The infant cries as it feels the pains of colic. The boy has his hurts. Middle age is not exempt, and old age is often a climax of pain. Suffering has characterized all ages in the history of the race. In pictures on ancient walls men are being driven as slaves under the lash and mourners sorrow over their dead. The whole evolutionary process in all its stages seems to have been characterized by suffering.

Suffering springs from various causes. It may be due to ignorance. The thirsty man did not know that there were typhoid germs in the cool water; the hungry child did not know that the berries were poisonous; the busy man who was killed in the street did not know that the wire he touched was a live wire. But they all suffered and died just the same.

Suffering may be due to carelessness, either our own carelessness or that of others. Men, women and children are every day being crippled or killed by carelessness in automobile traffic.

The evil will of man is a constant and vicious cause of the most serious forms of suffering. Because of it, murders are committed daily; wars with all their aftermath of suffering are waged; industrial oppression grinds the life out of hopeless men and women. Through the evil human will syphilitic babies are born, mere wrecks of existence, blind, deformed, idiotic. Out of the evil human will spring envy, ingratitude, cold indifference, "greetings where no kindness is," and all these constantly produce human suffering. How can we think that there is a good God inciting human progress when man, his chief product, is evil?

Terrible calamities in the natural world, wholly uninfluenced by man, sweep hundreds of thousands to death. The Japanese earthquake in a few seconds kills thousands and the tidal wave sweeps human beings like flies into the sea. My neighbor, a missionary from India, after many years of high sacrificial living sits in his automobile by the lake, and in a few moments is hurled by the storm into a pile of automobile wreckage at the water's edge. What can we say to his family about the goodness and mercy of God? From our modern standpoint it appears more and more evident that there is one force behind all phenomena. In that case, all these prolific causes of suffering, at least in the natural world, are in some way connected with the one Force that we call God. How then can there be what has been called "a friend behind phenomena" when phenomena are so unfriendly? Was the learned professor right when he said that the great war would do away with all foolish talk about a Heavenly Father? Many are saying that a Being who would stop all this suffering if he could, but cannot, is too weak to be called God; and that a Being who could stop it, but will not, is too wicked to be called God.

II

Two preliminary questions concerning the nature of suffering call for attention.

How serious a matter is death? It is death that is prominent in the most tragic forms of suffering. In the earthquake a multitude of people died within a few moments. In the great war millions died within a few dark years. In all the evolutionary process there has been an age-long record of violent deaths. Death, from many causes, is a constant phenomenon, moment after moment, age after age. If to die is not so serious a matter as we have sometimes thought, then a large and tragic part of suffering is less serious than we had supposed. All that we really know about death is that it means disappearance—not necessarily non-existence and waste. To Jesus the horrible thing was the evil will and not death. He urged all his disciples to go out boldly to death as he himself proposed to do. Charles Frohman, going down to death on the Lusitania, is reported to have siad: "Why should we fear death? It is the most beautiful adventure in life."[1] Is there any chance for life after death, as Mr. Frohman hoped? Does the great law of recuperation, of recovery, operate after death as we know it often does in life? Will the syphilitic baby have opportunity for healthy development after death? May the millions of young men who died in the great war have careers opening before them after death?

How came the evil will of man to be? How deep and horrible is the mysterious abyss out of which this most prolific cause of suffering arose? If it could be shown to be an essential feature of an upward evolution, the suffering occasioned by it would not seem the complete denial of a vast good will.

The essential evil of the evil will lies in its assertion of itself regardless of any other. It simply says: "What I want I take." Personality is a high and tremendous form of concentrated force. Perhaps in a lower stage of the evolution of personality it was necessary that this tremendous and relentless self-assertion should be dominant. In evolution it seems often to happen that something essential to progress up to a certain point, if it survives that point, becomes a hindrance to further progress and ought therefore to cease. For a while it is good but afterward becomes an evil. This seems to have been true in the case of human slavery and perhaps, also, of war. So it may be true that the dominance of fierce self-assertion was once essential to the evolution of personality, but that its continuance in our present stage of evolution is wholly evil and must be overcome. These considerations tend to make the fact of human suffering seem at least somewhat less dark than it would otherwise be.

III

Two considerations that lighten the problem still further wait for consideration. Suffering is only one phase of a great enterprise. We often wholly misunderstand a situation if we concentrate attention only on one phase of it. I know an aged man, who has lain blind and helpless on his bed for several years. If one were to

[1] Snowden, *Christian Belief in Immortality*, p. 174.

concentrate attention on the single fact of his suffering he would utterly fail to understand the situation. This man's mind is clear; in thought he travels intelligently over the earth; his uplifted spirit gives cheer to any discouraged friend who comes to his bedside. His life is rich and strong. A Marathon racer in the Olympic contest may near the end of his course be in physical agony, but this single fact of physical pain may be only an item in a great national triumph that fills his soul with patriotic joy.

The great enterprise, in which the suffering of men and lower animals is but one item, is the evolution of a wise, powerful, honest and friendly race of men. As a matter of fact, suffering has not ruined the enterprise. The race has advanced. Friendliness and power have gained ground, brutality and weakness have abated. We judge of the power behind a process by the product of the process. *The product here has not been a growing evil but a growing good.*

A second consideration making the problem at least less oppressive is the growing realization that God is sharing the suffering of men. The vast Force which is so triumphantly able to evolve life and give it ever larger scope and power, is taking its part in the great experience of pain. This is a necessary inference from the Christian idea of evolution. An essential feature of this idea is that the life of God is in the very process of evolution giving it vitality and direction. The suffering of God is also a necessary inference from Jesus' idea of the Fatherhood of God. A true father must of necessity suffer with his children. In the revelation of the life of God made through the life of Jesus, suffering has its place. Suffering is one element in the composite consciousness that Christian thought attributes to God.

IV

The Christian idea of the relation of suffering to human progress further concerns us.

In the long run suffering leads to good character and power. By good character is meant an instructed good will, a good will expressing itself in efficient action.

Not all suffering leads to better individual character. The little baby's pain may have no bearing on its character. Too intense suffering in any one's case may benumb and weaken and degrade. But in general it seems true that when men have suffered enough themselves, or have seen others suffer, they will certainly rise up to discover and remove the cause of the suffering. They will be moved to take their part in God's creative evolution.

When men have suffered enough from disease physicians and chemists will surely discover the causes of disease and the way to overcome them. When men have suffered enough from famine, there will be discovered new ways of irrigation, new fertilizers and new methods of speedily transporting food from regions of plenty. When men have suffered enough from earthquakes, they will learn to build against them, to detect the slight beginnings long before they reach their climax. When they have suffered enough from the fury of great storms, they will perhaps learn, as Sir Oliver Lodge has prophesied, to control the weather, to deflect the rush of wind, or break the tidal wave by the use of powerful explosives. When men have suffered enough from war they will learn to discover and remove the causes of war. As Professor Robinson has said, it may require the destruction of the great cities of the world before men learn this lesson. When men have suffered enough from the evil will of man in all its malicious ingenuity of expression, they will learn to overcome the evil will. Jesus in his great Christian enterprise has undertaken nothing less than this.

That is, men are being driven by human suffering in all its forms to discover the laws of the evolution of life and to take their part in the creative activity of God. The apparent roughness of God is teaching men to feel at home in a vast universe of colossal energy, in a universe in which "fierce fires are burning in a million million suns." Men must learn to use these terrific forces. The situation is like that of a little boy frightened by the fierce furnace fires in the great plant which he must control when he grows up. Does this mean that suffering will forever be essential to progress? Not necessarily. Difficulty may be always essential to progress through human effort, but not necessarily suffering.

We do not, then, need to be discouraged by the fact of suffering, nor to talk foolishly about there not being any God. A Being powerful enough to bring life up from small beginnings to its present dimensions and wonderful prospect is a Being powerful enough to be called God; and a Being good enough to suffer with advancing life is a Being good enough to be called God.

So we may suffer bravely when our turn comes, or what is more difficult, watch without utter dismay the suffering of those whom we love. These sufferers are contributing to the sum total of suffering that will lead to the cure. They are as worthy of esteem as are the men who finally discover the remedy. They are pushing life forward to larger power and better purpose. They are making contribution in a fundamental way to human progress.

CHRISTIAN PRAYER AS A FORCE
IN HUMAN PROGRESS

Lecture IV

CHRISTIAN PRAYER AS A FORCE
IN HUMAN PROGRESS

IN the religion that Jesus possessed and desired to share with all men prayer was a vital element. He is portrayed to us in the Christian scriptures as praying at his baptism, as praying over the sick and the dead, as praying in the dark garden, on the cross, while ascending into the heavens, and in the heavens as offering continual prayer to God for us men.

I

What do we mean by prayer? If spiritual photography were possible, exactly what would it show to be taking place when a man is praying? In general when a man is praying he is trying to have conscious intercourse with God. The nature of the intercourse depends upon the nature of God. Is God a form of being that is stirred by the desires of the praying man?

We have conceived God to be a Life vast and strong, close up and active, subtly pushing all things on by an evolutionary process toward a good goal; and that goal, so far as this earth is concerned, we have conceived to be a creative race of men, wise, powerful, sincere and friendly.

II

Now, in general, what sort of things could a man expect to reach out and get from such a Life, from such a Vast Good Will?[1]

[1]Cf. also Herman, *Creative Prayer*, Ch. VI in which the author sets off from a like viewpoint. The treatment is a helpful supplement to Dean Bosworth's thought in this Lecture. The method of Herman, however, is that of devotional dissertation rather than of careful inquiry.

"How can prayer benefit anyone beyond the person who prays? How can prayer on behalf of others be effectual without infringing upon their free-will? . . . If prayer admittedly cannot change natural law, why should we expect it to change the laws which govern the moral and intellectual nature of those we pray for?

"To have the will of God, the mind of Christ, concerning ourselves and the world,

Perhaps we should rather say, reach down in and get, for it is in the depths of our personalities that we strike the roots of our being into the Life of God.

We could not expect to get anything from God that it would be contrary to his nature to give, nothing that would be against the deep trend of his vast purpose. Therefore, in the first place, we could expect nothing that would weaken man's creative power. God's purpose is to evolve a strong, creative race, a strong resourceful race. So we could expect nothing that would make life easy for men, no exemption from difficulties, from suffering, from problems, from a certain degree of mistake and failure that might lie on the road to ultimate success. We could not expect God to be always tender with us, but rather to handle us roughly at times as we certainly find him doing.

We could not expect to get from God through prayer anything that would be to the disadvantage of another person, for this would hinder the development of an honest and friendly world. It would hinder the development of a civilization in which each man shall wish for all the others such a fair chance at all good things as a man would like his brother to have. The firm set of God's Will is toward such a result and no prayer could change it. A high minded, socially minded manufacturer would not grant his son's request for money to use in starting a sweat shop. A patriot would not give his son money with which to finance a traitorous attack on his nation.

To put the matter positively, what a man might expect to receive from the Life of God in answer to prayer would be something to share with another person, something that would in this way help in the evolution of a brotherly world. There can be no selfish praying, no praying that ignores others. Such prayer might be pagan prayer; it would not be Christian prayer. Prayer might

---

and to have them not merely by way of intellectual assent or moral appreciation, but by a vital appropriation that assimilates us to our Lord, is to have the key to apostolic power. Apart from such assimilation, we constantly relapse into a pessimistic view of the prospects of the Kingdom of God upon earth. We see evil triumphant and goodness mocked. . . Day by day the voice of the Church, nay, the voice of religion itself, seems to count for less in the popular mind. . . But when we turn from our own interpretation of facts to Christ's vision of the world, we find ourselves breathing in another atmosphere. We look this way and that, and all the time the Lord of the harvest is passing unseen through the field, laden with the sheaves of His prolific Passion." pp. 154, 172-173.

often be for something that a man could use for himself, but only in order to make himself more efficient in the great evolutionary push toward a brotherly world. Prayer "in Christ's name" means prayer in Christ's spirit, which is the spirit of devotion to God's great purpose to produce a friendly world.

We are therefore not surprised to find that Jesus' clearest and simplest illustration of the nature of prayer involves three persons, namely, a man in prayer getting something from God to share with a friend in need. A man at midnight heard knocking on his door. When he opened his door he found a friend standing out in the darkness, tired by his long journey and hungry. In his humble household he had no food for his hungry friend, but he went to the home of a well-to-do friend near by, wakened him from sleep and said to him, "Friend, lend me three loaves, for a friend of mine is come to me from a journey and I have nothing to set before him." The well-to-do neighbor finally gave him "as much as he needed," and he took it back to share with his hungry visitor.

We naturally ask, what might pass from the Life of God into the life of a praying man to be shared by him with others? The answer is quickly at hand: the two supreme values of life, namely feeling and thought.

By feeling is meant not a mere superficial emotion but that fundamental element in personality which is the basis of will and thought, and which gives character to every act. It is that in the true artist's work which makes it so superior to the work of an exact copyist. It is that which differentiates the true musician's performance from that of one whose technique may be perfect but who lacks the artist's feeling. Edward Carpenter, in his book, *Civilization; Its Cause and Cure,* in emphasizing the fundamental importance of feeling, calls attention to the fact that even so abstract a study as geometry rests on feeling. All the propositions to be proven rest upon axioms, and these axioms are simply feeling. We simply feel that the whole is equal to the sum of all its parts, and that things equal to the same thing are equal to each other. It is in the sphere of feeling that we find courage, hope, loving interest, morale. The presence of the proper feeling means success, its absence means failure. Your friend comes to you in utter discouragement, hungry and tired from the journey of life. So men often came to Jesus' door. You can do very little if anything directly for him. But you can unobtrusively reach down into the Life of God in your own soul and say; "Friend, lend me three loaves, for a friend of mine has come to me from a journey and I have nothing to set before him." Then you find rising within you a wealth of hope and courage which you share with him and he goes out from his interview with you to success instead of to failure. Your contact with the Life of God in prayer has brought your own capacity for feeling into exercise. The result has been a working together with God.

The other fundamental value in life is thought. If the business man in a crisis can hit upon the right thought, he will save his business. If the mother whose family life is in peril can get the right idea, she can keep the home from being wrecked. If the physician can think right he will make a true diagnosis and devise the proper remedy. If the scientist with his scientific imagination can hit upon the right idea, he will know along what line to institute his experiments. When your friend comes to you in utter perplexity, not knowing what to do in the emergency that presses upon him, you have very little wisdom. But, here again, you reach down into the Life of God and ask for ideas, for thoughts, to share with your friend in need. Your own mind becomes unusually active. Ideas come to you which surprise you. The ideas are the product of your mind working together with the mind of God. When in response to such simple and unobtrusive prayer, you find the needed feeling and thought repeatedly rising within you, you finally conclude that Jesus drew his homely illustration out of a vast reality, out of his own experience with God and out of the possible experience of all people who pray in friendly simplicity, of all people who look in to God and say "Friend"; who look out around all the circle of human relations and at every point say "friend of mine"; who, in the words of Jesus, 'as they stand praying forgive, if they have anything against anybody.'

III

How do these supreme values pass from the Life of God into the life of a praying man? In accordance with psychic law; in accordance with the laws, or conditions that prevail when feeling and thought pass from one human life into another human life.

There seem to be cases in which, in answer to prayer, thought and feeling from God arise in a third person's mind. A man in need of money for some benevolent enterprise asks God for it, and a third person finds herself strongly moved to send money to the person who prayed. Such a case occurred in my circle of acquaintances. This might seem to be a case of telepathy; the strong desire in the mind of the one who prayed directly affected the person who sent the money. But telepathy does not eliminate the Life of God. Telepathy requires some connecting medium between the two human minds and also, it would seem, some power connecting the mind of the one who prays with some particular person rather than with others.

IV

Would God ever wait before doing a good thing for one person until some other person asked him to do it? It would seem that generally he would not. But under certain circumstances it is conceivable that he might. The man in need may not have found God and learned how to draw from the Vast Life. In Jesus' illustration, the tired hungry traveler seemed not to know the way to the house of the well-to-do man with plenty. Furthermore it may work to the advantage of the great cause of brotherhood among men, if good things sometimes come from the Life of God into a needy man's life by way of another man who prays.

V

Could the forces of nature be affected by God in answer to prayer? Can we with good courage pray for rain? Theoretically yes, for we find the forces of nature to be exceedingly susceptible to the manipulation of personal human wills and therefore, we might infer, directly responsive to the will of God. But practically we feel that the sphere of so called natural forces has been left to man for his mastery. Man develops knowledge and power by being left to himself in his dealing with these forces. If, when he desired to fly through the air, he had nothing to do but pray for levitation, the power and joy of human achievement would be impossible. His life would become poor and cheap. He would be deprived of the unspeakable joy of *working* together with God in a creative evolution.

There is plenty of room left for prayer in the sphere of psychic relations. Here the situations are almost without number in which God can answer prayer by putting thought and feeling into the mind of a man in accordance with psychic law, putting thought and feeling into the human mind in such a way as to stimulate the man's own power of thought and feeling and so to strengthen him rather than weaken him.

VI

How does Christian Prayer contribute to Human Progress?

Friendly Christian prayer is a conscious opening of the soul to God. It is an appeal to God for incitement to such feeling and thought in one's self or in another as will make us creative in and for the great world group. It is an appeal to God in the concrete instances of human relationships for those high values, right feeling and true thought which will enable us to join creatively in the great push of mankind toward a wise, honest and friendly world. It brings us into conscious active alliance with the great creative working force of the universe, the will of God.

Evolution advances when organisms fit into their environment. A praying personality is fitting into the environing Life of a Living God. Prayer is the normal activity of a healthy soul, living a full life. It stimulates creative activity. A scientist praying over a problem may get a suggestion that incites to an experiment that turns out to be fruitful. An artist may get some gleam of beauty that he works into a shape that blesses all who see it. One of my friends once asked the artist Hoffman who was his model for the boy Jesus in his famous picture. He gave the name of the one who served as model for the figure, but the face, he said, came in answer to prayer. A plain man feeling out in prayer for some better way to do his job gets a half idea that he works out in a way that makes him more fruitfully creative in some detail of the world's work.

There is need of experimenting with prayer. We are in a wonderful environment. We are in the midst of a net work of human minds and wills all resting in the vast creative Life of God. This gives a wonderful opportunity for experiment. Theorizing about prayer helps, but only as it clears the way for experiment. Professor H. S. Jennings of Johns Hopkins University in an address delivered in December, 1926, and reported in *Science,* spoke a word that is as true in religion as it is in science.

The man of science must accept as the final word John Hunter's maxim: "Don't think; try"! Thinking is an instrument, a very fallible instrument, for helping to decide what to try, but the *last* word must be *try.*[2]

Since responsibility for using the evolutionary process intelligently and creatively is now placed on man he needs more than ever before to pray. He needs not so much to think as to try.

[2]*Science,* New Series Vol. LXV, Jan. 14, 1927, p. 21[2].

THE CHRISTIAN WAY OF LIVING
AND HUMAN PROGRESS

Lecture V

THE CHRISTIAN WAY OF LIVING
AND HUMAN PROGRESS

JESUS stands out in history as the instigator of a certain way of living. He lived it; he taught it; he believed in it so thoroughly that he proposed to make it universal. His way of living was not like that of a religious order with many rules for the details of conduct. It was rather a certain disposition, or way of feeling on which he laid emphasis. He pointed out a few general ways in which this disposition would naturally express itself in the conditions that prevailed in his day.

We have to make three inquiries: What was this way of living? Will it work in modern life? Does it contribute to human progress, that is, does it advance the great evolution of life?

I

General statements of Jesus' way of living and their meaning demand attention at the outset.

"Thou shalt love the Lord thy God with all thy heart." What does this statement mean? We have seen that to love a person means wanting to have to do with him; wanting to see him realize his deepest desire; wanting to work with him for the realization of his deepest desire. Therefore to love God, who is a vast Good Will set toward the evolution of a wise, powerful, honest and friendly civilization, means to work with him at any cost and to the utmost for the realization of this deep desire. The vast force of the Will, or Life, of God is set toward a social result. To love him is to join him in his great evolutionary push toward this social result. So Jesus coupled with his first great teaching a second, "like unto it"—"Thou shalt love thy neighbor as thyself." That is, Jesus stood for a *religious* movement of the soul toward God necessarily involving an *ethical* movement of the soul toward men. In

43

Jesus' experience and teaching religion and ethics become practically one and the same thing in principle.

Can men be profoundly set toward a worthy social result without any awareness of God? Some men seem to be, but generally in such cases it is the traditional theological God of whom they have no awareness. They generally feel that in their social devotion they are working with the deep trend of the evolution of life. They are working consciously with this trend and so are essentially religious. We probably need to realize that there is much genuine, though unrecognized, religion in human life. This seems to be implied in the New Testament picture of the Judgment Day when many cried out in surprise that they could not remember ever having expressed any such religious devotion to the Christ as he credited to them. Such persons, especially in the face of great discouragements, would be immensely helped by realizing that this deep evolutionary trend in life is consciously sympathetic, and very likely multitudes would make no persistent, fruitful effort at all along social lines without such realization. Jesus was sure that this socially sympathetic Life was all about men and he proposed primarily to show his followers how to become aware of it. He proposed to share with men his own awareness of the socializing Life of God.

II

How, according to Jesus' teaching, do we become aware of the Life of God? A preliminary question is, How do we become aware of any unseen force? The answer to this question is simple: We adjust ourselves in action to the supposed nature of the force and if the force be really present, it then makes itself felt. Electricity is invisibly present in the atmosphere about us, but we do not feel it until we adjust ourselves in appropriate action to what we have learned about its nature. Then it breaks out in light and heat or some other form that we can feel. What then is the nature of God and how do we adjust ourselves to it in appropriate action? We come back once more, as so often before, to Jesus' idea of the nature of God, namely, a vast Good Will close up to every man's life saying in many ways: "I want you, I want you to work with me for a powerful, honest and friendly world." A word which Jesus often used to describe this adjustment in action to the nature of God, was "faith," or "belief." "Have faith in God" he said. What is it to have faith in, or to believe in, a person who is doing some big thing? It is to approve of the big thing and to set one's self with all his might to work at the big thing with him. Faith, or belief, in God, then, is the reaching out of the whole man to work with the unseen energy of God at any cost and to the utmost in creating a wise, powerful, honest and friendly world.

This involves, first of all, meaning ourselves to become wise, powerful, honest and friendly. It means to set one's heart on being wise; to determine, so far as may be, to understand; to find out the reasons for things; and to know the meaning of all the words we use. An illustration of this disposition and also of the way in which it leads to finding and working with God appears in the boyhood experience of Abraham Lincoln. He said of himself: "I remember how when a mere child I used to get irritated when anybody talked to me in a way I could not understand . . . I can remember going to my little bedroom after hearing the neighbors talk of an evening with my father, and spending no small part of the night trying to make out what was the meaning of their to me dark sayings. I could not sleep, although I tried to, when I got on such a hunt for an idea, until I had caught it, and when I thought I had got it, I was not satisfied until I had repeated it over, until I had put it in language plain enough, as I thought, for any boy to understand. This was a kind of passion with me and it has stuck by me for I am never easy now when I am handling a thought until I have bounded it north and bounded it south and bounded it east and bounded it west."

This effort to adjust one's self in action to the nature of the unseen Will of God means also starting out to develop power. It means determining to do something well; to be efficient in some occupation, in business, in the management of a home. It is the Will of God that men should have power over all the forces of nature. Behind all inventions that increase the power of men is the instigating Will of God.

The effort to increase power is so in accord with the Will of God unfolding in human life, that it sometimes leads to astounding results. The Wright brothers whom I have personally known, are said to have set out definitely to increase the power of man, and to have tried to do this along various lines without marked success, until finally they concentrated attention in the aviation problem and contributed to its solution in a way that has enlarged the power of man to an extent that no one is yet able to realize.

The effort to adjust one's self in action to the Will of God means also starting out to be entirely sincere. It represses all desire to seem to know more than we really do know; all desire to seem to have more—or less—than we really do have; all desire to seem to be better than we really are meaning, at any cost, to become.

This effort involves setting out to be entirely friendly. It involves much friendly forgiving. It is through forgiving, seventy times seven times, all through the years, that forgiving becomes a fixed habit of life and so life feels its way into a fixed consciousness of the vast forgiving Life of God. It means friendly apologizing. Jesus drew an illustration from temple life of the futility of trying to become aware of God without first apologizing to an injured fellow man. He pictured the man who had perhaps made a long journey by land and sea to Jerusalem, and who stood by the altar of God, gift in hand and priest by his side, ready to lift up his gift to God. Suddenly, with a shock, there came to him the thought of some man in his distant home city whom he had wronged. This unrighted wrong made it impossible to go on with the delivery of his gift to God: "If thou art offering thy gift at the altar and there rememberest that thy brother hath aught against thee, leave there thy gift by the altar; first be reconciled to thy brother; then come and offer thy gift."

The development of the friendly disposition involves much friendly praying, over and over saying to God, "Friend, lend me three loaves for a friend of mine has come to me from a journey and I have nothing to set before him." It involves friendliness in business, not only as emphasis of the friendly side of all legitimate business whose function it is to meet the needs of the community, but also an eagerness to discover methods of business more friendly than those that sometimes prevail in the present business world. It means putting the friendly element in business above the element of financial profit. Ruskin once said: "If your fee is first with you and your work second, then fee is your master and the lord of all fee who is the devil; if your work is first with you and your fee second, then work is your master and the lord of all work who is God." An American manufacturer has lately said: "The shop is the mainstay of all the finer things which the home represents. If we want the home to be happy, we must contrive to keep the shop busy. The whole justification of the profits made by the shop is that they are used to make doubly secure the homes dependent on that shop, and to create more jobs for other men. If profits go to swell a personal fortune, that is one thing; if they go to provide a sounder basis for business, better working conditions, better wages, more extended employment,—that is quite another thing. Capital thus employed should not be carelessly tampered with. It is for the service of all, though it may be under the direction of one."[1]

The effort to adjust to the Life of God through some form of friendly action, includes all the small details of daily life at home and on the street, in all business and social contacts, in what Wordsworth calls:

> That best portion of a good man's life,
> His little, nameless, unremembered acts
> Of kindness and of love.[2]

III

If then we are proceeding scientifically when we endeavor through these fundamental forms of action to adjust ourselves to the nature of the unseen Force we call the Will of God, and so seek to become aware of him, what sort of feeling should we recognize as awareness of God? When we adjust ourselves in action to the invisible electric force in the atmosphere about us we feel something, it may be a certain shock, or a certain sensation of light or heat, or motion on the electric car. What is the feeling that we should identify as feeling God? It must be something that everybody of any age or occupation or temperament can have, for the Life of God is close up to everybody. It must therefore be something rather commonplace, though vital and fundamental.

[1]Ford, *My Life and Work*, pp. 163-4
[2]Wordsworth, "Lines Above Tintern Abbey", cf. *Complete Poetical Works*, Cambridge Ed., 1904, p. 91[2].

It is what we have already considered in another connection, namely, the experience that Jesus called "soul rest." This means, it would seem, a deep growing satisfaction. It is the satisfaction that is experienced in learning to understand; the satisfaction that comes when a difficult problem is solved; when the experiment has succeeded. There is joy in the Life of God over the advance so made in human understanding and this joy of God has penetrated our lives. Or there is deep satisfaction over some expression of honesty, over work honestly done, over wrong doing honestly acknowledged and put away. Or there is deep satisfaction in friendship. In general there is the deep satisfaction produced by pushing life forward, by creating lasting values. This satisfaction is primarily in the vast underlying Life of God. As this joy of God rises in human hearts, they experience awareness of God; they feel that they are doing what all the highest Life in and around them has called upon them to do, and is setting itself to do.

IV

This sense of God may come suddenly or gradually. The most important personal relations of life may begin suddenly at a day and hour always remembered; or they may begin obscurely and only gradually come to be recognized. The sense of God may come after great struggle and strain, in temptation, in overwhelming trouble, in the burden of responsibility almost too heavy to be borne, just as a man may come to an awareness of the fresh air that is all about him only after a desperate struggle for breath. Or his awareness of God may come after peaceful reflection, as a man becomes aware of the fresh air about him by being instructed regarding its hygienic function and by quietly feeling it fill his lungs and purify his blood in his early morning walk.

The point of this discussion is that Jesus' wonderful way of living was conceived by him to proceed from an awareness of God, that he could teach men to experience. The great fact of his own life and the prospective life of all men consisted in awareness of the enfolding Life of God, but of a Life of God, as has been said, that was set toward a social result.

V

What now is the nature of this social result? What is the Christian way of living in human relationships?

First of all, what does it mean to "love your neighbor as yourself?" It means wanting him to have a chance to be his best as much as you want such a chance for yourself, wanting to share with him, as far as possible, all the advantages that you possess.

It does not mean treating all men alike but rather treating each man in such a way as to help him make his largest contribution to the common good, to the forward push of life. For instance, a physician in time of pestilence will be surrounded by special safeguards not afforded to ordinary men.

It does not mean making things too easy for our neighbor. We would not want things made too easy for ourselves. It would not be good either for ourselves or the other man.

It does not mean ignoring one's self. Jesus said, "Love your neighbor *as* yourself." To ignore one's self is to ignore a value established by God through a long and expensive process of evolution. To ignore one's self is to deprive the common good of a valuable asset. We are under just as great obligation to make the most of ourselves for the common good as to help our neighbors make the most of themselves for the common good. To ignore ourselves is to make an assault on our neighbor's self respect. We should lose our own self respect if we let our neighbor ignore himself in his treatment of us. We ought not, therefore, to inflict on him treatment that would lessen his self respect. It is *bad for him* to have us ignore ourselves. We do not stand on the threshold of his life and commit suicide there, but we summon him to come out and join us in working for the forward push of life.

We do often sacrifice our lower interests entirely for the higher interests of others. We sacrifice physical life for the freedom of the nation, or the husband sacrifices life for the honor of his wife. But we do this for ourselves. We sacrifice physical life for our own spiritual integrity. We are always sacrificing our own lower interests for the sake of maintaining our own higher interests. We expect others to sacrifice their lower interests for the sake of our higher interests. It is right that I should deprive myself of certain lower physical comforts in order to pay for my brother's education. It is also right for him, in turn, by similar sacrifice to help me get my education. The common good needs the educated powers of both of us.

It is true that a faithful physician may sometimes sacrifice his own physical life to save the physical life of another man. A fireman will do the same. This is because the highest interest of the community requires that there shall be certain classes of men whose profession requires them to do this.

Does loving one's neighbor as himself eliminate competition? In the present state of society it would seem not to do so. Competition constitutes the only practicable way of finding out where each individual can make his largest contribution to the common good. In making up an athletic team there seems no other way to determine who are the men best fitted to win athletic success for the college; or in business, what baker can make the best and cheapest bread for the community; or in scientific research what student can make the best use of the fellowship to be awarded for graduate study. The competition of course must be absolutely fair but it must be real, no man holding back his best effort; otherwise the common good would suffer.

Furthermore everyone in a Christian competition should help the defeated man find the place where he can do his best for the common good, and the defeated man must not be sore and sullen. A Christian enthusiasm for the common good should sweeten all competition. There is need of emphasizing again the fact that in the teaching of Jesus, the common good is not the abstraction that often appears in philosophical teaching and that has no great moving power over ordinary minds. Jesus sought, as we have already seen, to kindle a warm sense of the active Will of God in the heart, stirring the whole being to work with it gladly and triumphantly for the welfare of all concerned.

VI

What does it mean to "love your enemy?" It means wanting him to become the best that his nature indicates he might be. It means wanting him to get over his ill will, for his personality will be wrecked should his ill will persist. Therefore loving an enemy means doing everything possible to change him into a friend. It involves an apology if an apology be due to him. It means rebuking him if the fault be his: "If thy brother sin against thee rebuke him."

What does it mean to "deny one's self?" "If any one would be my disciple, let him deny himself." It means denying to one's self the right to the supreme place in thought and action. It is the refusal to say "What I want I take, regardless of the interest of others." It brings the other man's interests abreast of our own and inquires "What will be good for both of us?" We must not endeavor to lord it over others, neither must we encourage others to lord it over us, for this would be developing in them the evil disposition we are overcoming in ourselves.

What does it mean to be everybody's bond-servant—"Whoever would be first among you, shall be bond-servant of all?" This is a strong way of forbidding the tyrannical spirit; in the context the strong men among the "Gentiles," for instance the Roman officials, are said to "lord it over" their subjects. Evidently one should be the bond-servant of those about him only so far as it is good for them to have a bond-servant. A man should treat another in such a way as to stimulate in the other the two great elements of good character, namely, good will and vigorous action. The mother should not be the bond-servant of her daughter, nor the daughter the bond-servant of her mother. Neither should tyrannize over the other.

What is the meaning of the Golden Rule—"Do unto others as you would that others should do unto you?" It means, "Treat the other man as you would feel that he *ought* to treat you, if you and he changed places." The military officer ought to treat the common soldier as he would feel that an officer ought to treat him if he himself were a common soldier. It means that in all business transactions buyer and seller should treat each other as each would feel that he *ought* to be treated if buyer and seller changed places.

THE CHRISTIAN WAY OF LIVING
AND HUMAN PROGRESS
(*Continued*)

THE CHRISTIAN WAY OF LIVING
AND HUMAN PROGRESS

(*Continued*)

VII

THE RELATION OF JESUS' WAY OF LIVING TO HUMAN PROGRESS

WE have seen in general what Jesus' way of living was. What is the main contribution to human progress made by this way of living?

The disposition that is dominant in Jesus' way of living, and that really constitutes his way of living, is absolutely essential to human progress in its present stage. In lower stages of development life has made progress without any large measure of this disposition, perhaps with this disposition present only in germ form. But now human life has reached a stage of development beyond which it can make but little if any progress without the genuinely Christian disposition. This disposition, as we have seen, is an invincible good will. Nothing done to the property or person of the man of invincible good will can break down his good will and make him hate. He is ready at any cost to work with the will of God in creating a wise, powerful, honest and friendly world. The purpose of the Christian religion, truly conceived, is to fasten this disposition upon man as a fixed habit of life.

The Christian disposition will express itself differently at different stages in the evolution of society. Ways proper and right at one time may be utterly improper and wrong at another time. In the rudimentary stage of social organization at one time necessarily prevalent in American frontier life, lynch law seemed to contribute to social order, but when community life had developed to the point where regular courts and court officials had come into existence, lynchers were necessarily regarded as criminals.

The way in which the Christian disposition should express itself at any given point in social evolution is to a large extent determined by experiment. It is largely through experiment that we can ascertain the answers to these and many other questions: What is the proper length of a working day in different occupations? How ought we to distribute the responsibilities of management and ownership in the industrial process? Who ought to control capital? How ought profits to be distributed among stockholders, managers, and workmen? Ought the wage system to be abolished? Who ought to vote?

The teaching of Jesus proposes to fasten on men the sacrificial disposition requisite for the experiments essential to human progress. In all experiments there is an unavoidable risk of temporary loss. Being forced to experiment and to run this risk is a character-making process. Good will alone is not enough. An instructed good will is necessary, that is, a good will guided by experience gained through experiment. Men of this character are called by Jesus "the salt of the earth"; they keep civilization from decay. The great cohesive, constructive forces—faith, hope and love—work in them against the disruptive forces—suspicion, despair and hate. They are the super-men. They are the men who have the future in their keeping; they are "the meek who shall inherit the earth."

Jesus made two specific applications of his general teaching about the Christian way of living that we have not yet discussed. They are applications that at first glance perhaps do not seem contributory to human progress. They concern money and the use of force.

Is Jesus' teaching about money favorable to human progress? His teaching is characterized by certain remarkable omissions. It contains no urgent injunctions to get and save money; no wise sayings about thrift; nothing about endowing schools and hospitals or building factories and accumulating capital. On the contrary Jesus seems to have dreaded the possession of money either by himself or his disciples. He warns against laying up money on earth and urges men instead to lay up treasure in heaven. This treasure in heaven seems to consist in friendships. He distinctly urges men to use their money all up for others and become poor men and assures them that in this way they will make everlasting friends who will later be ready to receive them into the everlasting friendships of the other world. He represents money, or mammon, and God as irreconcilable rivals for the devotion of men. "You cannot serve God and mammon," he said. This seems a way of saying "You cannot devote yourselves to money and to friendship."

It is not difficult to see why Jesus regarded the possession of money as detrimental to the development of friendship which he considered to be the chief value in human life.[1] The possession of money gives opportunity to gratify and so to strengthen the selfish instincts which are the denial of friendship. It is difficult for a rich man to have, or to be, a true friend. He lacks the keen sense of needing others which is the basis for friendship. His money gives him large power to break other men down in business and social relations. His habits of life are so different from those of other men that he cannot live with them, on the level, as friends live together. If, in an effort to associate with them, he goes without the comforts to which he is accustomed, he will often be restless, and if he attempts to provide for his poorer associates the luxuries to which he is accustomed, an element of patronage enters into the situation which spoils friendship. All of his social relationships are apt to be insincere and artificial. Poorer people feel a sense of being at a disadvantage in his presence that makes them dislike to be with him, or they are wondering how much they can get out of him for themselves or for some cause that they represent. *They do not sincerely want him just for what he is, nor does he want them.* When the rich associate with the rich their intercourse is apt to be characterized by certain subtle comparisons and social competitions that are ruinous to simple sincere friendship. Furthermore, the accumulation and care of riches absorb attention and leave little leisure for the development of friendship. The development of democracy in our modern world may possibly be bringing rich and poor together with less sense of superiority and inferiority, but the difficulty still remains.

What would be the effect on human progress if Jesus' dread of large personal fortunes should prevail? In some ways at least it would stimulate progress. Bitterness over the shocking contrast

[1]Cf. Bosworth, *Life and Teaching of Jesus,* pp. 160-162, 180f.; also in this volume, Address XVI, "The New Testament Conception of the Disciple and His Money."

between luxurious living and abject poverty would to some extent abate. Large amounts of money would be turned to the support of public enterprises. Capital, which seems essential to progress, would more and more be managed by groups of men and cease to constitute huge personal fortunes. This change is already taking place through quiet processes of orderly industrial development, especially through the more extensive purchase of stock by employes in large corporations.[2]

VIII

Is Jesus' teaching about not resisting evil favorable to human progress? The spirit of his teaching on this subject is perfectly clear. It requires an invincible, unlimited, good will. The form in which this idea is expressed raises the question just asked. Men are commanded always to lend to every one who wishes to borrow, to give to everyone who asks, to invite a second insult, and not to resist evil, that is, apparently not to use force.

Yet Jesus urged men to the form of resistance involved in protest: "If thy brother sin against thee, rebuke him." He himself rebuked with a fierceness of invective rarely paralleled elsewhere in literature and he is reported to have used physical force in reforming the trade abuses tolerated by the priests in the Jerusalem temple precincts.

We know that physical force is a natural way to express spiritual meaning. The friendly spirit naturally expresses itself with the physical force of a vigorous hand clasp, and the indignant spirit also expresses itself with a physical blow administered by the same hand. That is, physical force in itself has no moral quality. The moral quality is found in the disposition with which physical force is used.

We cannot escape from the conscientious conviction that we must sometimes resist and refuse. We must use physical force to prevent a suicide; to keep a drunken man from beating his little boy to death. We must not always give what people ask for. We must not lend a man a revolver with which to commit murder. The banker must not lend to everybody who appears at the cashier's window asking for a loan. To do so would be as bad for the borrower as for the lender.

[2]Cf. Carver, *The Present Industrial Revolution.*

Why did Jesus put his teaching into this extreme form, specifying concrete actions that it seems so unwise to perform? It is necessary to remember that this form of expression would not have been misleading to those who first listened to his words. They knew how to understand such language and to catch the spirit which such words were intended to convey. In modern life we constantly trust people to understand what we mean by injunctions that ought not to be literally obeyed. We urge our children with utmost earnestness to be kind to dumb animals, but we trust them to understand that this language does not forbid destroying the rattlesnake, the malarial mosquito, and the rats that spread bubonic plague. We do not hesitate to destroy minute forms of animal life by boiling the water and pasteurizing the milk.

It is also possible that these extreme forms of expression may have been in part due to the idea that the end of the age was at hand; that the Judgment Day was impending. With such a prospect certain actions might be right that would otherwise be unjustifiable. When a man is hurrying to his wedding or to the death bed of his child, he cannot stop to expostulate with the small boys who throw stones at him, although ordinarily it might be his duty to do so.

It seems clear that we are left to decide for ourselves when we shall do more good by yielding and giving instead of resisting and refusing. The necessity of refusing makes character. The dominant motive must always be the desire to do good, and never the desire to keep a good thing from another or to secure personal revenge.

Jesus' way of living, then, involves the development in the heart of an invincible good will, commonly called love. This steady good will is produced by a growing awareness of the Life of God, pulsing through all things with an unvarying love. Men are in the main left to decide for themselves how to express this good will in the different ways appropriate in the different stages of an evolving social order. Men learn by experience how to discharge their responsibility for advancing this evolution and they gain their experience through a series of experiments which generally involve risk and sacrifice. The Christian way of living makes a profoundly important contribution to human progress by generating the sacrificial spirit requisite for these experiments.

THE CONTRIBUTION OF JESUS' PERSONALITY
TO HUMAN PROGRESS

Lecture VII

THE CONTRIBUTION OF JESUS'
PERSONALITY TO HUMAN PROGRESS

WHAT is there about the personality of Jesus, as distinguished from his ideas, that stimulates human progress?

Professor Bousset has said: In no other religion has a personality ever won a significance in any way approaching that of Christ's in the Christian religion. He maintained his power over his disciples' souls beyond death and the grave . . . and wherever Christianity has struck out a new path in her journey it has been because the personality of Jesus had again become living and a ray from its Being had once more illumined the world.[1]

There had been progress in the world before Jesus was born. Human life had climbed long and far in the period between the cave man and Plato. Socrates, Plato, Aristotle and the Hebrew Prophets had certainly given speed and direction to the upward evolution of human life. What contribution has been made by the personality of Jesus?

I

Who was, or is, Jesus?

Two preliminary considerations need to be noted. The first is that we have to *live* our way into the answer. We begin to learn who he was by doing what he said. We follow his directions for finding God and our success makes our hearts grow warm with what seems to us to be his kindling presence. His own chief concern was not for the intellectual recognition of his dignity but for the doing of what he said: "Why call ye me Lord, Lord, and do not the things that I say?"

The second preliminary consideration is that we do not need

[1]Bousset, *What Is Religion*, pp. 236-238.

to understand the metaphysical relation of his personality to God in order to be transformed in character by his influence. I do not understand the metaphysical relation of my mother's personality to God but nevertheless her personality has had a powerful influence in shaping my character.

To return to our inquiry: Who was, or is, Jesus? We are helped by asking: How do we tell who anyone is? When a stranger presents himself what do we need to know about him in order to tell who he is? We ask his name, but his name itself gives us no information. We learn his father's name, and if we already know his father well this information gives us some help; but a son is sometimes very unlike his father. He tells us that he comes from London; but London is a great city and many different kinds of people live there. He tells us that he is entitled to be called "Doctor," but there are many very different kinds of men to whom this title is applied and in any case the mere title gives no clear information about personal character. We learn that his deepest feeling and desire are the feeling that he could paint a picture that would bless all men who might see it, and the desire to do it. This gives us vitally important information about him. He seems to have an artist's soul and to have high ideals. One further point remains regarding which we need information in order to know who he is; Can he paint the picture? That is, in order to tell who a person is we need to know his deepest feeling and desire and the corroboration afforded them by what he shows himself able to do.

In the case of Jesus, we know that this personal name was common among the Jews. We know that he is called the "Son of God," and that he is said to have come from heaven; but many persons are supposed to be in heaven and many of its inhabitants are called "sons of God." We know that he is called the "Christ," or the "Messiah," words which mean "anointed," and designate one appointed by an official anointing to any one of several important offices. These titles tell us nothing very definite about who Jesus really was. We know that he is said to have been born of a virgin without the agency of any human male; but we should not know in advance what kind of product to expect from such a process. We should need to examine the product in order to find out. In making this examination we most naturally inquire: What were his deepest feeling and desire? The answer to this question is reasonably clear in the Gospels and is fundamentally revealing. He felt in the very depths of his being the force that we call the Will of God in all its moral fulness of power. His deepest desire was to work with the Will of God to the utmost and to lead other men to do the same. He finally came to feel that God laid on him the responsibility of leading the human race into full and active accord with the Will of God. We have repeatedly discussed the Will of God and its goal. Jesus felt finally convinced that God laid on him the responsibility of leading the human race into the life of knowledge and power, honesty and friendliness, that he and his people had learned to call the Kingdom, or Reign, of God.

The name of such a person was *"The* Messiah," or *"The* Christ." Among all those appointed by an anointing to various offices, the one appointed to this supreme office was *"The* Anointed." As the nation looked forward to the appearance of such a character various ideal careers were attributed to him in the popular imagination. Various ideas regarding the goal of the Will of God prevailed among the people. It would be interesting to discuss these various conjectures, to discover if possible how Jesus proceeded to form his own ideals and how he came to the conclusion that God meant him to assume Messianic leadership in their realization, but this would lead us too far from the purpose of the present discussion.

As Jesus yielded fully to the vast Will of God and to the ideal which he felt to be its goal, he became such an expression of the Will of God in terms of human life and—as it turned out—human death and immortal spiritual presence as rightfully to constrain all men to become his loyal and obedient followers. He grew into this position of authoritative power through hard experience. One of the early Christian documents describes the process: "Who in the days of his flesh, having offered up prayers and supplications with strong crying and tears unto him that was able to save him out of death, and having been heard for his godly fear, though he was a Son, yet learned obedience by the things which he suffered;

and having been made perfect, he became unto all them that obey him the author of eternal salvation."[2]

The evolution of life had reached a stage in which the Life of God could lift itself up in such a personality.

II

After the death of Jesus a remarkable situation arose. The corroboration of his deepest feeling and desire began to appear, in what he showed himself able to do. Wherever men committed themselves at any cost to his three great ideas about God and life, and let their affections follow him out into the unseen world, there flowed into them a mighty tide of spiritual incentive. They felt the beginnings of a great ethical success which filled them with deep content and enthusiasm. This experience took different forms according to temperament, habits of thought and religious fashions, but its essential nature was a triumphant, fearless good will. The dark fears that lay so heavily on the spirits of men in the first century lost their power to oppress. These men and women felt the loving Life of God rise within them with a power that no persecution could break down. They were able to love to the uttermost. The Life of God, or "the Spirit of God," produced within them "love, joy, peace, long suffering, kindness, goodness, faithfulness, meekness, self-control."

What is it then to "believe in Jesus Christ," which is the traditional form of the Christian message? To believe in a person means to accept him, for good reasons, as what he is represented to be and to treat him accordingly. That is, in the case of a leader, to accept his great ideas, to work for their realization at any cost and to come as close as may be possible to the personality of the leader himself. The result of this in the case of the leadership of Jesus is "salvation," that is, being saved from a daily life of increasing selfishness, and its moral ruin to a daily life of increasing unselfishness, knowledge, power, honesty and friendliness, with all the fulness of life that these words imply. It means being *saved to a creative career.*

[2]Hebrews, 5: 7–8.

III

Is Jesus still living in the world and working on the lives of men for their emancipation from the power of the evil will? Have men experience of connection with the living spirit of Jesus?

We do not know what influences are playing upon us to produce the consciousness of the present moment. There may be memories, visible contacts with persons or things immediately around us, and perhaps invisible personal contacts which we do not distinctly recognize, though they may nevertheless be powerful. We know that we live largely in the sphere of things and persons that we are not seeing. We are remembering persons who are in the various homes of our acquaintance; we are thinking of things that have happened; we are anticipating things that will happen and of persons that we shall meet. A comparatively small part of the consciousness of a given moment is due to things visibly present in our immediate environment. Strictly speaking, what we are directly conscious of may be only a certain deep contentment, or satisfaction. We then proceed to make an intellectual interpretation of this satisfaction. If we have established what seems to us a reasonable idea of God we may attribute this deep contentment to the presence of the Life of God.

Do we also have reason to attribute any of our experience to the presence of Jesus? We take into account Jesus' own conviction of Messianic leadership in the life of men; his own passionate devotion to the life of men, and his love of being with them; his own conviction of immortality, which in this case would be a conviction of immortal connection with the great human enterprise. We take intellectual account also of the fact that men have seemed to themselves to have spiritual connection with Jesus, men of different temperaments and culture, generation after generation and in the face of the strict scientific scrutiny of experience. We take account of the fact that especially in times of great trouble and distress men often find themselves convinced that the Spirit of Christ walks with them. Dr. Albert Schweitzer, speaking out of deep and varied experience has said:

He comes to us as One unknown, without a name, as of old, by the lakeside, He came to those men who knew Him not. He speaks to us the same word: "Follow thou me!" and sets us to the tasks which He has to fulfill for our time. He commands. And to those who obey Him, whether they be wise or simple, He will reveal Himself in the toils, the conflicts, the sufferings which they shall pass through in His fellowship, and, as an ineffable mystery, they shall learn in their own experience Who He is.[3]

IV

What contribution is made by the personality of Jesus to human progress?

There is first of all his clear vision of the goal of human progress. This he saw in its simplicity. It was not involved with a mass of superfluous and inferior matter. There is also his warm sense of God, of the inner urge of the Will of God toward this goal; and his deep sense of his own supreme leadership in the human movement toward this goal.

There has apparently proceeded from his personality power to gather men about himself and hold them. The Life of God has so lifted itself up in him as to fix him in human experience past and present as one who, by virtue of what he was and is, shapes our idea of God himself. There has seemed to proceed from his personality a living, lasting incentive to creative activity in the evolutionary push for an honest and friendly world.

Our clear recognition of an evolutionary process may at first seem to make Jesus seem unnecessary. I have been asked this question: "As you understand the world and as the process of evolution develops, does not Jesus become less and less necessary? Does not the idea of a divine Christ become superfluous and is not the need of a Savior eliminated?" Knowledge of the evolutionary process lays new responsibility upon us, a heavier responsibility than any we have hitherto been called on to bear, responsibility for using the process intelligently and with utter good will toward future generations. With this new sense of responsibility laid on us, more than ever we need Jesus as a powerful source of inspiration and incentive. The evolutionary process does not save anyone. It simply shows us what the situation is in which we need saving. It is a situation in which we may join creatively in an upward development, or be left behind.

[3]Schweitzer, *The Quest of the Historical Jesus,* p. 401.

Perhaps it seems that the race might some time in the future outgrow the personality of Jesus. He was a manifestation of God at a definite time in human history and the race may be expected in the future to go far beyond all the phenomena of that time. This idea overlooks the fact that Jesus himself, as an immortal, living leader may be conceived as moving forward and keeping always in advance of humanity's vanguard, an eternal contributor to human progress.

THE RELATION OF JESUS' DEATH
TO HUMAN PROGRESS

Lecture VIII

THE RELATION OF JESUS' DEATH
TO HUMAN PROGRESS

THE death of so good a person in such a horrible way has always challenged the attention of the Christian section of the world. There have been other noble deaths, for instance, the death of Socrates. But Socrates is not supposed to have been so good a man as Jesus and the method of his execution was certainly not so horrible. His death was a dignified death, speedy and probably painless. The benumbing poison was administered by a regretful, apologetic executioner. He was surrounded by sympathizing friends engaged with lofty conversation with him almost to the end. It was a gentlemanly death. Jesus died in torture, in utter disgrace, abandoned by his friends and surrounded by jeering enemies. What did it all mean?

I

First of all, what meaning did Jesus himself see in his death? Did he think it would be of advantage to anyone? And if so, of what advantage? His death must have been a profound religious experience. What was he thinking about during the hours on the cross? What was going on in his soul?

Jesus had gradually become convinced that God willed him to be the Messianic leader of his nation and so, of course, of the world; for the Jew always thought of his nation as meant by God to dominate the world in righteousness, to secure world wide obedience to the law of God given through Moses.

In the course of this developing messianic consciousness it had become clear to Jesus that his messianic career involved a violent messianic death. This idea was foreign to Jewish thought. There were those who expected the Messiah to live for a certain period and then die a peaceful death, but no one expected him to

73

die a violent death in defeat and shame. In *IV Esdras* he is pictured as living 400 years. At the end of these four centuries he would die peacefully and all the inhabitants of the earth would die with him. After a week of silence, like that which preceded the original creation, there would be a general resurrection and the New Age would begin.[1]

Jesus felt that he would be executed not because the hostile ecclesiastical machine, priests and scribes, was too powerful an enemy. They were not too powerful for God. God had often overcome greater odds, for instance in the brilliant Maccabean victories two centuries before.

Jesus seems to have reached the conclusion that he must die because of an inner feeling that God willed it, which found corroboration in certain passages of Scripture. Since no one else had found such meaning in these scriptures we conclude that Jesus' inner feeling preceded his peculiar interpretation of the scriptures.

What did Jesus think to have been God's reason for putting a violent death into the messianic career? There is only meagre general evidence available at this point. Three statements stand out in the teaching of Jesus. He said that he was to give his Life as a "ransom for many."[2] That is, his death would be something that would liberate many. It would introduce multitudes into the liberty of the New Age, or the Kingdom of God. At the Last Supper he spoke of his body in a way that seemed to liken it to the paschal lamb,[3] the killing of which had marked the passage of ancient Israel from Egyptian bondage into liberty. Also at the Last Supper he spoke of his blood as "covenant blood," or "blood of the new covenant." This new covenant was commonly thought of as destined to be made on the threshold of the New Age when multitudes would enter into its liberty and when all men from the least to the greatest would know God.[4]

II

It was believed in Jesus' day, how generally we do not know, that the execution of holy men could ransom or liberate a nation, although even in circles where this idea prevailed there seems to have been no thought of a messianic death. The splendid age

[1] IV Esdras 7: 26-44.   [2] Mk. 10:45.   [3] Mk. 14:22.   [4] Jeremiah 31:31.

of national liberty beginning soon after 167 B. C. had been introduced by the horrible execution of nine people, an old priestly
scribe, a widow and her seven sons. All of them had been put
to death after hideous torture because they refused to depart from
the law of Moses and identify themselves with the national religion by means of which the Seleucid king hoped to unify and
solidify his empire. The youngest son, after having witnessed the
torture and death of his six older brothers, said: "I, as my brothers, give up both body and soul for the laws of our fathers, calling upon God that he may speedily become propitious to the nation ... and that in me and my brothers thou (the Seleucid King)
mayst stay the wrath of the Almighty which has been justly
brought upon our whole race."[5] It is said of the nine martyrs that
"through them was their country purified."[6] The old scribe Elea-
zar, prayed: "Make my blood their purification and take my soul
to ransom their souls."[7] The author of IV Maccabees says of them
all: "Our country was purified, they having as it were become a
ransom for our nation's sin, and through the blood of these
righteous men and the propitiation of their death divine Providence delivered Israel."[8] The famous tragedy of these martyr
deaths was in every one's mind in Jesus' day.

Did Jesus perhaps feel that his messianic execution would break
the heart of the people into a great national repentance such as
John the Baptist had called for and such as was currently expected
to introduce the New Age of the Kingdom of God?

Jesus considered his execution to be an experience that all his
disciples must share. He pictured to them a procession of men
each with the horizontal bar of his cross on his shoulder all going
out to execution; himself leading at the head of the procession:
"If any man would be my disciple, let him take up his cross and
follow me."[9]

The death of Jesus (soon followed by a resurrection) for a while
seemed likely to sweep the people into a great national repentance.
On one day 3000 declared themselves to be penitent disciples of
Jesus. But the penitential movement was checked by the obsti-
nacy of the ecclesiastical machine and by a great flaming up of

[5]II Maccabees 7. [7]IV Maccabees 6:29. [9]Mk. 8:34.
[6]IV Maccabees 1: 7–12. [8]IV Maccabees 17:22.

racial jealousy as the Christian movement began to get a start among non-Jews. The Jews as a nation raised the cry: "The Kingdom of God for the people of God," and steeled themselves against the whole Christian movement with its liberal tendencies.

However a remarkable phenomenon in personal religious experience emerged which has persisted ever since. This was discussed in the last lecture. People who were brought to repentance by the tragedy of the messianic death, who adopted the Messiah's way of living, and who let their personal devotion follow him out into the unseen world as their living Lord, experienced moral liberation from bondage to the selfish habit. They felt flowing into them out of the unseen world a great tide of moral incentive. They experienced an exultant sense of power to achieve an everlasting ethical success.

The problem for Christian thought is this: What rational connection is there between this experience of moral liberation, or ransom, and the execution of Jesus? In the history of Christian thought various answers have been given that have proved to be only temporarily and partially satisfactory. They have been answers in terms of the assumptions temporarily current in the thought world that produced them. This thought world, with its assumptions, passed away, and so, of course, these answers wore out; they became obsolete.

If there were time, it would be interesting to discuss the various answers given by Paul to this insistent question. As he traveled over the Roman Empire, wanting to become all things to all men that he might by all means save some,[10] he devised various ways of explaining the messianic crucifixion to different types of mind and previous religious experience. We shall return later to his most fundamental presentation.

Two illustrations taken from the long history of Christian thought on this subject will serve to show why certain theories were for a time useful and afterward ceased to be so.[11] For a long period it was assumed that Satan had certain vested rights in mankind. Before men could be freed from his control, or ransomed, it

---

[10] I Cor. 9:22.
[11] Cf. Shailer Mathews in *The American Journal of Theology*, Apr., 1921; Rashdall, *The Idea of the Atonement in Christian Theology.*

was necessary that he should be paid a suitable price, for the surrender of these rights. The price which God paid him was the person of God's Son. After Satan had received this price he found he could not hold it. The Son of God was more powerful than he was and broke away from him by a resurrection so that he really got no permanent remuneration for what he surrendered. The axiomatic assumptions on which this theory was based in time passed out of human thought and the theory ceased to be useful.

At a later stage in the development of human thought it was assumed without question that any injury to a man's honor made it necessary to afford him "satisfaction." Sin was a grievous injury to God's honor; therefore some one must offer him "satisfaction." No ordinary man was competent to do this, so God introduced Christ into the world as a being of infinite value. When God saw this superior being die on the cross, his honor was "satisfied." But feudal ideas have passed away. We are not impressed by a man who goes about demanding "satisfaction" for an insult. Dueling is no longer assumed to be a necessity among gentlemen of honor. We are much more impressed by the conduct of a man who is big enough to forgive an insult without exacting "satisfaction." The theory has ceased to be useful in our effort to understand God in his relation to the death of Jesus.

III

Paul's most fundamental explanation of the death of Jesus is implied in these words: "God was in Christ reconciling the world unto himself."[12] The same idea runs through the Gospel of John in such utterances as, "He that hath seen me hath seen the Father."[13] That is, the Life of God lifted itself up unhindered in the personality of Jesus. The consciousness of God pressed up into the consciousness of Jesus. One element in the consciousness of God was pain occasioned by the brutal selfishness of his human children.[14] This pain was directly shared by Jesus. His religious experience in connection with his death indicates extreme mental distress. It was mental distress amounting to agony that he felt in the dark Garden. His death occurred sooner than would have been expected if its main cause had been the physical suffering involved

[12]II Cor. 5: 18-21.   [13]John 14:9   [14]Cf. Lecture III.

in crucifixion. The crucified are said sometimes to have lived for days. It is natural to conclude that his speedy death was largely due to the spiritual suffering involved in sharing the feeling of God over the wrong doing of his human children.

This was no artificial, or official, imposition of the Life of God upon the soul of Jesus. It arose naturally out of Jesus' vital connection with the life of his countrymen and the Life of God. The soul of Jesus had always been aflame with the Life and Will of God. Now in these last hours when the crisis was at hand and the leaders of the ancient people of God were moving through the darkness to strike down the conscious expression of the Life of God, this element of pain in the consciousness of the Living God filled the spirit of Jesus with its holy passion. God was not doing something *to* Jesus, but something *in* Jesus. "God was in Christ." The utmost that a father can do to reform a son who has gone wrong is to show the son how he feels in the depths of his heart about the son's wrong doing. The single hour in which he brings visibly to the surface the deep intensity of his soul's holy passion is the hour which has no equal in morally moving power. The death hour of Jesus was such a time. "God was in Christ reconciling the world unto himself." Men have never been able to escape from the power of this hour. As they see its deep meaning more and more clearly, generation after generation, there is enlargement of its power to produce repentance, to reconcile men to God, to ransom them from bondage to the evil selfish will.

IV

What contribution does the death of Jesus make to human progress?

In general, it furnishes the supreme incentive in overcoming the selfishness that retards the progress of the human race toward its goal.

More specifically, it shows all the world the desperate ugliness of human selfishness. As we understand more exactly the situation in which the death of Jesus occurred we see clearly that it was occasioned by selfishness, the selfishness of scribes, priests and the Roman procurator. Because Jesus, in giving supreme expression to the good will of God, interfered with their getting what they wanted they struck him down with murderous hate. Jesus stood between a powerful theological, ecclesiastical, political machine and the gratification of its selfish desire for power; consequently with great glee it crucified the life out of him. If there were time to analyze the situation it would appear that not all scribes and priests were of this type; there were those to whom it seemed a religious and patriotic necessity to put Jesus down, but the dominant leaders were not of this sort. The priests and rabbis who walked in their long robes about the cross chuckling and gloating over their success were men of evil will. The selfishness that was in them, revealed in this dramatic repulsiveness to all the world, is essentially the same thing that is found in any selfish man in any age. We all see written large in this event the story of our own lives. The man with an inconspicuous cancerous pimple somewhere on his body may look at a repulsive case of highly developed cancer and realize the nature of his own disease.

If we look now at Jesus instead of at his assailants, the death of Jesus shows us how we must feel toward the evil doers of the community if we would work creatively with the Life of God in liberating men from the selfish habit that retards human progress. The supreme pain of the cross was the pain of the Life of God in the soul of Jesus. Jesus was convinced that this redemptive pain in the Life of God must rise also in the souls of his disciples. They must be "crucified in Christ." When we read in the newspapers about the criminal acts committed in the community, we are not to be merely unfeeling spectators. We should feel about these evil doers some measure of the very pain of God and let them know that we feel it. The church is not set simply to denounce bad men but to suffer the pain of God in their behalf. We have made selfish use of the cross. We have thought only of what we could get out of it for ourselves in terms of personal salvation. We have let this sense of personal salvation become a kind of anaesthetic that has dulled the pain of God that should have risen in our souls. *The church as a whole has yet to enter upon its great career of redemptive suffering.* Some sections of the church have already begun to walk the way of redemptive loving suffering.

V

The death of Jesus shows us not simply how disciples must feel, but it shows us also how we must make concrete sacrifice of definite values if we would work creatively with the Will of God in the sacrificial experiment essential to the progress of social evolution. Men in professions or other occupations in which success is measured in terms of money-income must be prepared so to do the work of these occupations as to sacrifice some income and sometimes much income. It may even be necessary sometimes to experience professional failure. As a professional Jewish Messiah Jesus was a failure. We must all sacrifice something and some of us may at any time be caught in a situation where we must sacrifice much. An editor who proposes to conduct a newspaper according to the principles of Jesus may suffer considerable diminution of income. To print only true news; to advocate no cause harmful to the common good; to advertise no harmful or useless article may result in meagre income. The lawyer who never tries to clear a guilty man but only to make for him a fair presentation of all ameliorating circumstances; who is willing to take the cases of poor people for the meagre fees that they are able to pay; who will settle inexpensively out of court so far as possible; who will work hard to secure the passage of good laws, though he be not paid for it, this Christian lawyer may make large financial sacrifices. The business man who gives always a square deal may make less money than a more unscrupulous competitor.

This sacrificial spirit incited by an intelligent understanding of the Cross of Christ preserves civilization. It nerves men to take their part in the great push of God in human progress toward a wise, powerful, honest and friendly world.

THE CHRISTIAN IDEA OF LIFE AFTER
DEATH AND HUMAN PROGRESS

Lecture IX

THE CHRISTIAN IDEA
OF LIFE AFTER DEATH AND
HUMAN PROGRESS

THE teaching of Jesus presents the prospect of a desirable existence after death for men of good will. It is called an eternal, or age-long life, a life running out into the ages of the everlasting Reign of God. For men of evil will it predicts a mysterious wreckage of personality in the Gehenna of fire. The terms in which these ideas are presented are those that were current in the Jewish apocalyptic literature of Jesus' day. In the present lecture we are to consider only the future life of the men of good will.

Can we conceive a view of the future life of men of good will that will be true to the essential teaching of Jesus and that will stimulate human progress?

It is sometimes asserted that the Christian view of immortality retards progress. Professor Leuba of Bryn Mawr College has said: "The modern belief of immortality costs more than it is worth. . . . Its disappearance from among the most civilized nations would be, on the whole, a gain."[1]

Is there a Christian view of immortality against which this objection has no force?

I

THREE QUESTIONS

Can we conceive a kind of existence after death that would seem desirable if it should prove feasible?

Is there any likelihood that there will be such a life after death?

[1]Leuba, *The Belief in God and Immortality,* pp. 290-291.

How would the expectation of such life affect human progress?

There is a logical propriety in taking up the questions in this order, for modern experience is teaching us that any really good thing may be regarded as practicable. Men long felt the desirability of flying swiftly through the air. For centuries it seemed an utter impossibility. One of the most distinguished scientists of modern times some twenty-five years ago felt not one iota of confidence that men would ever travel through the air by any other means than balloons. But now aeroplanes are so common that we often hurry on our way without looking up to see them when we hear them singing in the air above us. No really good thing is to be regarded as impossible. We are constantly seeing larger meaning in the words spoken by the rich employer to his servant in Jesus' parable of life: "I will set you over many things."

What then would be a desirable future life?

In the first place it would be some higher stage in the development of the present life. In the long evolution of life as we trace its history, there has been a rising life. This rising life has been along lines of advance indicated in lower stages of development. The best and highest forms of life in the lower stage have been the prophecy of that which was destined to become common and characteristic in the next higher stage.

We need, therefore, to see what is highest and best in life as we now know it and on the basis of what we see now conjecture what might be outstanding characteristics of life in the future.

Among the very best things that life in its present stage brings us is interesting work. The instinct to do work, to do business, to make things happen, is deep seated in human life. As life advances new forms of work are constantly appearing. Specialization is everywhere demanded by life. There must be many different kinds of physicians and lawyers. As knowledge advances there must be many different kinds of teachers. A single invention like the automobile calls into existence a dozen or more new forms of manufacturing and business. Furthermore, life in its present stage is more and more making it necessary for men to work together. Men are finding it necessary to work together in labor organizations, to combine in the joint ownership of capital through stocks and bonds, to work together in scientific societies.

Medical specialists are grouping their offices, and lawyers of different kinds are uniting in the same firms. Nations are uniting in leagues. All different forms of high grade work demand co-operative effort.

This co-operative effort involves a growing spirit of devotion to the common good. It may be the good of a small group, of a national or of an international group.

Moreover there is a growing sense among men of working together with a unified unseen energy. They may shrink from calling it God or attributing consciousness to it. But their conviction of its unity expresses itself in the idea of the universality of law. Many scientists go farther. Lord Kelvin spoke for many of his fellow scientists when he said:

> I cannot admit that with regard to the origin of life, science neither affirms nor denies Creative Power. It is not in dead matter that we live and move and have our being, but in the creating and directing power which science compels us to accept as an article of belief . . . If you think strongly enough you will be forced by science to the belief in God which is the foundation of all religion.

If we let these highest and best features of the present life shape our conjectures regarding a possible higher stage of life in the future we shall conceive it to be a high form of civilization in which multitudes of men work together with profound enthusiasm for the common good, with a deepening sense of God and his Christ. In this civilization vast enterprises will be originated and carried forward. Extensive expeditions will be organized; difficult problems will be solved; great sacrifices will be gladly made. There will be many failures followed by ultimate successes. There will be much hearty laughter. Men will be engaged in building the civilization of heaven, and working together with great gladness on the unfinished universe of God.

II

This conception of the future life is not liable to the reproach which is sometimes brought against other forms of the idea. It does not conceive of the future life as a reward for sacrifice in the present life. Those who must be bribed to live unselfishly here the promise of reward in the future life are certainly inferior to those who do right now without any such bribe. The future life as we have imagined it is simply a continued chance to keep on making whatever sacrificial effort may be called for by the common good in the future life. Any right minded man would regret the conclusion that there is no future life if he found himself obliged to reach such a conclusion. If he did not regret and resent such a conclusion he would be revealed as a person who is perfectly willing to stop working for the common good. No one who has really experienced the deep joy of living for the common welfare in this life can help resenting the idea that such activity must end, with physical death. Men like Professor Huxley and Herbert Spencer who felt themselves obliged to reach this conclusion protested against it. Herbert Spencer called it a "strange and repugnant conclusion."[2] Professor Huxley said: "It flashes across me at times with a sort of horror that in 1900 I shall probably know no more of what is going on than I did in 1800."[3]

Should we include the possession of some kind of body in our picture of a desirable future life? Since work on an environment is an essential feature of a desirable life, it would seem to follow that there must be a body to serve as a means of operating on an environment. The Christian apostle Paul conceived of a spirit-body of a higher order than the present flesh and blood body. Probably he conceived it to be a body responsive to the demands of "spirit" and adjustable to the conditions of a "spirit" world, whatever the nature of "spirit" may be. Ought we perhaps to think of personality in its present form as being a soul-body rather than a soul and body and as continuing, after what we call death, to be a soul-body that has simply sloughed off in death a temporary phase of itself?

Where ought we to think that a desirable future life would be lived? Should we think of it as localized in some other planet? Or as all about us in the mysterious environment which we perceive so imperfectly with our present organs of perception? These very organs show that there are potential colors and sounds that our physical eyes and ears do not perceive. We know that lower orders of life live in a world that they apparently do not perceive.

[2]Spencer, *Facts and Comments*, p. 301.
[3]Huxley, *Life and Letters of Thomas H. Huxley*, II, p. 67.

The oyster is in the world of the fish but does not know it. The fish is in the world of the horse but does not know it. The man on the horse's back is in a physical world of physical forces which the horse seems unable to recognize or manipulate. So we men may have all about us a world of which we have no adequate perception. "Our eyes are dense and dim, and cannot see it as it is." All this is in the realm of speculation. We are simply endeavoring to conceive of a kind of future life that would seem to us desirable, whether feasible or not.

III

Is there any likelihood that there will be some such life after death?

Is there anything in the nature of personality, as we now know it, that is decisively for or against the probability of the survival of consciousness after death?

What we call the body evidently disintegrates in physical death. Does personality in some form, whether with or without some sort of body, survive this dissolution? Certain phenomena of personal existence indicate the entire dependence of the so-called mind upon the body. It is through the body that the mind makes its most obvious connections with the world around it. Because the so-called mind depends on the body for so much, it is supposed that it depends upon the body for everything and therefore could not exist without the body. On the other hand, there are some things that indicate the independence of the mind. The mind or will uses the brain as an instrument or tool. Something in the personality decides to pack away a new language in the brain. This something knows that a section of the brain can be so used and determines by severe study day after day to produce this result in the brain. Such phenomena and others lead men like Professor Bergson to conclude that the mind is something much more than the body, that it is like a cone the mere apex of which touches the brain and so receives impressions from the physical world.[4] Physicians like Dr. J. A. Hadfield, surgeon in the British Army, find evidence of the superiority of mind to body in the fact that mental emotions produce physical effects; that through hypnotism physi-

[4]Bergson, *Mind Energy,* p. 73, etc.

cal pain is eliminated; that through mental suggestion blisters are produced. He finds in the increasing ascendency of mind over body, both in the development of the individual embryo and in social evolution a reason for conjecturing that the mind will finally be able to dispense with the body altogether.[5]

It seems right to say that there is nothing in the nature of personality as we know it now which decisively forbids all possibility of life after death, if reason for such a conjecture should appear elsewhere.

Are there any real communications from the dead? It is not easy to answer this question because we do not know what influences may be operating upon us to produce consciousness at any particular moment. We know that we are in the midst of a mysterious environment the nature of which we do not clearly understand. It is not inconceivable that our dead friends may be influencing us in all the warp and woof of our daily living. But do we receive any specific recognizable word from them? Most of us would have to reply that we do not. We find certain distinguished men like Sir Oliver Lodge in whose integrity and scientific judgment we have confidence, declaring with conviction that they do receive communication from the dead. But such conviction is not widespread. Certainly, however, no one would be willing to close the case against immortality, because conscious communication with the dead is not an established fact. We are too keenly aware of the mystery of our environment and of the mystery of personality to be willing to do this.

IV

We are therefore thrown back upon certain general considerations that have been recognized as making the future life possible or probable.

First of all it seems to us unjust that those who sacrifice so much to produce a better order of life should have no part in that better order. We do not feel this injustice so much in the case of those who live in comfort and make no painful sacrifice. But multitudes do experience great and unrelieved privation in the onward

[5]Referred to in Streeter, *Reality,* pp. 280, 339n, 343. Cf. also Streeter, *Immortality,* p. 17.

press of life toward a better order. It seems to us particularly unjust that Jesus should not survive death to have any participation in the life he sacrificed so much to secure for men.

It seems to us also a shameful waste of supreme values when high character, developed at great cost, is utterly extinguished by death. A man after long discipline has learned to love and live the unselfish life; he wants to continue living it after he dies and is capable of doing so. Why should he in a moment become nothing? Especially when we think of man as the result of a long evolutionary process, it seems intolerably wasteful to extinguish him in death.

Perhaps we could forget the apparent injustice and overlook the waste in view of the fact that nevertheless a higher race is being evolved. Individuals make their contribution to the life of the race and then become extinct at death. The fruit of their effort is conserved in the lives of those who succeed them.

The validity of this idea depends upon the future of the race. What will ultimately become of the human race? If the planet on which the human race lives should ultimately become uninhabitable then there would be nothing left of the long evolution of life. If individual men live on after death, then, no matter what ultimately becomes of the planet, countless generations of valuable human beings will have been preserved and this planet with its precious human civilization will have made a contribution to the life of the universe to which it sustains such intimate physical relationship.

It may be that the planet will never become uninhabitable, or that the human race might find some way to migrate before the earth should become unfit for life. Our present ventures into the air might be preliminary to a general migration! However, so far as we can see, there could never be a perfect civilization at any time or anywhere if belief in personal immortality should cease. Neither on this planet nor on any other could men push far on toward higher stages of civilization, if it should be realized that men do not continue to live after death, that death is the end of friendship. *A perfect civilization, or a civilization continually approaching perfection, is one in which all members are growing toward perfection of relationship.* Perfection of relationship means perfection of love. If this great love is developed and then the person loved is known to have been utterly extinguished in death great and hopeless suffering will result and no perfection of civilization will be possible. It is probable that men would refuse to love in any high degree when they realized that those loved ones were certain to be destroyed, in which case no perfect civilization would be possible. Love would be confined to its lower forms. Friendships high in quality and degree could not thrive. Men are sure to find out the facts ultimately. If it be a fact that there is no personal immortality, men will finally be sure of it and adjust life to the narrow dimensions imposed upon it by an absolutely certain mortality.

Personal immortality of some sort is a practical certainty for those who hold the Christian idea of God. Two things are involved in this idea, love and power. This combination of love and power in the case of God is symbolized by the word "Father." We have seen that love means wanting a person, wanting to be with him, wanting to see him become the best his nature is capable of being, wanting to work with him in pushing life forward. Since the fatherly God loves individuals he would be constantly sorrowing if they drop out of existence in an endless series of deaths. Something of great value that he had produced by the long expensive process of evolution and very much wanted to keep he would be steadily and hopelessly losing. It might be supposed that he would be indifferent to this loss because he knows that others are constantly being born. But the Christian idea of God involves the certainty that he loves these very ones who are about to die; that no others can permanently take their place with him. This is the basic meaning of individuality. A mother's love necessarily involves sorrow for the loss of her dead child, and her sorrow does not disappear with the assurance that other children will be born to her.

Personal immortality is necessarily involved in the Christian conviction of the power of God as well as the love of God. It would be an utterly un-Christian type of God that had not power enough to keep his friends in existence. It is unthinkable that the friendship of a man with God should be utterly destroyed in an instant by the crashing of a bullet through the man's brain. The

God who has power enough to bring life up to the high form of individual existence with all its high aspirations, surely has power enough to maintain that existence after the incident of physical death. The Christian proposition of the Fatherhood of God has as its necessary corollary the immortality of the child of God. It was upon this view of the case that Jesus seems to have rested his own triumphant conviction of immortality. "God," he said, "is not a God of dead persons, but of living."

V

How would the expectation of such a future life affect human progress?

Human progress, as we have seen, is secured when men work creatively in the evolution of an intelligent, powerful, honest and friendly civilization. The elements in such effort are intelligent, effective work and reliable invincible good will. Looking forward to such a life after death as we have described leads a man to do the best work of which he is capable now. The way in which he does his work here and now determines his chance for work in the life after death. Slovenly habits of work here mean, in the nature of the case, a lessened fitness for the high opportunities that we suppose will confront men there. It is as if the superintendent of a large hospital should visit a student in the midst of his medical course and promise him a desirable position later in the great hospital if he does his work well in the medical school. Or it is as if a student in an engineering school should be visited by the manager of a great manufacturing plant and should be promised large opportunity later if he succeeds in his work as a student. That is, the kind of work we are to have in the future life depends on the way in which we do the work we have here and now.

Looking forward to such a future life incites a man to develop the invincible reliable good will essential to human progress now. He knows that only men of reliable good will can find footing in the enterprises of the life to come. His chance for high grade work then depends upon his learning to be a man of reliable good will now. He must learn to get along with all kinds of people here and now, for there will doubtless be all kinds of people in the larger world of the future life. There is no reason to suppose that death removes all disagreeable peculiarities of temperament and differences of culture.

The expectation of such a life leading on into larger opportunities and greater responsibilities makes small things seem small and lose their power to irritate. Irritation due to the small frictions of life hinders progress now. It tends to spoil the fine work and the fine friendships that are essential to the best progress. But when one learns to see irritating circumstances against the background of an eternal career, a new patience begins to possess his soul. Nervous haste gives way to the leisurely temper that goes forward without haste and without weariness. The man of the immortal hope has come under the glad spell of eternity.

In general, the expectation of such a future gives an uplifting sense of the bigness of life and importance of personality which lead us to do our utmost. Life stretches out to an extent that seems suitable to the vastness of the universe. The people with whom we have to do assume an importance commensurate with the size of the universe in which they live and the problems which they study with an ever deepening interest.

We see, then, that daily life here and now is a situation devised and evolved by the infinite ingenuity of God to prepare men for a vast inheritance of power in the future by teaching them to use power in an honest and friendly way. And so we push on now to do our utmost along the great lines of human progress that we may be fit for a place as everlasting creators in the unfinished universe of God.

Section II

Studies

THE STORY OF PAUL'S LIFE

THE STORY OF PAUL'S LIFE

A BOY IN THE TARSUS GHETTO

NOT many years after the humble carpenter's wife tended her first-born in the manger of a Bethlehem *khan* (inn), an old aristocratic family of Pharisees welcomed a baby boy into their ample home in the ghetto of Tarsus, the beautiful capital of the great Roman province, Cilicia. They were of the tribe of Benjamin, and gave the boy the name of their famous tribal ancestor, King Saul. The father was also a Roman citizen, and gave his young son in addition the Roman name, Paulus. The family possessed Tarsian citizenship as well, and must therefore have been sufficiently well-to-do to meet the property qualification for citizenship in Tarsus. As loyal Tarsians they were probably somewhat influenced by the distinguished university and general educational atmosphere of the city, even though cherishing conservative Pharisaic family traditions. Acts 21:39

Acts 23:6

In the home this Pharisaic family, unlike many far from the fatherland, still spoke the Aramaic of Palestine as well as Greek ("a Hebrew of Hebrews"). And in accordance with Jewish thrift, Saul, like other boys of the ghetto, was taught a trade. He learned to cut and stitch the coarse canvas of the province into tents. Phil. 3:5

Acts 18:3

A STUDENT IN THE HOLY CITY

At the age of perhaps thirteen or fifteen, the lad left the brilliant city with the clear, beautiful Cydnus river running through it and the fertile plains lying about it, and came to the rather bleak and waterless Judæan plateau of the fatherland. But he came to the city of his dreams, the Holy City! The sensitive, highstrung lad wandered through the beautiful, white marble colonnades about Jehovah's House. He saw the smoke rise from the great altar, heard the silver trumpets of the priests calling to prayer, saw the richly robed temple officials, and kneeled with the multitudes on the pavement at the hour of incense. He heard the great rabbis teach in the synagogues. The influence of his family secured for him a place among the students of one of the most famous of them. With other ardent young Pharisees, he gave himself up in passionate devotion to the study of the law of Moses. The dignified, appreciative patrons of budding rabbinic genius smiled upon the young Benjamite from Tarsus when they saw him outstrip-

Gal.
1:14

ping his fellow-students.

A Fierce Defender of the Law

Probably Saul from time to time made long visits to the Tarsus home. On his return from one of these visits, he found Jerusalem

Mk.
3:21

agitated over a strange religious madness that had come upon some of its inhabitants. A seemingly deluded Messianic aspirant had gained a large popular following. The fanatic had been a severe critic of the rabbis, and was himself reported to have been lax in the observance of the holy law. The men who were Saul's ideals of religious propriety and orthodoxy had publicly declared Jesus to be in league with Satan. God had endorsed this declaration by openly cursing him,—Jesus had met his death in naked shame on the accursed cross.

Matt.
27:62f.

His followers, however, instead of being dispersed by this catastrophe, pretended that God had raised him from the dead, and began industriously to organize a rapidly spreading Messianic movement in the name of Jesus. Many of the adherents of this new movement denied any lack of reverence for the law, but one of the most persuasive of their leaders, a man named Stephen, seemed surely to have asserted that Jesus would return to destroy the temple and abrogate its sacred ritual. The supreme court of the nation promptly put him to death, and young Rabbi Saul, who had been prominent in securing his execution, began a most rigorous campaign of extermination throughout the city. Every day he was busily engaged in the synagogue courts passionately calling

Acts
26:11

upon Nazarenes to curse Jesus or die. When the movement seemed to be thoroughly demoralized in Jerusalem, Saul determined to visit the ghetto of every large city to which any of these renegade enemies of the law might have fled, and rid it of the Nazarene pest.

THE TRANSFORMING INTERVIEW WITH JESUS

The first city which Rabbi Saul proposed to visit was Damascus. But just before he reached the city, he had an experience that absolutely and permanently transformed him. He saw Jesus himself standing in glory unmistakably Messianic on the threshold of his soul, and heard his voice in homely Aramaic speech, resounding through all the inner chambers of his being. Jesus was indeed alive as the Nazarenes had said, and was therefore God's Messiah. To Rabbi Saul's amazement, Jesus did not destroy him on the spot, nor did he even blind him for life, but he treated him with kindness, and in the days immediately following produced in him the conviction that he was to be honored with important responsibility for the propagation of the Messianic movement. This filled the young rabbi with profound gratitude. He then and there became "Jesus Christ's bond-slave." Moreover, his experience with Jesus turned out to be no temporary interview, but the beginning of a permanent sense of the spiritual presence of Jesus, which he carried with him through all subsequent years. This initial interview with Jesus seems to have occurred a year or two after the death of Jesus,—that is, in the year A.D. 30 or 31.

Acts 26:14

AN EVANGELIST AMONG HIS COUNTRYMEN

Rabbi Saul at once began to speak with enthusiasm for the Nazarenes to his countrymen in the Damascus synagogues, but soon withdrew into Arabia,—perhaps some portion of Arabia that was in the immediate vicinity of Damascus. He returned to Damascus from this short sojourn in Arabia, and three years after the interview with Jesus went back again to the Holy City. The purpose of this visit to Jerusalem was twofold. He wished to communicate with Peter, the leader of the Nazarenes. He probably wished to describe to Peter his sense of appointment by Jesus to important responsibility in connection with the Messianic movement, and to come to some understanding with Peter about the discharge of this responsibility. Furthermore, it seemed to him that he could, by the story of his Damascus experience, win the rabbis of Jerusalem to the new movement.

Gal. 1:17

Gal. 1:18

Gal. 1:18

In this latter expectation he was bitterly disappointed. After

Acts 22:17-20

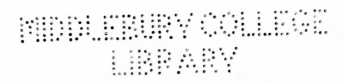

Gal. 1:18
Acts 9:29

only two weeks, he was obliged to leave the city in order to avoid assassination. He went back to his friends in Tarsus. If his father was still living, the interview must have been a painful one. His father felt that the money spent on his son's education had been far worse than wasted. Saul had disgraced the proud family, disappointed their love, and outraged their deepest religious convictions.

What the young Nazarene rabbi did in these next years is not

Gal. 1:21

clear. He evidently preached in Syria and Cilicia, and probably for ten or twelve years (A.D. 34–44). This preaching was mainly among Jews, for the author of Acts says nothing about Saul's connection with Gentile evangelization at this time, although the book of Acts purports to show how Gentile evangelization began. Saul's own account of his life in the first chapter of Galatians is sometimes thought to indicate that he did begin extensive work among Gentiles immediately after the Damascus experience. The narrative in Galatians, however, is extremely condensed, and does not necessarily demand such an interpretation.

Saul had learned in Damascus that he was to be connected with some general turning of the Gentile world to the Messianic movement of Jesus. He would naturally have thought that the Gentile world would come into the Messianic movement as Jewish proselytes. The twelve apostles evidently thought that Jesus' command

Matt. 28:19

to disciple all nations would be fulfilled by making Jewish Christian proselytes of them, and they waited before beginning to obey the command for some general turning of Gentiles to Judaism. It would naturally have seemed to them that they could not urge Gentiles to become Jewish Christian proselytes until the Jews themselves, as a nation, had identified themselves with Jesus' Messianic movement. This was probably Saul's view also.

He doubtless often found in his synagogue audiences a little group of Gentiles who worshiped Jehovah without becoming Jewish proselytes. Perhaps he discovered that they were interested in his message about the Messianic kingdom of Jesus, and he may have encouraged them to think that they too could believe in Jesus. According to the author of Acts there were certain venture-

Acts
11:19–21

some preachers who did just this in one great Syrian city, Antioch. Gentile Christians appear a little later in other parts of Syria

and Cilicia, and they may have been a by-product of Saul's preach- Acts 15:23
ing, as well as of the preaching of these other men whom the author of Acts brings into prominence, and who probably preached
in other cities than Antioch.

But in the main, these years (A.D. 34–44) were spent among his
own countrymen, preaching in many synagogues and gradually
making the readjustment in his Pharisaic theology necessitated by
his new Christian viewpoint. Many of the hardships mentioned in
II Corinthians 11:24–27 may have been endured in this period. He
suffered shipwreck on some coasting vessel. He was slowly acquir- v. 25
ing the experience that fitted him for twenty years of action to follow, more vital and far-reaching in its influence upon the life
of the world than has been the action of any man who has since
lived.

THE APOSTLE TO THE GENTILE WORLD

These years of preparatory evangelization terminated in a year
of rich experience with the large church in Antioch, whose mem- Acts 11:25, 26
bership included both Christian Jews and a considerable number
of Christian Gentiles who, though not Jewish proselytes, had been
regular attendants upon the Jewish synagogue before they ever
heard of Christianity. From this church as a new center, Saul began his great work as an apostle to the Gentile world.

In the Roman Province Galatia.—A company of Antioch brothers stood on the wharf and waved farewell to Saul and Barnabas,
and the latter's young kinsman, John Mark of Jerusalem. The
travelers preached their way through the Jewish communities of
the lumber camps and mining towns of Cyprus, the old island
home of Barnabas, and the scene of some previous Christian Acts 4:36
Acts 11:20
preaching. After an exciting experience with a Roman procurator, Acts
they sailed across to the mainland. There Paul found his health 13:4-13
breaking, but rather than return to Antioch he determined to
search for more healthful surroundings in the highlands of South Gal. 4:13
Galatia. John Mark, who perhaps shared the prejudice of the Jerusalem Christians against Paul, and also resented the increasing Acts 9:26
leadership of Paul in a group of which his honored kinsman
Barnabas seemed to him to be rightful leader, was not in a mood
to follow a sick man on any wild chase after health through the

brigand-infested passes and swollen streams of the Taurus mountains. He consequently turned back to Jerusalem.

In four great cities of South Galatia, and their outlying districts, Paul and Barnabas established Christian churches. At first they preached only to Jews and to the Jehovah-worshiping Gentiles in the synagogue, as they had learned to do in Syria. But here in South Galatia, as Professor Ramsay has shown, the author of Acts represents Paul and Barnabas to have discovered that any Gentile _{Acts} without previous connection with the synagogue, and without expectation of future connection with it, could nevertheless become a Christian. This work in Galatia probably occurred between the years A.D. 45 and 49.

Acts 13:44-49

Rumors of the radical step taken by Paul and Barnabas greatly disturbed an ultra conservative minority in the Jerusalem church. They raised the cry: "The Messiah's Kingdom for the Messiah's People!" and started out forthwith on a campaign to convince all Gentile Christians that their Christian hope was vain unless by circumcision they were incorporated into the body of the Messiah's people. This determined band of narrow-minded enthusiasts was stopped by Paul and Barnabas at Antioch on the Orontes, and was persuaded to submit the matter to the leading Nazarenes to be assembled in Jerusalem for its consideration. This Jerusalem meeting, held probably in the year A.D. 48 or 49, declared decisively against the contention of this minority. They seem to have left it uncertain, however, whether uncircumcised Gentile Christians *might not be better Christians if* they should be circumcised, and whether uncircumcised Gentile Christians could expect to enjoy free social intercourse with Jewish Christians. The first of these uncertainties led, in South Galatia, to the situation discussed in the Epistle to the Galatians, and the second to the misunderstanding and severe reproaches alluded to in Galatians 2:11–14.

Acts 15:1, 2

Acts 15:22, 29

In the Roman Provinces Macedonia and Achaia.—During a period of between two and three years following the Jerusalem Council alluded to above, Paul, assisted part of the time at least by Luke, Silas, and Timothy, carried on extensive operations among the Gentiles of Macedonia and Achaia. He selected strategically located cities. In each case his work began naturally in the ghetto

Acts 16-18

where a prepared audience always awaited him, but it soon disconnected itself from the synagogue.

In Philippi he gathered a group of Christians, small but always peculiarly sympathetic with him and his needs. A larger group was formed in the great commercial center, Thessalonica, which quickly became famous all through the Levant and beyond. Paul was driven out of this city by its officials before his work was done, and slipped away to the quiet town of Berea, hoping soon to have opportunity to return to Thessalonica and complete his work, but "Satan hindered" him. Driven out from Berea by plots of assassination, he spent a few weeks in Athens, preaching in the ghetto and debating with the university professors and students in the *agora,* but with little result. From the university city he went on to the commercial metropolis, Corinth. He came to the great city with many misgivings, especially after his comparative failure in the university town. He had reason to feel misgivings, for it was the most difficult piece of work he ever attempted. Once in its course his magnificent courage failed him. He was about to leave the city, fearing assassination or lynching, but his Lord made him stay, and finally he won here his chief apostolic triumph.

Phil.
1:3-5
2:12
4:15-18
I Thess.
1:8

I Thess.
2:17, 18

Acts
17:17,
18, 32-34
I Cor.
2:1-3

Acts
18:9, 10

During this period he wrote from Corinth his two letters to the Thessalonian Christians, and at the close of the period from the home church in Syrian Antioch, his indignant but tender letter to the Galatian churches.[1]

In the Roman Province Asia.—Paul had long planned to work in Asia, but had not felt that God was ready to send him there. Now for about three years, perhaps from A.D. 52 to 55, Paul conducted a campaign with Ephesus as his headquarters, which affected the life of the entire province. During this period the headstrong church in Corinth, Paul's perplexity as well as his pride, made him perhaps the most serious trouble of his life. This trouble may have had something to do with producing the attack of illness, from which for a time he had no hope of recovering. Pharisaic Christians, presumably from Jerusalem, and one especially offensive man in particular, appeared in Corinth, and nearly

Acts 16:6
Acts 20:31

Acts
19:10

II Cor.
1:8-10

II Cor.
11:4

---

[1]Unless, indeed, this letter was written in Athens or Corinth, before those to the Thessalonians.

persuaded the church to disown all connection with Paul. From Paul's letters to the Corinthians, one written from Ephesus and the other from Macedonia, it seems that Paul sent several messengers to Corinth, and made one flying visit himself. He, or more probably his messenger, Timothy, was grievously insulted by some member of the church, and for a time the church sympathized with the offender. A very vigorous letter from Paul, which for a

II Cor. 7:5–12 2:5–10 time he regretted writing, and of which the last four chapters of our II Corinthians are perhaps a portion, brought them to terms.

Acts 20:2, 3 The winter succeeding this vigorous correspondence Paul spent in Corinth. From a letter written to the Christians in Rome at the end of this winter in Corinth, it appears that Paul planned next to establish a mission in Spain, and hoped to use the Roman church as a base of supplies. Also during all this general period of his work, money was being collected in all the Gentile churches from

I Cor. 16:1 Galatia westward, as a conciliatory gift to the Jewish Christians in Jerusalem. Paul hoped by means of this expression of good will to bind the Jewish and Gentile churches together before he left this part of the world. If he could only be so fortunate as to see this result secured, he could with good courage undertake on the western edge of the world to finish his apostolic commission to

Rom. 15:18–33 the Gentiles of the Empire, and so be ready for his Lord's return.

The Prisoner of Jesus Christ

Just at this critical period, when every ounce of energy and every minute of time seemed needed for this last and crowning work of his life, Paul suddenly found himself in prison. This was no new experience, for he had been in prisons oft, but this imprisonment dragged on finally through five long years. It began in the Roman barracks of Jerusalem, near which he was rescued by Roman soldiers from the Jewish mob that was savagely pounding him to death in the street. The imprisonment continued for two years in Cæsarea, included a perilous voyage to Italy with shipwreck, and two years more in Rome waiting for the decision of the Emperor, to whom he had, as a Roman citizen, made appeal.

The reason for his countrymen's hatred of him was his old insistence that *Gentiles need not become Jews in order to become Christians.* The acceptance of Jesus' Messiahship had ceased to be a mortal sin in the eyes of orthodox Jews. They were even ready gladly to tolerate Christianity if, by requiring circumcision of its Gentile converts, it would allow itself to serve as a feeder for Juda- ism. But this perversion of Christianity Paul uncompromisingly resisted. He would not allow Christianity to degenerate into a Jewish sect. He saw in it *a world religion* for which Judaism had been simply a temporary preparation, and in which Judaism must itself be merged. Gal. 5:11 6:12

These dreary years in prison were, nevertheless, not the least fruitful in Paul's fruitful life. From his prison house, through his lieutenants and his letters, he effectively inspired Christians all over the empire to be true to Jesus Christ. His literary productions in this period have vastly enriched the religious thought of the world. They consist of four letters, two to the Christians of Philippi and Colosse, and the so-called Epistle to the Ephesians, and the beautiful personal note to Philemon. Eph. 4:1 Col. 4:18

THE END

How Paul's life ended, the New Testament does not tell. The book of Acts does not give the result of his appeal to Caesar, but leaves him in the city of Rome after two years of imprisonment, during which time he had been "teaching the things of the Lord Jesus" with all his life-long "boldness." No date in the life of Paul can be established with unquestioned exactness. Quite possibly these two years in Rome were 59–61.[2] There is some reason for supposing that these two years of prison life ended with Paul's release, and were followed by another period of missionary activity in which the East was revisited, according to the expectation expressed in Philippians and Philemon, and the Spanish mission established. To this period would then be assigned the letter to Titus and the first of the two to Timothy. On this hypothesis Paul was arrested and brought to Rome as a prisoner a second time, during which imprisonment the second letter to Timothy was written, shortly before his death. Acts 28:30, 31 Phil. 2:23, 24 Philemon 22

In the year 64 or 65, after the great fire in Rome,[3] he who had for many years "died daily," found himself finally facing a Roman

---

[2]So Turner in Hastings' *Dictionary of the Bible,* or A.D. 60–62, Ramsay.
[3]By another reckoning in the year 67.

headsman. The most famous Roman citizen who ever lived was about to die, sentenced by the most infamous of Rome's emperors. But something of far more profound significance was about to happen. The great apostle of Jesus Christ was about to pass into the unseen world, and make devoutly triumphant report to his Lord.

PAUL THE FOUNDER AND HIS FOUNDATION

XI

PAUL THE FOUNDER AND
HIS FOUNDATION

W E have come together tonight to remember a master
workman who laid here, patiently and wisely, a foundation on which others are now with equal patience
and wisdom building a superstructure. On a recent "Founder's
Day" attention was directed to the life and services of this master workman. Tonight I think we shall be doing what Dr. Schauffler would have us do if we go far back to a master workman
of the first Christian decades who loved to think of himself as a
Founder by the grace of God. "According to the grace of God that I Cor.
has been given to me," he said, "as a wise master-builder, I have ${}^{3:10}_{v.\ 11.}$
laid a foundation." What that foundation was he never wearied
of telling: "Other foundation can no man lay than that which is
laid, which is Jesus the Christ." Paul the Founder and Jesus Christ,
his Foundation.

Paul's life work was to put Jesus Christ under the lives of
men. Or, to drop the figure, Paul's mind and life were absolutely
dominated by the personality of Jesus Christ, and his ambition
was to make this personality dominant in the life of every other
man. The question of the hour is: What did Jesus Christ mean
to Paul? What was Paul's idea of Jesus Christ?

The name Jesus Christ is made up of two parts, a personal
name and a title. The personal name is "Jesus," sometimes appearing in the form "Joshua" or "Jeshuah"—a commonplace personal name among the ancient Jews and in some countries still
almost as common as "George" and "William" in our country.
The title is "Christ" or "The Christ," that is the anointed or
kingly man. We say Christ Jesus or King Jesus as we say Kaiser
Wilhelm or King George.

In the days before Paul began his career as a founder, while he was still an orthodox non-Christian Jew he had an idea of the Christ and also an idea of Jesus. He had always looked forward to a time when the Christ would appear, and he had recently heard much about the Galilean Jew named "Jesus"; but to put these two names together and say "Christ Jesus," as some of his countrymen were doing seemed to him horrible blasphemy. If we would rightly understand what Paul's idea of Christ Jesus finally was, we must first ask two questions about him in the period before he became a Christian: What did he at that time think of Christ? What did he at that time think of Jesus? Picture him, if you will, on the morning of that day which was second in importance to but one other day in all his life,—I mean the day on which at high noon as he was riding his donkey along the hot Syrian road near Damascus, Christ Jesus stood in his path as Lord and put him under gently omnipotent arrest, a day second only to that on which, years afterward from some spot near the walls of Rome, he went to be at home with this same Lord.

The first question, then, is this: As Paul was riding across the plain toward Damascus what idea of the Christ was it that filled his mind? Paul was what the Jews called a Rabbi—that is, a Rab, a great man or master because of his knowledge of the Law of Moses. Saul was a young rabbi but was already famous among the students who flocked to the Holy City to study Moses under the great teachers of the Law. What idea of the Christ did these great rabbis of Jerusalem have as they talked together walking through the colonnades of the temple courts or sitting in the synagogues? It is difficult to tell for the ideas which people had of the coming Christ were very various and confused. Some thought that there never would be a Christ and that the popular expectation of a Christ was superstitious fanaticism. Others hoped that there never would be, for he would only disturb things that were better left alone. The high priest and his adherents were well satisfied with things as they were. Their revenues were large and the powerful Romans were their generous patrons. They felt no need of a Christ.

But by far the larger part of the nation expected a Christ. Some thought that from a branch of David's family now scattered here and there over the land, living in poverty and having only some local village prestige, a son would be born, grow to manhood, call the nation about his standard, give it liberty and lead it into righteousness. Others had a different idea. They thought that the Christ was in heaven where he had been kept by God from time everlasting and that he would on some great day suddenly descend from out the sky in glory with a great shout, perhaps stop for a moment over Jehovah's holy temple and then leap from its top down among the worshipping thousands of the people to purify them and destroy their enemies. We know that Paul had an idea somewhat like this after he became a Christian and this fact perhaps indicates that before he became a Christian he was one of those who held that the Christ was already existent in the heavens.

There probably were Jews who tried to combine these two views—*David's Son* and *The Christ from Heaven*. They may have thought that the Christ from Heaven would take possession of the body of some obscure man among the descendants of David, for it was a common idea that beings from the Spirit world did take possession of human bodies. Demons were thought to go in and out of the bodies of men. Herod thought that the spirit Mt. 14:1-2 of the dead Baptist had returned and taken possession of the body Mt. of Jesus. Many thought that the spirit of one of the old dead proph- 16:14 ets had taken possession of the body of Jesus. This son of David into whose human body the Christ had entered and who was hidden away among the people might suddenly appear as a great reformer or possibly he might shine out in heavenly glory. There would certainly be a sudden emergence of some sort from obscur- Jo. 7:27 ity. "When the Christ cometh no one knoweth whence he is," the people of Jerusalem said according to John's Gospel. As has been said, the ideas of the Jews about the coming Christ were very confused and vague,—as much so as are our ideas about the end of the world or what heaven will be like.

While we do not know in full detail what conception of the Christ we may ascribe to young Rabbi Saul, one thing is certain. Since he was a Pharisee, a son and grandson of Pharisees, his chief interest was in the Mosaic Law. He says himself that he was famous for devotion to the law among the law students of Gal. 1:14 Jerusalem. "I advanced in the Jew's religion beyond many of mine own age among my countrymen, being more exceedingly zealous for the traditions of my fathers." His ambition was to see every individual in the nation scrupulously obedient to the law of Moses as the rabbis understood it,—keeping the Sabbath perfectly, fasting every Monday and Thursday, giving a tenth of all his income. Really the chief need of a Christ that many rabbis felt was to help them enforce the Law; to secure such political freedom from foreign rule as would make it easy for the people to obey the Law; to root out of the nation all who would not do what the rabbis said the Law of Moses commanded; in other words the Christ would give the rabbis a clear field. He would be their all-powerful assistant and patron.

If we may suppose that an idea which is reported in the Talmud some centuries after Saul's time really prevailed as early as Saul's day, then we know that Saul and his fellow rabbis felt that the reason the Christ's coming had been so long delayed was the fact that the people were impenitent and kept the law so imperfectly. The Talmud says, that if the nation would only repent and keep two Sabbaths perfectly, the Christ would come. That this idea did prevail in Saul's day is indicated by one statement in the New Acts 3:19-20 Testament. Peter said, "Repent ye, therefore . . . that the Lord may send the Christ who has been appointed for you." If Rabbi Saul held this view, then his fierce indignation against the Nazarenes is explained as I shall show in a moment.

Our answer to the first question, then, is this: During the busy months just preceding the great crisis in his life near Damascus, the idea of the Christ that filled Paul's mind was probably this: The Christ was a glorious being living with God in the highest heaven. Some day when his people were prepared for him by penitence and the obedient keeping of the holy Law of Moses, this glorious Christ would appear in the earth. He might appear in the body of some man of the David family or he might come swift and straight from the heavens. He would gather the holy nation about him, establish them in the Law of Moses, and make them a great missionary people who would go to the earth's end and teach all men everywhere to keep the Law of Moses and become faithful Jewish proselytes. Those who would not keep the Law of Moses would in some way be destroyed from the earth perhaps by physical force such as Saul was now using upon the

Nazarenes or in the twinkling of an eye by a fiery gust of God's wrath from the heavens. No earthly power—not even that of Roman legions—would be able to stand before these hosts of righteous missionary Jews and their allies led by the mighty Christ.

Or, perhaps Saul did not think that the Christ would engage in any such missionary campaign as this, but rather that so soon as the Jews scattered all over the world, gave themselves up without reserve to keeping the Law of Moses, the Christ in his heavenly glory and without any merciful missionary campaign among the Gentiles would instantly destroy all God's enemies, call the righteous from their graves, transform the bodies of righteous men living on the earth and the earth itself into the heavenly glory of the spirit world. The new heaven and the new earth would be instantly revealed. God himself would come down from the highest heaven and tabernacle with his glorified and holy Jewish people. Whether or not the Christ would first conduct a missionary campaign among foreign nations, he would finally and in some way put an end to this present evil world of flesh and blood, for flesh and blood could not inherit the kingdom of God. This world of flesh and blood with its decaying trees, crumbling rocks, and perishable human bodies—this earth and air through which Satan and his angels freely ranged, would be displaced by an eternal spirit world no longer under bondage to sin, decay and death. The spirit world above in which God, his Christ, and the holy angels lived would swallow up the world of flesh and blood in glory.

We have asked what was Saul's idea of the Christ, and we can now ask the second question: What was young Rabbi Saul's idea of Jesus as he rode across the Syrian plain under the hot forenoon sun? One sentence gives the reply: Jesus was the arch enemy of the Christ. Jesus had opposed the rabbis in their efforts to secure from the nation such obedience to the Law of Moses as would bring the Christ from heaven to earth. Some of Jesus' friends would have said that he had not opposed the Law of Moses, but only the rabbis' interpretation of the Law of Moses. But the rabbis were sure that their interpretation of the Law of Moses was the true one, and that to oppose their teaching was to oppose the

Law itself. We are apt to feel sure that the fundamental truths of our creeds and of our theology are taught in the Bible, and when we find those who oppose our creeds and our theology we are apt to say without hesitation that they are opposing the teaching of the Bible. So the rabbis felt about any who opposed their teaching. They were expert students of the Law, and they were sure that they understood the Law.

What did Saul think that he knew about Jesus? He thought he knew that Jesus had encouraged people to disobey the Law of Moses. The rabbis were trying to get all the people to keep the two fast days in each week, and Jesus had said that it was absurd to expect his friends to do this. The rabbis were trying hard to get all the people to keep the Sabbath. Jesus, they said, did not properly keep the Sabbath himself and defended others for not keeping it. For instance, he was reported to have cured people on the Sabbath who had chronic diseases of long standing, who were in no special danger and might just as well have been cured on other days. The President of one of the Galilean synagogues on one occasion, expressed the indignation of all the rabbis at Jesus' conduct. There was a woman who had a spirit of infirmity eighteen years and could in no wise lift herself. When Jesus saw her he laid his hands on her and immediately she was made straight and glorified God. The President of the synagogue being moved with indignation because Jesus had healed on the Sabbath, answered and said to the multitude, "There are six days in which men ought to work; in them, therefore, come and be healed and not on the day of the Sabbath." Jesus' attitude toward the Sabbath had seemed to the rabbis so outrageously wicked that they had early in his career tried to enlist the Herod party to act with them in securing his trial and execution as a Sabbath breaker. He had encouraged bad people, publicans and sinners, who did not keep the Law to think that they could enter the Kingdom of God.

On the other hand, Jesus had become extremely popular as a prophet among the masses of the people. Some, as we have noted, thought him to be a reincarnation of one of the great prophets of the past, Elijah or Jeremiah. His remarkable power to cast out devils from the demonized added to his popularity. This popularity made him seem to the rabbis a most dangerous man. A funda-

Lu. 13:11

v. 14

Mk. 3:6

Mt. 21:31

mentally irreligious man was deluding the people into thinking him to be a great prophet and religious guide. The Jerusalem rabbis, the best men young Rabbi Saul knew, his honored theological professors, publicly declared that Jesus was in league with Satan and that his power over demons was given to him by Satan himself. This man in league with Satan, had become intoxicated with his own popularity and finally had encouraged a blasphemous idea which began to spread among the people, namely, that he was the Christ. There seemed to be danger that on the great Passover feast when Jerusalem was filled with thousands of his adherents, Jesus would formally declare himself to be the Christ. To prevent this the rabbis and priests acting together but from different motives, arrested him secretly by night the day before the feast began, sentenced him to death and executed him before the crowd found out what was going on. *Mk. 3:22f.*

In the course of this midnight trial the court asked Jesus whether he considered himself to be the Christ, and when he distinctly declared that he did, the court in horror instantly condemned him to death. Then God cursed him. For six hours he hung in naked shame on a cross and all the rabbis knew that everyone who hangs on a tree is cursed of God. Even his most intimate friends who had come to believe him to be the Christ gave up their belief as they saw the awful evidence that God's curse rested upon him. *Gal. 3:13 Deut. 21:23*

The peril to true religion now seemed to the rabbis to be safely past. But to their dismay, after a few days the man's followers began to assert that he was alive. These ignorant men found some statements in the Scriptures to which they gave a new and, in the eyes of the rabbis, utterly unwarrantable interpretation. These passages were asserted to predict that the Christ when he did appear would die, be raised from the dead, ascend to heaven, and then after a little time come back to judge the world and to do the other things that so many of the Jews expected the Christ to do. Strangely enough this apparently absurd story rapidly gained ground, especially as those who believed it began to live lives of amazing friendliness and generosity, in the spirit of the man's own life and deeds. "The multitude of them that believed were of one heart and one soul; and not one of them said that aught *Lu. 24:45f. Acts 2:23f. v. 31* *Acts 4:32-33* of the things that he possessed was his own; but they had all things common. And with great power gave the apostles their witness of the resurrection of the Lord Jesus." One of the most effective speakers in the new Jesus movement began to assert that when Jesus returned as the Christ to judge the world, as he soon would, there would be an end of the temple service and of all the Mosaic Law which concerned the temple administration. That is, in the new age there would be no temple. The rabbis sprang to the front, arrested this man as they had Jesus, and in holy horror at his blasphemy, without waiting for all the formalities of sentence and execution, practically lynched him. The death of Stephen was like the taste of blood to a tiger and a furious persecution of the Nazarenes began which included women as well as men. Young Rabbi Saul, full of pious horror, was foremost among those who undertook to stamp out the pestilential movement. "Entering into every house, and dragging men and women committed them to prison."

Acts 8:3

But now the Jesus movement began to show new possibilities of peril to true religion. The Nazarenes who fled from Jerusalem went to the ghettos of various foreign cities. The pestilence was simply spreading. It was like scattering smallpox patients from some infected center and putting each in a place where he would be a new center of contagion. These Jews who lived outside Palestine in foreign cities were always in special danger of losing something of their devotion to Moses. They were surrounded on every side by pagan life and worship. They were always doing business with pagans and there was greater danger than in the homeland that the edge would be taken off from their loyalty to Moses. Now, if this dangerous Nazarene heresy, with its tendency to depreciate the importance of keeping the Law of Moses, should get a foothold in the ghettos of the foreign cities, no one could calculate the danger that would be done.

The problem before Rabbi Saul was to secure devoted obedience to the Mosaic Law on the part of all Jews both in the homeland and in the principal ghettos of all the great cities of the Roman Empire. There would be no coming of the Christ until such obedience was secured. Since the Nazarene movement wherever it spread threatened to make the Jews lax in their law keeping, the Nazarene movement imperiled the Messianic hope. Unless the

Nazarene movement were destroyed the Christ would not come from heaven and the holy ideal of religion which the good men of Israel were cherishing would never be realized. The great hope of a glorious future for Israel could never be realized so long as the Jesus movement was allowed to exist. This was the view of the case that was in Saul's mind as he rode toward Damascus.

It is not in place here to discuss whether or not Saul had ever experienced misgivings about the correctness of his view or any dissatisfaction with his own restless religious life as contrasted with the radiant hope and the deep peace of the Nazarenes whom he arrested and helped to sentence to death. Instead we have next to inquire what it was that revolutionized his whole outlook upon life. According to the account attributed to him by the author of Acts he suddenly found himself in the midst of an overwhelming light. It must have seemed to him that the heavenly Spirit world with its unspeakable glory had broken into this world of flesh, as he had expected it to do whenever the Christ should be revealed from heaven. Could it be that the judgment day was here and that the Christ had come without waiting for Israel to be a law-keeping nation? Had the Christ come without waiting for the blasphemous Jesus movement to be stamped out? Acts 9:3

Then from the midst of the heavenly glory he heard a voice that went sounding down into the depths of his soul speaking the dialect that he had learned in the home of his infancy. "Saul, Saul, why are you persecuting me?" "Who are you, Sir?" he said in terror. To his horror, the voice replied, "I am Jesus of Nazareth, whom you are persecuting." Jesus, then, the horrible blasphemer, who had been cursed on the cross by God, was in heavenly glory and possessed of the Christ's own power to make heavenly glory break into the world of flesh! He was now demonstrating his power to do it. Saul was experiencing the Christ's judgment day. What would the Christ do to him on this judgment day? The voice tells him to go on his way to his intended destination and find out there. He rises up a sinful man blinded by the glory of the Christ's judgment day and yet not destroyed by it. He is still on the earth among men whose hands of flesh he feels as in amazement they lead him into the city. For three days he sat in darkness, neither eating nor drinking, the guest of some leader of the ghetto Acts 9:4-5 who had doubtless made ample but necessary preparations for the entertainment of his distinguished guest from Jerusalem.

What now did Saul think of Jesus Christ? He has learned to put the two names together. Jesus, the name of blasphemy and shame, belongs with Christ, the name of holiness and glory. He can say Jesus Christ.

He knows that Jesus Christ is kind. He is a friendly person. One of the severest criticisms passed by the rabbis upon Jesus was that he consorted in a friendly way with the most outrageous law-breakers,—the publicans and sinners who made no effort to keep the Law. Saul, who now has strong sense of being a sinner,—even "the chief of sinners"—of having done great wrong in fight-ing against God's Christ and killing his faithful followers, now finds that Jesus Christ is really a friend of sinners. Jesus Christ has not destroyed his persecutor. He has not blinded him for life. Neither has he scotched him and let him go free with a warning never to persecute again. Instead Jesus has honored him with a high commission. Saul's great longing to prepare the peo-ple for the Christ's coming was to be utilized by Jesus, only in place of preparing for it by destroying the Jesus movement, he is to do it *through* the Jesus movement and become a great leader in that movement. This friendliness of Jesus Christ was what Paul later described by the word "grace." Grace is a beautiful kindness that makes its recipient glad, and "the grace of our Lord Jesus Christ" was a phrase that ever afterward had an inexhaustible meaning for Paul.

I Tim.
1:15

But Saul soon discovered that his interview with Jesus Christ did not end. The blinding glory fortunately passed away, but his sense of the presence of Jesus did not pass away. Saul had been introduced into a new world. The world of spirit, which to his mind was in God's high heaven above the world of flesh, had opened to him and had not closed again against him. Flesh man though he still was, he lived in the world of spirit. The Jesus Christ of the spirit world stayed with him. "Christ liveth in me," was his description of himself thenceforth. In later life Paul used one sentence that described vividly the way he felt during this experience in Damascus. He said that "Jesus Christ laid hold of him." He had a strong sense of being powerfully gripped by a

Gal.
2:20

Phil.
3:12

mighty personality, who never after relaxed his hold upon him. This unrelaxing grip gave him the indomitable purpose, strong as iron, with which he pushed on against and over all conceivable difficulties. "I push forward," he wrote from a Roman prison, "that I may lay hold of that for which Christ laid hold of me." Because of this strong grip of the personality of Jesus Christ upon him, he dared to undertake any enterprise no matter how vast. "I can do all things through Christ which strengtheneth me," he said, and went from city to city, from peril to peril, undismayed. Phil. 4:13
Whenever he saw a company of men coming down a city street, he never knew but that they were coming to seize him. He never passed a dark gateway in the evening without feeling that someone might be lurking there to assassinate him. "I die daily," was his fearless confession,—fearless because the Lord who walked with him had taken away his fear of death and of all that hostile men could do. I Cor. 15:31

It was out of this experience of Jesus Christ's vital hold upon him that Paul's great teaching regarding righteousness through faith was born. When Paul settled down thankfully to follow the leadership of the friendly Christ in Damascus, he found himself in a strangely peaceful frame of mind. He had never before known such rest and grateful contentment. It was such peace as he very well knew could come only to one who had been made righteous, that is to say, right with God. That which made him righteous was certainly no deeds of pious law-keeping, for the experience of peace came to him when he was in the midst of an unrighteous fight against God's Christ. Without doubt what gave him peace was his humble, thankful acquiescence in the control which Jesus Christ assumed over his life. He accepted Jesus as Christ and treated him as the Christ ought to be treated, namely, with humble, submissive love. To treat Jesus Christ in this way evidently made him right with God, for it brought him such peace as only the righteous man can experience. This was ever after his idea of faith, and of righteousness through faith. To have faith, or to believe, in Jesus Christ, was to accept him as Lord and treat him accordingly, namely, thankfully to give one's life up to his control.

This idea of righteousness through faith he afterwards found

corroborated in the Scriptures, especially where the Scriptures
describe the religious experience of Abraham, the founder of the
Hebrew nation. Abraham simply believed in God, and his belief
was accounted righteousness. Faith to Paul was always the vital
reaching out of the believer's spirit in penitent, submissive love to
find the spirit of the unseen but ever-present Lord Jesus Christ.
On the basis of his own Damascus experience with Jesus, continued in a life of daily fellowship with Jesus and corroborated by
Scripture statements regarding Abraham which he now interpreted in the light of his own experience, he went everywhere
preaching the message of faith in Christ. It seemed to him a very
simple message which anyone might understand. "The word is
nigh thee," he said, "in thy mouth and in thy heart, the word
of faith which we preach: that if thou shalt confess with thy
mouth Jesus as Lord, and shalt believe in thy heart that God
raised him from the dead, thou shalt be saved."

Other questions about Jesus Christ were raised by Paul's religious experience and were answered in the light of that experience. For instance, he must have begun at once to ask why the
glorious Christ from the heavenly spirit world should die the
shameful death of a God-cursed flesh-man. This is a question he
had doubtless put in derision to many a Nazarene on trial for his
faith in Jesus. The Nazarenes probably were perplexed and gave
various answers. But they had all agreed that in some way his
death was predicted in the Scriptures and that it was for our sins.
When Paul in later years wrote to the Christians in Corinth, he
referred to the fundamental ideas which he found prevailing in
the Christian community, when he became a Christian and which
he had himself in turn passed on to the earliest Christians in
Corinth. "I make known to you the gospel which I preached to
you. . . For I delivered to you among principal truths what I also
had received, that Christ died for our sins according to the Scriptures."

How the Christ's death was thought of by the primitive
Christians to be connected with our sins does not appear in this
statement. Paul, later, in stating his own view of the connection
uses several illustrations which perhaps represent the various
phases of the subject that presented themselves to his mind at dif-

Ro. 4:3 (margin)
Ro. 10:8–9 (margin)
I Cor. 15:1–3 (margin)

ferent times. His most fundamental idea is that in the death of Christ, God was revealing his own love in such a way as to reconcile men to himself. In the discussion of the death of Christ which occurs in his second letter to the Corinthian Christians he says of it that "God was in Christ reconciling the world unto himself." This conception seems a natural outgrowth of the idea which Paul held before he became a Christian and which also appears in the early preaching attributed to Peter in the third chapter of Acts, namely, that the coming of the Christ from heaven to inaugurate the new spirit age will not occur until large numbers have repented and become obedient to God. To hasten their penitence and obedience, God sent forth his Christ to be by his death such a revelation of God's love as would bring men to penitent obedience. When his death had produced its full effect, then God would send his Christ a second time from heaven to establish the new age. ^{II Cor. 5:19}

Paul's idea of the function of Mosaic Law was revolutionized by his experience with Jesus at Damascus. Evidently since God meant to make men righteous through their faith in Jesus Christ, it was theoretically probable that he did not mean to accomplish this end through the Mosaic Law. In practice also this became evident. The most perfect law-keepers that Paul knew, the pious Jerusalem rabbis, had not been made righteous by their law-keeping. Their law-keeping had not prevented them from becoming the murderers of God's Christ and his followers. They were in the foremost van of the world's sinners. Paul looked back to the time when he was with them as the time when he was the chief of sinners. If the law, then, was not God's means on which God relied for making men righteous, what was it for? Paul's answer was simple. The law was God's means of making men realize how bad they were and making them regard penitent faith as their only resource. Now that the Christ had by his death turned men to penitence and faith more effectively than the law could do, and by his resurrection became the ever-present object of faith, the function of the law was ended. Christ was the end of the law for righteousness. ^{Ro. 10:4}

All Paul's conception of future life centered in his personal experience with Jesus Christ. It was the powerful personality of Jesus Christ that would bring the spirit world into the world of

flesh with an irresistible glory that would swallow up the world
of flesh in the twinkling of an eye. "Now this I say, brothers, that
flesh and blood cannot inherit the kingdom of God, . . . but we
shall all be changed in a moment, in the twinkling of an eye, at
the last trumpet." The life of the spirit age that would then begin
could all be summed up for Paul in terms of a developing friendship with Jesus Christ. "The Lord himself shall descend from
heaven with a shout, accompanied by the archangel's voice and
the sounding of God's trumpet, and we shall be always with the
Lord."

I Cor.
15:50–52

I Thess.
4:16–17

I have gone at some length over this ground tonight for two
reasons. *First,* because such a Biblical study may be of some
interest to the students of the Bible Training School, and *second,* because it reveals the secret of success in the personal evangelism for which this Bible Training School prepares its students.
However widely modern conceptions of the nature of the world
may differ from those that prevailed in the first century, the
essential nature of Christian evangelism has not changed since
Paul's day. It is still *personal experience with Jesus Christ* that
gives the evangelist his sense of mission in his work and the
inspiration for undertaking it. He goes out as Paul did to introduce other men into an experience with Jesus Christ like in kind,
if not in detail, to that which is bringing him enlarging moral
emancipation, a deepening peace, and a growing enthusiasm.

THE SEARCH FOR A RELIGION

XII

THE SEARCH FOR A RELIGION

HOW should a man proceed to search for a satisfactory religion? The article on "Religion Now" by Mr. Clutton-Brock in the July issue of *The Atlantic Monthly* emphasizes the sense of the need of religion that is rising with insistence in the minds of many who seem to find little to satisfy them in the religion presented by various sections of the Christian church.

Many men are conscious of a new passion for reality. The war and its results have made it necessary to decide what are the real values which men will readily die to maintain in the world. Men who have been desperately struggling to preserve what they have felt in their inmost souls to be the political and economic foundations of civilization must have a religion that appeals to their thought as fundamental reality. It must be, as Mr. Clutton-Brock says: "a building of our own thought in which we can be at home." The builder may find much in the experience of others recorded in literature and embodied in institutions past and present which will prove useful building material, but *he must build his own "home."* It must be a truly democratic "home," in which all sorts of people could live together with some sense of being a family, and in which would be conserved every real interest of human life. It must be a "home" which could be enlarged without destroying its unity; a "home" in which one could anticipate living permanently with no fear of outgrowing his quarters.

What the relation of the church to such a religion would be is another and secondary question. The prime question is, How should an earnest man prosecute the search for such a religion,— a search for an enlarging and increasingly satisfactory religious experience?

I

The sincere searcher for a religion would naturally, first of all, consult the best men and women he knows, that is, the men and women who possess the highest character, in order to ascertain whether or not they are having any experience that could properly be called religious. We were never before so sure as now that *an alleged religion which does not issue in moral character is not worth considering.* The prime elements in such character are honesty and invincible friendliness, expressing themselves in increasingly efficient action. The persons we would like to consult about religion are those to whom a father on his death-bed would, in his necessity, willingly entrust his little motherless children and their property.

II

The man in the western world searching for a religion would naturally make a thorough examination of the Christian religion. It is the form of religion that is immediately at hand and that purports to have wrought itself, at least to a limited extent, into the best life of the western world. It seems to have produced a certain desirable type of civilization, ideals and institutions, that we call Christian. The greatness of its influence is implied in some of our severest criticism of it. We criticize it for failing to prevent the most devastating war in history. This implies that it had done so much for the western world as to give us reason for expecting it to prevent war.

Furthermore, the Christian religion appears to be, at least at present, the most active and effective in the group of the world's redemptive religions, the religions that propose to redeem men from sin, by which we mean, from bondage to the evil will. It has always been possible to find large numbers of Christian men effectively redeemed from moral filth ever since the early days when Paul, the Christian missionary, enumerated to his converts I Cor. the unmentionable vices of the slums of Corinth, with the tri-6:11 umphant comment: "Such were some of you: but ye were washed, but ye were sanctified."

III

In examining the Christian religion, it becomes at once evident that its outstanding feature is the personality, the religious experience and teaching of Jesus Christ.

The character of Jesus has always been a challenge to the curiosity and conscience of mankind. Men have been perplexed to know how to explain and classify him; and multitudes, good and bad, among all classes of society, have found in his life and teaching an incentive to better living. The man searching for a religion finds in him an outstanding religious leader, but one lacking certain qualities that are ordinarily considered essential to leadership. He trained no soldiers; he wrote no books; he was no aged sage but died in comparative youth; he was no recluse but lived in the open, a workman, either as employer or employee or both; he did not found, at least directly, any institution, for the Christian church sprang up after his death, apparently through force of circumstances.

Without attempting at first any critical analysis of the literary sources of information about Jesus, it appears to the inquirer that through all these sources *there runs the story of a profound religious experience* which Jesus proposed to share freely with all men. He went hopefully about among the notoriously irreligious, confident that they were capable of sharing his own religious experience.

IV

An analysis of this religious experience shows that it centered about certain germ ideas. These germ ideas, conceived in the terms of current presuppositions, have grown fruitfully in the experience of men whenever they have been allowed re-statement in terms of the changing presuppositions of developing thought. These ideas entering into human experience generation after generation seem destined to be permanent because they have turned out, like everything vital, to be *capable of indefinite change without loss of identity.* They seem more and more clearly to be in line with the central trend of human evolution in thought and life.

There are three of these central germ ideas. None of them originated with Jesus but the inquirer recognizes them to have been
conceived by him in harmonious combination and with unusual
elimination of the erroneous or subordinate ideas that often ac-
company them elsewhere. Furthermore, they seem to have been
experienced by him with unusual thoroughness and to have received from him in some way a degree of self-propagating, permanent character kindling power not found elsewhere.

V

The first of these germ ideas was the Fatherhood of God. This
is an expression which implied recognition of dependence upon
God for being; recognition of superiority, providence, and loving personal relationship with men, a relationship which called
for a life of faith and prayer on the part of men. To Jesus the
Fatherhood of God seems not to have been a mystical dogma, *but*
Mt. *a great fact of experience* which he proposed to share with all
7:7–8 men: "Ask and *ye* shall receive; seek and *ye* shall find; knock and
it shall be opened unto *you.*" "Everyone that asketh receiveth." In
the thought of Jesus this fatherly power is always giving itself,
revealing itself, opening itself to human approach, seeking expression for itself in human life.

To many men of our day this means that there is a vast Power
all about us,

> "Nearer than we can think and farther off
> Than any mind can fathom"

feeling, thinking, willing to produce the true and the beautiful,
which in the sphere of personal life are the honest and the
friendly. To understand the nature of the metaphysical relationship between this Power and ourselves is to solve the, as yet, un-
solved problem of personality. *This Power is near enough to give
us personal being and keep it going, yet distinct enough from us
to give us a chance to be ourselves.* This Power, working for
truth and beauty, honesty and friendliness, is always pressing upward out of the depths of personality in order to gain expression
for itself in the human life of individuals and in all social customs and institutions. It calls for "faith," which is not believing the incredible but is rather the reaching out of the soul to

work with this unseen Energy in good will and to the utmost for the common good. As the soul opens itself in faith and prayer this Power proves itself to be ready, in accordance with psychic law, to pour into the soul its own honest and friendly feeling, its own honest and friendly thinking and willing, in such abundance as to push these great elements of enlarging life out into victorious action.[1]

VI

The second great idea that appears in the religious experience and teaching of Jesus was *his vision of the task of humanity,* the great human enterprise which he called in current Jewish phraseology "the Kingdom of God." This was a germ idea capable of a development that involved changing forms without loss of identity. More and more it means to multitudes of modern men the production on the earth of a civilization in which the peoples of all nations and classes, in all stages of upward moral development, may work together in growing honesty and friendliness as the brotherly sons of God to master all the forces of nature for the common good. It involves the mastery of the resources of the natural world; and the development of the latent powers of human personality in the interest of truth and beauty.

The Kingdom of God is an enterprise in which the human race comes to a sense of its unity, to a realization that it is an organism, perhaps a biological organism, as professor Nicolai in his *Biology of War* has lately maintained; in any case an organism in which no part can dominate, but in which all parts must work for the health of the organism as a whole. In these war and post-war days more than ever before is it swiftly becoming evident that the human race is an organism destined in the course of its evolution to reach a point at which it must become a conscious cooperative brotherhood, or else perish. It is an evolution in which the law of the survival of the fittest prevails, but in which *the fittest are those who respond to the demand for cooperative brotherhood.*

This evolutionary process, which men have discovered, does not bear us all securely forward to a certain goal in an easy, care-free

---

[1]For a more complete study of the attitude of mind and life called "faith" in a growing relationship, cf. Ch. XV, pp. 171f.

existence. It is a process in which the unseen, evolving energy of God is found to be challenging us to a cooperation with itself that involves always something of sacrificial effort and at times sacrificial struggle to the utmost. When Jesus, in his profound religious experience, found the evolving consciousness of God arising within him, challenging him to cooperation in sacrifice for the better world order of the Kingdom of God, he had his Gethsemane and Calvary. These are realities from which men who enter into the life of God cannot be excluded, and which Jesus proposed to share with all those seeking vital religious experience.

VII

The third great germ idea in the religious experience of Jesus was the persistence of a purposeful individual life after physical death. He was sure of it for himself and therefore for others. As this idea has developed it has conceived of life in the unseen world as a democracy, a civilization constantly receiving reinforcements from the human race, in which brotherly men under other conditions than those which prevail here continue to work together upon the unfinished universe of God in the interest of truth and beauty.

A selfish conception of life after death, such as bliss measured out as reward for present sacrifice, makes little appeal to men who have learned to work vigorously, and when necessary sacrificially, with others for the common good. But no man who has tasted the joy of such work *can fail to resent the idea that death ends his chance at life ever-afterward*. If he could face this possibility with complacency or indifference he would have to confess himself culpably indifferent to the common good.

VIII

These three fundamental ideas found in the religious experience and teaching of Jesus were apparently accompanied by a unique sense of God-given responsibility for permanent leadership which would continue unimpaired after his emergence through death into the unseen world. This conviction was an inevitable accompaniment of the assurance of personal immortality which had been worked out so securely in his own religious experience. He anticipated continuing with men in the strength of his immortal spirit as their leader in preparing for the Kingdom of God. Through the power of his immortal spirit he would share with them his own active faith in the Fatherhood of God, his own sense of human brotherhood, his own victorious certainty of immortality.

Since the beginning of the Christian movement, as men have adopted the ideals of Jesus and let their affections follow him out into the unseen world, something has come back to them that has kindled ethical passion and religious devotion in their hearts. To those of distinct mystical temperament this experience has seemed to involve direct, inspirational connection with the immortal spirit of Jesus. In the case of others it has been rather a slowly growing awareness of the reality and nearness of an unseen spiritual world of which they more and more feel themselves to be an indestructible part. In both types of temperament it has been *a character kindling experience.*

In the early Christian centuries, as this experience penetrated different spheres of thought and life, it seemed so wonderful to its possessors that they appropriated for Jesus the highest religious titles with which they were familiar. Without any sense of unfitness or irreverence, they applied to him the title, Lord. They saw in him the kind of Christ in which men could believe—the Jesus kind of Christ. Thus has he come to be known to Christians everywhere as the Lord Jesus Christ.

*   *   *

What shall a modern man do, then, in the search for a religion? It would seem to be reasonable for him to adopt these fundamental ideas, which were wrought out in the experience of Jesus and were persistently corroborated by the experience of many subsequent generations. Such an honest, open-minded man might well take as the working hypothesis of his life: the daily practice of the Fatherhood of God in all departments of his life; the daily practice of human brotherhood, working in all practical ways to secure for every other man such a fair chance at all good things as a man would like his brother to have; the daily practice of immortality.

The call to the religious life so conceived is the call to a great adventure in and for experience connected with the personality of Jesus, an adventure which by its very nature involves democratic relations of honesty and good will with all men, and devout outreach into the unseen world. If there is some higher type of religion, such a course of action would certainly be a step toward it.[2] In a rational moral universe progress is made by working hard and faithfully the best clews available.

---

[2]Herbert Spencer has commented: "The democratic form of government is the highest form of government; but because of this it requires the highest type of human nature —a type nowhere at present existing." (Ed.)

THE CENTRAL IDEA
IN THE CHRISTIAN RELIGION

XIII

THE CENTRAL IDEA
IN THE CHRISTIAN RELIGION[1]

THE essence of religion in its higher forms is an experience of the soul with God, especially of the soul in its relation to other souls, reaching out together with them after God. Theology aims to describe systematically the phenomena of religious experience. Religious experience furnishes the facts; theology endeavors to describe and understand the facts.

The Christian religion is the experience of men who have sought God under the leadership of Jesus Christ. Christian theology aims to describe systematically the phenomena of Christian experience. Christian theology is often and rightly thought of as largely concerned with the Bible. This is because the Bible is the report of experience with God on the part of certain preëminent religious pioneers of humanity and especially because it reports the religious experience of Jesus Christ and the men whom he originally influenced.

Christian theology has not always kept close to the phenomena of Christian experience, but in this present discussion it will be assumed that its proper function is to analyze and interpret Christian experience.

Christian experience has many phases and Christian theology must therefore discuss many topics. The purpose of the hour is to ascertain, if possible, what is the central idea in the Christian religion.

The inquiry seems appropriate to the occasion. The world is in

[1]The original title of this address was, "The Central Idea of Christian Theology." An examination of Doctor Bosworth's summary, however, together with the emphases recurring throughout the Study, has made the revised title seem appropriate. From the viewpoint that the heart of the matter is religion based essentially on experience; that theology is the orderly explanation of that experience and its implications, it becomes clear that the central interest here considered is *religion*. The major part of the address was published in *The Biblical World*, Vol. XLI, pp. 11f. (Ed.)

the midst of a thorough re-examination of foundations. This re-examination covers practically every area of life and has come to involve a vigorous attack upon some things that have long seemed to many to be a part of the foundations but that seem to others to be simply encumbering debris. A part of the work of re-examination must necessarily be done in the underground passages of scholastic research. The people on the surface naturally become nervously apprehensive regarding the operations below, especially in view of various reports that come up to them from those workers whose shafts have gone deepest and who have been longest at the work. In the religious situation it is the business of theological teachers and students to discriminate as clearly as they can between foundation and debris, to sympathize both with the faithful workers below and the apprehensive people above. In other words, the business of religious thought today is to outline a reasonable, constructive, conquering conception of Christianity which its students may preach with conviction and enthusiasm. In this process the first thing to do is to discover if possible the central idea in the Christian religion.

The central idea is not necessarily the idea most conspicuous at a given moment. Some casual remark in a sermon, by reason of peculiar local conditions, often becomes more conspicuous than the central idea of the discourse. The idea of a crucified king was so disconcerting to Jewish patriotism and so offensive to the Greek aesthetic sense that it became for a time the most conspicuous feature of primitive Christian teaching. The Jewish and Greek challenge to Christianity at this particular point aroused in Paul the conscientiously defiant determination to preach a crucified Christ. While for this reason the death of Christ was perhaps for a time dramatically the most conspicuous feature of Paul's thought, it is not so clear that it was logically the central thought.

The central idea is not always the one that seems for the moment most practically useful. The most clamorous need of the age may lead the Christian thinkers of that age, who are naturally eager to present Christianity as the panacea for all human ills, to represent as the central Christian idea the phase of Christianity that will most practically meet this need. But the age may be deceived in thinking that its most *clamant* need is its *central* need, and Christian thinkers may be correspondingly confused in their effort to select the central Christian idea.

In our own day we are so keenly conscious of social and industrial injustice that we are inclined to represent as the central idea of Christian theology the broad brotherhood of man; or to give height and depth to this broad idea by restating it as the impartial and universal Fatherhood of God. Yet we should have occasion to question this statement closely before we let it pass, at least without explication, as a final statement.

It may seem doubtful whether the theologians of any single age can hope so to free themselves from all biasing considerations as to see with unerring vision straight to the center of Christian experience and thought. No age, however, can be excused from endeavoring to do so, and the present age enjoys advantages that give it hope of unusual success. The achievements in many departments of life and knowledge during the last century have given Christian thinkers of today a point of view, a spirit, and a method that make it easier than it once was to see deeply and clearly into the real nature of Christianity. The human mind may not have become keener but unfolding life has made the task easier.

If the central idea, then, is not necessarily either the most conspicuous or the one for the moment most practically useful, what are its characteristics?

CONTINUITY

First of all, it must be *one that is found in germ at the beginning of Christianity and that has been running through Christian experience ever since,* changing its form perhaps but not losing its identity. As Professor Eucken would say, it is something that is not the product of the *Zeitgeist,* but of the *Geist der Zeiten,* not of the spirit of the age, but of the spirit of the ages.

In the teaching of Jesus, the founder of Christianity, and of the men of the apostolic age who mediated his thought to the world of their day, we should expect to find this idea in the form of a regulative germ. It will appear there in germ, for, as has been generally recognized, the Christian Scriptures are not reflective philosophical treatises, containing careful analytical statements of truth that can be passed down from generation to generation as final in their form. If the Scriptures had been such, they would long ago have ceased to be interesting. They are rather, in the most valuable sections, a spontaneous report of deep personal experience with God, a report called out often by critical emergencies or special needs, and made with a view to propagating this religious experience in the lives of others.

This experience is reported in a way that has appealed for centuries with unparalleled and unabating power to all who seek religious experience, but also in a way that lays upon each generation the responsibility of determining the comparative value of the various phases of experience reported in the Scriptures. For instance, we have in the second chapter of the Book of Acts the report of a wonderful experience on the first Pentecost after the death of Jesus, near the beginning of the Christian movement. It was an experience having various phases and conditioned by various circumstances of temperament, previous habits of thought and life. In the Book of Acts this experience is reported to have repeated itself on several occasions soon after, but it is not an experience which has been repeated in its most dramatic features regularly through the Christian centuries. When Christian people today try to speak with Pentecostal tongues, as some in Ohio have recently done, they do not receive the approval of the Christian church. Upon each generation there is laid the responsibility of determining what the central feature of this experience really was and whether or not it can be properly repeated in modern Christian experience. My point is that God has not seen fit to put into the Christian Scriptures a statement of the central idea of Christianity in a form which is final for every subsequent age. There is no chapter and verse to which all Christians unhesitatingly turn for such a statement. Each generation must do its best to make such a statement for itself.

Yet this central idea must be one whose regulative germ is found in the Christian Scriptures. There is that within a germ which determines what the subsequent development shall be. The subsequent developments may be in form very unlike the original germ. To a casual observer, an oak tree is very unlike an acorn but the oak tree is really in the acorn. The germ in the acorn is absolutely regulative of all the development that is to follow.

Whatever of good or evil which the climate and soil may supply to the tree, an oak it will always be so long as it continues to be at all. This, then, is clearly one characteristic that the central idea in the Christian religion must possess: it must be an idea present as a regulative germ at the beginning of Christian experience reported in the Scriptures and one whose development may be traced in the developing Christian experience of the centuries since.

INDESTRUCTIBILITY

Closely related to this is another characteristic. If Christianity is to be the final religion, its central idea must be *one that can last as long as men continue to have a religious nature.* It must not only have accompanied them through all the centuries of the past, but it must keep on with them in the future. It must be an idea that men will not outgrow, an idea that is capable of indefinite future growth without losing its identity, an idea that men can carry with them through a long course of development and find still always pushing them forward with unabating motive power.

OF SUPERIOR QUALITY

The central idea in the Christian religion must be *one that can dominate and conserve all the interests of life.* It must dominate all of life. All highly developed religions by their very nature must claim to be dominant. They are either supreme or are nothing, for God who is the soul of religion is either supreme or he is nothing. Religion is not one interest among several, but it is by its very nature the chief interest and the one that gives significance to all others. The Christian religion does not differ from other religions in this respect. It claims sovereignty over all of human life. It can make good this claim only by having as its central idea an idea that will be recognized as *rightfully* dominant in all of life. Therefore it must be an idea that conserves all vital human interests. The moment that any real human interest in any department of life is jeopardized by an alleged central idea of Christianity, that moment the idea loses its right to be considered central, or, if it is really central, then Christianity so conceived is itself discredited.

Constructiveness

This conception of the central idea of Christianity as one that can dominate, and conserve all human interests at once brings a closely related characteristic into view. *It must recognize man's divine call to work creatively on his environment.* Men, especially in modern times, are characterized by a passionate purpose to subdue their environment. The spirit of man feels itself set by an irresistible inner impulse to master the forces that sometimes play about it with a fascinating fury of power and at other times move with the quiet majesty of inexhaustible strength. These forces challenge man to understand them and to co-operate with them in the further shaping of the world. In response to this challenge he has not only discovered in their action a process of continuous creation by evolution running back through countless ages,—a discovery which is itself a wonderful achievement,—but he now proposes nothing less than, in conjunction with these forces, to take an intelligent share himself in the process of evolutionary creation. He will not only create new fruits and flowers but he will so change social conditions as to create new types of human life.

The modern prophets of humanity can see in these deep stirrings of the human soul the beginnings of a new career for humanity. The human creature will prove himself made in the image of the Creator by becoming himself a voluntary, purposeful creator, and with no clearly marked limit to the range of his creative operations. This creative career opens not only before the great creative geniuses of humanity but before all the men who do the common work of the world. Where one genius presses forward to enlarge the scope of creative human activity by showing a new opportunity, there ten thousand push forward after him to use the opportunity. Mr. Edison by a single step forward in the mastery of electric force may bring into view a new field of activity that calls for a million workmen to occupy it.

This passion for the creative mastery of environment, expressing itself in science, art and industry, is so central and vital in the nature of man, that it must find recognition in any statement of the central idea in the Christian religion. It is not enough to say that Christian thought must adjust itself to all permanent advances made in any department of knowledge. It is not merely the much discussed adjustment between Christian theology and science that is to be sought, as if these two were diverse interests seeking reconciliation. Something deeper than this is demanded. The human passion for the exercise of creative power which underlies all science and art and industry must be recognized as central in the nature of man and so must be incorporated into the central idea in the Christian religion.

This emphasis upon creative activity vitally differentiates the Christian religion from the great religions of India whose ideal is peacefully resigned to inaction with the hope of losing personal consciousness in Nirvana. Candor requires our recognizing that there have been times in the history of Christian thought also, when this emphasis on action has been resented. Christianity has sometimes seemed to Christian thinkers to be set in enmity against the world and to be chiefly concerned to get men happily out of the world after having had as little as possible to do with it. And yet Christianity has always been at heart an insistent call to action; a call to the emphasis and the development of personality through action.

Unity in the Spiritual

The central idea in the Christian religion must be *one that shall present to men the unity and nearness of a friendly spiritual world.* That is, it must hold before men the idea of an unseen friendly God, and a vast sphere of his unseen operation. One aspect of this unseen spiritual world may well be the so-called material world that men see and work upon with such passionate enthusiasm, but this material world is only an aspect of something greater into which men work their way through scientific research, through creative art and industry and most of all through responsive spiritual activity within the soul.

It is the very essence of all religions to hold before the minds of men the idea of God. They conceive the nature of God variously and present various methods of human approach to God. The Christian religion, chiefly under the influence of Jesus, uses the symbolic word "Father" to describe the friendly unseen God. It represents the unseen Father to be invariably near to his human children doing for, with and through them all the things that the growing significance of the word "Father" has led men to think that the unseen Father would wish to accomplish. In the Christian centuries this idea has taken various and sometimes strange forms. In calling God a personal God men have sometimes forgotten their real ignorance of what the word "personal" means and have thought of him simply as an infinitely expanded human personality. They have ascribed to him artificial and repellent attributes. But nevertheless this germ idea of the Heavenly Father, so wonderfully presented in the life and teaching of Jesus, has run vitally through the experience of the Christian centuries, changing its form but retaining its identity and increasing its influence. The unity and nearness of a friendly spiritual world is a part of the central idea in the Christian religion.

Redemptive Religion

The central idea in the Christian religion must be so stated as to *present the redemptive character of Christianity*. Christianity belongs with the redemptive religions of the world and considers itself to be by far the most efficient of them. It is the great redemptive religion of the world. That is, it proposes *to redeem or free men from the burden of guilt and fear*. In modern times something has been accomplished in analyzing the sense of guilt. Probably this age is able to see more clearly than some other ages, the real nature and source of guilt. Christian teaching has sometimes developed an artificial sense of sin. Men have felt guilty in view of certain tendencies and phenomena in their bodies and souls for which they did not need to feel guilty. These phenomena were necessarily characteristic of beings rising from the dominance of the animal to dominance of the spiritual element in them. But there has resulted from this analysis of the sense of guilt a more intelligent affirmation of what guilt really is, of its universal presence in human life and of the necessity of some kind of redemption from it.

Guilt is more and more clearly seen to result from actively warring against or pulling sluggishly down as a dead weight on the rising civilization of invincible good will purposed by God for the life of the world. He is guilty who will not respect his neighbors' interests as conscientiously as he respects his own, who stifles the instinctive cry of his own spiritual nature for friendly intercourse with others and encourages the savage animal instinct which proposes to take what it wants regardless of the interests of others. From this awful sin that is both suicidal and anarchistic, that wars against the higher self, against other men and God, Christianity proposes to redeem men.

This purpose came clearly out at the beginning in the career of Jesus, especially in the death with which that career seemed for a time to have ended. This is not the place to discuss what it was in the career and especially in the death of Jesus that was so powerfully redemptive.[2] The variety of theories on the subject, which have been formed in the history of Christian thought, is sufficient to prove that here again we have an idea that appeared in the beginning as a germ and that has been unfolding in more or less fruitful forms ever since. The central idea of Christian theology is not necessarily identified with any one of these theories. The process of redemption has been going on through the Christian centuries, and at the forefront of Christian thought today stands the ancient proposal to redeem man from the power and guilt of the selfish life. In redemption from guilt is involved also enlarging redemption from that fear which all profound natures more or less keenly feel, fear of the mystery of the universe, fear of the mysterious abysses that yawn within the soul.

That which has become clearer than it once was is the purpose of the redemption. A new meaning is given to the traditional Christian word "salvation," by a better understanding of *that to which* men are saved. Men are saved to a career in which they work creatively together upon their material environment and together make gain in their acquaintance with the real and ever present spiritual world of the Heavenly Father. For success in such a career men must be redeemed from bondage to the selfish habit because such a career involves unselfish co-operation with God and men. Men must be redeemed to a life in which there is growing realization of the ideals of sonship and brotherhood.

---

[2]This will be found in Vol. I, pp. 289f.; in this volume, Address XXI, "The Gospel of Forgiveness," pp. 251f. (Ed.)

ACKNOWLEDGED IMMORTALITY

The central idea in Christianity must involve *recognition of man's immortality*. Man's desire for life after death is ages old. In modern times the present life has been so filled with the opportunity for achievement that men have sometimes seemed to be engrossed in the present to the exclusion of any thought about a life to come. The present life has seemed to them to afford ample opportunity for the gratification of legitimate ambition. But closer scrutiny of human experience shows that men do not rest content with the present life. The more full of opportunity the present life is seen to be, the more valuable it becomes and *the more intolerable is the thought that it should end abruptly, and incomplete with so-called death*. Even men who do not believe in immortality look forward with dread to the time when they must lay their fascinating work down. They experience the ineradicable native longing of the soul for immortality, the deep seriousness of which they sometimes unsuccessfully strive to disguise. Twelve years before Professor Huxley's death, with characteristic honesty and humor he ended a letter to John Morley concerning this.[3]

It is not simply the opportunity for fascinating achievement in the present life that makes men want more of it after death. As human friendship grows more perfect in family and neighborhood life, with the rising tide of good will in the world, the more painful is the thought of its cessation at death.

The conception of immortality that has sometimes seemed likely to displace the traditional idea of personal immortality, is the conception of racial immortality. Each generation of individuals, this conception argues, makes some contribution to the progress of the race and then in death ceases to exist, but the race goes on becoming more and more perfect in its civilization. An analysis of this idea reveals its utter inadequacy. A perfect civilization is one whose members are all perfectly related to each other. To be perfectly related to each other means to love each other. In the perfect civilization men will love each other with a depth of affection far surpassing that which they now feel. But the more perfectly they love each other, the more horrible will become the

[3]Cf. Huxley, *Life and Letters of Thomas Henry Huxley*, Vol. II, p. 67.

death that hopelessly blots out of existence the person so intensely loved. The so-called perfect civilization, on the basis of this theory, becomes something that can be anticipated only with dread. To describe such a civilization as perfect would be grim and awful irony. The only alternative is to recognize the fact that the perfection of friendship which evolution teaches us must constitute the perfection of the ultimate civilization logically involves personal immortality.

Therefore the promise of personal immortality with which primitive Christianity appealed so powerfully to the Greco-Roman world, appeals with equal power to the wistful hearts and logical sense of modern man. The well grounded expectation of personal immortality is the unabashed possession of modern Christianity and must find recognition in any statement of its central idea.

The content of the immortal life, however, must be stated in terms that will appeal to the modern man. A chief reason for the indifference to immortality that sometimes appears on the surface is the fact that the traditional descriptions of the life to come are not such as to make the future life seem greatly worth while. Crowns, harps, songs, golden streets, ecstatic worship and other figurative representations that appealed to the harassed imagination of the Mediterranean World in the first century awaken little enthusiasm in the twentieth century. Men of the Occident, and of the Orient as well, desire the joy of action, obstacles to be overcome, great enterprises to be undertaken, hard problems to be solved. If the modern man once becomes convinced that anything is really desirable, he has no serious difficulty in considering it to be attainable. Modern Christian thought is shaping a picture of the future life which does seem desirable and which will therefore more and more kindle an enthusiastic expectation of life to come.

The elements in this picture of the future life are furnished by three outstanding facts of the present life: man's capacity for creative activity; his capacity for friendly combination with other men; and the unfinished character of the universe. The planet on which we live is an unfinished planet, and, as we have already noted, man is becoming conscious of creative power with which to carry on the unfinished work, with which to change environment and shape life especially through enterprises that require the friendly co-operation of large numbers of men.

But to the eyes of the modern man this planet is but a speck in a vast universe, and this vast universe is an unfinished universe; its worlds are in the making. The human mind finds intellectual rest only as it thinks of the universe in terms of personal significance, that is, as furnishing a scene for personal activity. Men with capacity for personal creative activity which finds scope for itself on the earth necessarily try to interpret the universe from the standpoint of experience on the earth. *From some source personal beings like those developed on the earth must be poured into the unfinished universe.* It is not strange that earth-men peering out among the stars with their telescopes, seeing with the eye of faith the corpuscles of the atom, reaching out under strong inner compulsion for the unseen hand of God and for friendly co-operation with their fellow men, possessing a limitless ambition, should see their opportunity for endless life in the unfinished universe of God. The call to immortality sounds out to us from every point of the environing universe, as well as up from those inner depths where personality rests on God. It is the expectation of such an immortality that Christianity must extend to men in the statement of its central idea.

A LIVING CHRIST AND PERSONALITY

A statement of the central idea in the Christian religion must *recognize the personality of Jesus Christ.* It is he who stands out historically as the founder of Christianity and his title "Christ" has given to our religion its designating adjective. The Christian religion cannot state its central idea without reference to Jesus Christ. Jesus Christ stands out as the leader appointed by God to make the Christian religion, with its conservation of all human interests, dominant in the human race. The period of his leadership was not limited to the few months of activity in Palestine soon after the year 27 A.D., historically assigned to him. Christian thought has always regarded him as exercising active leadership after his death. He carried with him on into his immortal life the responsibility for making the Christian religion dominant in the race.

The nature of the experience soon after his death which convinced the disciples that he was still actively discharging this responsibility is not wholly clear. But it is perfectly clear that something occurred which gave them the triumphant conviction that their Lord was alive and possessed of spiritual energy sufficient for the conduct of his great enterprise. Through the centuries the Christian church has not ceased to look to him as its living leader and Lord. It has sometimes seen him obscurely. Christological dogmas have sometimes made him seem artificial and lifeless, but in various forms devotion to him as a living personality has run through the Christian centuries.

If the Christian enterprise seems much broader today than the first Christians supposed it to be, still it has not outgrown his leadership. He is represented in the Gospels to have assumed this leadership originally in the humble trust that God would make him equal to his task: "I can of myself do nothing." "The Father abiding in me doeth his works." If he has had need of larger powers than were his at the beginning, doubtless God has given them to him. The process of unfolding that has gone on in humanity may well have gone on also in him, the leader and soul of humanity. The Synoptic Gospels clearly teach that he passed through a process of development between childhood and manhood, and they contain no hint that this development ceased in manhood or that it suddenly leaped to a fixed infinity at the moment of his death. Jo. 5:30 Jo. 14:10

The Christian church has at various times tried to define, and must continue to try to define, his relation to God. The effort has never fully succeeded, because men do not yet know the real meaning of the metaphysical terms that would naturally be used in such definition. The words "personality," "man," and "God" lead into vast unexplored fields of thought. The central idea of Christian theology is not knit up with any existing metaphysical definition of the person of Christ. The Christian church has always felt and declared him to be a divine Lord and Saviour without being able, or finding it necessary for the practical purposes of Christian experience, to be more explicit.

That a metaphysical doctrine of the Trinity, always confessing itself to be incomprehensible, should so long be able to retain its place in Christian thought is largely explained by the fact that it has been a way, however vague, temporary, and inadequate, of recognizing the unique place which Jesus has actually maintained in centuries of Christian experience. Christian experience from the beginning down to the present time has found him to be a unique Ro. expression of the "power of God unto salvation," the matchless 1:16 personality through whose leadership God will establish his im- I Cor. mortal social order, and who, as Paul said, will finally "deliver 15:24 up the Kingdom to God."

In Summary

If we try now to gather up these characteristics of the central idea of the Christian religion, we may say that it is the idea of a Fatherly God working through Jesus Christ to redeem the human race from selfishness and give it immortal occupation in the development of the universe. It is the establishment by God of an unselfish human brotherhood under the redeeming leadership of Jesus Christ working together in love forever more in the development of the universe.

This idea has in it something of immediacy and concreteness, something definite to be done at once. At the same time it is big and vague enough to be an unfolding wonder forever more. In the immediate foreground it presents Jesus Christ with his program of an unselfish social order in God's name claiming for it every man and proposing to redeem every man from his destruc- Acts tive bondage to the selfish habit. The apostolic message, "Believe 16:31 on the Lord Jesus Christ and thou shalt be saved" is the message also of the modern preacher, although his conception of the nature of salvation may differ in some details from that of the Apostolic age. He sees stretching away in the limitless distance the vast human brotherhood working together undisturbed by death at the great tasks and problems presented by an unfolding universe. In the center of this brotherhood is still the figure of the Son of Ro. God, "a first-born among many brothers." 8:29

Each of the elements in the central idea here outlined has always been present in some form in Christian experience. In all the centuries of subtle theological discussion more or less convincing about points more or less important, Christian hearts of men, women, and children have felt the purifying, redeeming power of the spirit of Jesus, leading them into larger faith in the Heavenly Father and in each other; they have been doing together, on at least some small scale of co-operation, their daily work, as a task set for them by God; they have stood by their dead expecting to live with them again some time and some where.

The eager readiness with which these conceptions leap into the larger place made for them by modern thought may fill the heart of the Christian thinker with devout enthusiasm.

* * *

The consideration of the central idea in the Christian religion which I have here set forth is presented with no desire to fasten its particular form upon the minds of the students for whom this address has been primarily prepared. My purpose has rather been to incite each to realize for himself in the spirit of unhampered research which prevails among us, the meaning of Christianity, so that he may emerge from his period of study with a message as profound as human need, as simple as the love of God, as far reaching as eternity.

THE PERIOD OF DOUBT AMONG THE FRIENDS OF JESUS

A Study in the Life of Jesus

XIV

THE PERIOD OF DOUBT AMONG
THE FRIENDS OF JESUS

A Study in the Life of Jesus

I T is necessary first to sketch briefly Jesus' method of procedure in announcing his Messiahship, for only so do we see how the period of doubt was occasioned.

According to Matthew a voice from heaven at the baptism, applying to Jesus the Messianic title, Son of God, identified Jesus to John the Baptist as Messiah. According to the first chapter of John's Gospel, the Baptist introduced at least two, and probably more, of his disciples to Jesus as Messiah. There is evidence that the Baptist limited this explicit designation of Jesus as Messiah to an inner circle of his disciples, speaking of him to the main body simply as a very great personage from whom mighty works were to be expected. The evidence of this is the fact, that later, when John the Baptist and Jesus were working near each other in northern Judæa or southern Samaria, the Baptist's disciples came to him in a spirit of grieved loyalty, complaining that he who had been with them beyond Jordan, to whom their Rabbi had borne testi- Jo.
mony, was now drawing all men to himself. They would not have 3:25-26
resented the growing popularity of Jesus, if the Baptist had previously distinctly introduced him to them as the Messiah. They would surely have joined the company of Jesus, as did those to whom the Baptist did speak of Jesus' Messiahship.

Another indication that John spoke publicly of Jesus only as of a great personage is seen in the later attitude toward Jesus of the people east of the Jordan. Late in his ministry, when he was generally thought to be a Messianic aspirant, he went back to this region east of the Jordan where he had first received testimony from John. On the occasion of this visit, the people seem to have regarded him, not as one who had been designated by John as the Messiah, but as one from whom mighty works had been predicted. "John," they said, "did no sign: but all the things whatsoever John spake of this man were true." They then proceeded to believe in Jesus, presumably as Messiah, accepting the surmise that had now become current regarding him.

Jo.
10:40–41

It is to be observed that these two different, though wholly consistent, designations of Jesus are attributed to the Baptist, not the one in the Synoptic Gospels and the other in John's Gospel, but both in John's Gospel. The explanation of the phenomenon is to be sought in Jesus himself. The Synoptic Gospels teach very distinctly that Jesus was opposed to any general announcement of his Messiahship. He hushed the confessions of the affrighted demoniacs, who recognized him. When he sent his disciples out to preach, they made no mention of his Messiahship, but simply reiterated the Baptist's demand for repentance in preparation for the coming kingdom. Far on in the ministry, when Peter said unto him, "Thou art the Christ," "he charged them that they should tell no man of him." *It was to be the sacred secret of the inner circle.* We must surely think of Jesus and the Baptist as having had, in the early days of the ministry, considerable conference with each other; and, since Jesus was so strongly opposed to any public announcement of Messiahship, his wishes must have shaped the Baptist's course. The same stringent prohibition that he put upon all others who might be tempted to proclaim his Messiahship, he put also upon the Baptist.

Mk. 1:34

Mk. 6:12–13

Mk.
8:29–30

The Baptist, therefore, retained the great body of his disciples, and continued his work after the public appearance of Jesus, only making vigorous protest against the surmise, which his disciples' devotion to him was constantly prone to make, that he was himself the Christ. "Ye yourselves bear me witness, that I said, I am not the Christ, but, that I am sent before him." This attitude of extreme deference on the part of the Baptist to Jesus, together with the fact that a few of his most intimate disciples had attached themselves to Jesus, may well have suggested to the rest that John regarded Jesus as a possible Messiah. To produce so suggestive a situation would have been quite in harmony with Jesus' general policy, as will be shown later.

Jo.
3:28

This general reticence of Jesus, the Baptist, and the disciples, upon the subject of Jesus' Messiahship, explains the fact that, according both to the Synoptic Gospels and John's Gospel, the public at large, late in the ministry of Jesus, was in doubt as to whether he really regarded himself as the Messiah. At a time generally thought to be as late as six months before his death, Jesus questioned his disciples as to current popular opinion about himself. They replied, that there was great diversity of opinion, some supposing him to be a reincarnation of John the Baptist, now dead; others supposing him to be Elijah, or Jeremiah, or some other of the old prophets. Of course, if Jesus had announced himself as Messiah, this diversity of views would have been impossible. There could have been but two opinions. He would have been regarded either as the Messiah or as an impostor, for certainly Elijah would not *pretend* to be the Messiah.

Mk.
8:27-28

This same state of uncertainty at a late stage of the ministry is pictured also in John's Gospel. According to John 10:24, the Jerusalem Jews gathered about Jesus one winter day, in the temple area, and tried to extort from him a definite assertion on the subject. "How long dost thou hold us in suspense? If thou art the Christ, tell us plainly." Jesus replied, that he had told them, though evidently not by any such formal declaration as we are now discussing, but by the character of his works, a way of which more will be said further on. It is, furthermore, a familiar fact that at his final trial the prosecutors were unable to secure adequate evidence that he had ever distinctly asserted his Messiahship, and the case against him would have broken down, had not he himself made the requisite confession on the spot. There is evidence, then, both in the Synoptic Gospels and in John's Gospel, that Jesus repressed all public announcement of his Messiahship.

Mk.
14:55-63

It seems probable, also, that even in his intercourse with the inner circle of his own disciples, his assertions of Messiahship were neither explicit nor frequent. The first chapter of John's Gospel puts it beyond question that his first disciples, who were afterward members of the apostolic band, gathered about him with the conviction that he was the Messiah. Jesus seemed to encourage this conviction, not by a distinct statement, but by one of his characteristic suggestively obscure sayings, "Because I said unto thee, I

Jo.
1:50-51

saw thee underneath the fig-tree, believest thou? Thou shalt see greater things than these. . . . Verily, verily, I say unto you, Ye shall see the heaven opened, and the angels of God ascending and descending upon the Son of man."[1] They knew that he was re-

Jo.
4:25–26
Jo.
9:35–37

ported in Sychar to have said to a village woman, that he was the Messiah, and they may have known later of the distinct declaration of Messiahship made to the blind Jerusalem beggar that had been excommunicated from the synagogue. In general, however, in his intercourse with his disciples, he seems to have manifested a reticence about discussing his Messiahship that must often have perplexed them.

In connection with this mysterious avoidance of any distinct assertion of Messiahship, Jesus kept doing many things calculated to

Mk. 2:5
v. 28

Mt. 12:6

suggest that he thought himself to be the Messiah. He assumed authority to forgive sins; he assumed authority to abrogate the Sabbath law; he spoke of himself as one greater than the temple; above all, he asserted for himself an intimate and unique relation

Jo.
5:17–18

to God, by calling God in some special sense his Father.

Not all of these assumptions were currently recognized features of Messiahship. Indeed some of them would probably have seemed to the Jews, with their low conception of Messiahship, assumptions that no Messiah would have ventured to make. This may have been particularly true of Jesus' statements regarding his unique filial relation to God. While the title "Son of God" was a regularly recognized Messianic title, the Jews seem to have given it no such richness of meaning as Jesus expressed when discussing his filial relation to God. Therefore it may well have been that some of the discourses in John's Gospel referring to his filial relation to God in a way that is to us, and was to him, a clear implication of Messiahship, seemed to them such blasphemy as no Messiah would have uttered. In addition to these suggestive state-

Cf. Jo.
3:2

ments about himself, Jesus gave impressive exhibitions of power that were suggestive of Messiahship; although, taken by themselves, they were such as God might empower a prophet to make.

---

[1]It is assumed in all this discussion that the expression "Son of man" was not a current Messianic title, and that its use, therefore, was not an evident assertion of Messiahship.

In general, it may be said that Jesus did a great deal in public to produce the surmise that he was the Messiah, sometimes, especially among the Jerusalem leaders, according to John's Gospel, going to the very verge of explicit assertion; but that he scrupulously refrained from any decisive, formal, public avowal of Messiahship. The two unequivocal avowals mentioned in John's Gospel were both privately made to individuals when not even his disciples were present. He behaved in such a way as to draw the attention of the nation to himself, and yet he held the nation at arm's length, leaving it uncertain whether he really considered himself to be the Messiah. This strange method of procedure, so well calculated to arouse eager expectation, and yet for many months failing to gratify it, afforded the ground for what I have called the *period of doubt*. We have now to consider the different individuals or classes that doubted, discuss more particularly the ground of their doubt, and the measures taken by Jesus to remove it.

THE DOUBT OF JOHN THE BAPTIST

The first to be seriously troubled by this long-deferred announcement of Messiahship was, strangely enough, the Baptist himself. He that had been first to recognize, was first to doubt. Upon closer scrutiny, however, the Baptist's doubt does not appear so strange. Among the minor considerations that explain his doubt are these. He was the first of the circle of the friends of Jesus to suffer disaster, because of his connection with Jesus. He had gone fearlessly on with a vigorous popular campaign of preparation for the Messiah's kingdom, preaching reform impartially to high and low, and, in consequence, was now imprisoned in a fortress among the barren crags of Moab. He had been used to the wild, free, dervish life of the wilderness, and found his spirit growing moody in the unwonted and intolerable confinement of the prison. Furthermore, such inactive solitude, after the exhilaration of a period of great popularity, preaching to vast crowds upon subjects that profoundly moved him, produced a painful reaction. Like his great prototype, Elijah, who after the excitement of Carmel wanted to die, he, too, may have been greatly depressed in spirit. His depression was not helped by the apparent indifference

of Jesus, who organized no such movement for his release as a
Messiah might have been expected to originate.

But there must have been certain more fundamental doubts that
kept coming into his mind, and that he had not the health and
strength to put away. The first of these was Jesus' strange failure
to begin the work of judgment. The most prominent feature in
John's pungent preaching had been the prediction of judgment.
He had thrilled his audiences with most vivid and homely illustrations of the nearness of the Messianic Judge. The Messiah,
whose advent was now so imminent, was like a farmer making a
tour of inspection in his orchard, laying his axe down for a moment at the root of the tree, while deciding by a final examination of its branches, whether to spare it or cut it down. He was
like the farmer, whose foot was already upon the edge of the
threshing-floor, and whose uplifted hand held the winnowing-fan
ready to begin the separation of wheat from chaff, to garner the
one and burn the other.

Mt. 3:10

v. 12

John's heart had been hot with indignation against the great
sins of his age,—the religious hypocrisy and hard-hearted love of
money that he saw upon his occasional visits to Jerusalem, and
brooded over when he returned to his wilderness home. The Messiah would come in stern and awful wrath to smite the rotten
structure of this social system. But the months passed wearily on,
and Jesus gave no sign of a disposition to judge any one. He went
genially and sociably about among the people, attending their
weddings and dinner parties. His enemies, the Pharisees, were
contemptuously referring to him as a man overfond of good food
and fine wines,—"a gluttonous man and a winebibber." How
could a Messiah go socially about attending weddings and dinner
parties in the face of these awful evils of society that cried out to
heaven for judgment! Jesus was perhaps even reported in the
Machaerus prison[2] to have said that he came not to judge the
world! He was apparently proving deficient in what had been a
fundamental feature of the Baptist's conception of Messiahship.

Mt. 11:19

Another essential feature of the Baptist's conception of Messiah-

[2]Machaerus Citadel was located nine miles east of the Dead Sea. It is not mentioned
in N.T. Josephus, however, states that John Baptist was imprisoned and put to death
here by Herod Antipas. (cf. Mt. 14:3f.). "He (John) was sent a prisoner . . . to Machaerus. . . . and was there put to death." *Ant. XVIII*, 5, 2; *Wars VII*, 6, 2. (Ed.)

ship had been the Messiah's baptism with the Holy Spirit. "My Mt. 3:11
baptism," John kept saying, "is only a water baptism. His will be
a Holy Spirit baptism." But the months passed by, and Jesus baptized no one with the Spirit.

Furthermore the Baptist's faith must have been sorely tried by
a certain apparent aimlessness in the life of Jesus. Jesus failed to
take any decided steps toward the organization of a kingdom.
Although he gave startling exhibitions of power in the healing of
disease, he seemed unequal to the main emergency, with no adequate conception of what it devolved upon a Messiah to do. A
strange apparent hesitation had always characterized Jesus, and
must have been sorely perplexing to a man of John's positive temperament. At the very beginning, when Jesus met John in the
Jordan valley, he had manifested an inexplicable unreadiness to
embrace an opportunity. The crowds gathered by John were
eagerly expecting the Messiah, and were ready to be organized
into a kingdom. Everything seemed ready for the hand of a
strong, forceful Messianic leader, but Jesus, instead of seizing the
opportunity, strangely disappeared, and was not seen again for
some six weeks. He was reported to have gone away alone into the
wilderness.

The great festivals of the nation, when devout Jews came up to
Jerusalem from all over the Roman Empire, were choice opportunities for a Messiah to influence his people, but Jesus seemed sometimes to shrink from these occasions. It was this trait that made
his own family lose patience with him. "Now the feast of the Jo.
7:2-5
Jews, the feast of tabernacles, was at hand. His brethren therefore
said unto him, Depart hence, and go into Judæa, that thy disciples
also may behold thy works which thou doest. For no man doeth
anything in secret, and himself seeketh to be known openly. If
thou doest these things, manifest thyself to the world." He went
about country, village, and city healing sick people, visiting poor
people, and gratifying fond mothers, doubtless much to the an-
noyance of his disciples, by giving their little children his blessing.

And so it happened that two men of serious mien clambered
down the steeps of Moab, crossed the Jordan, and suddenly con-
fronted Jesus one day as he taught the people in the market, with Lu.
7:20
the abrupt query: "John the Baptist hath sent us unto thee, saying,

Art thou he that cometh, or look we for another?" Jesus' reply to the earnest question was characteristic. He bade the messengers

v. 21 watch him, while, for a busy hour, "he cured many of diseases and plagues and evil spirits; and on many that were blind he bestowed sight." Then he sent a message to John, devoid as usual, of any direct assertion of Messiahship. It was a description of what he was doing, in language suggestive of the Baptist's favorite prophet, the prophet in whom he had found the language that

Jo. 1:23 best expressed his sense of vocation, "I am the voice of one crying in the wilderness."

Isaiah had prophesied, as John had perhaps failed duly to notice, that a part of the glory of the Messianic age would consist in such healing of physical ailments as Jesus was then performing.

Isa. 35:5-6 "Then the eyes of the blind shall be opened, and the ears of the deaf shall be unstopped. Then shall the lame man leap as an hart, and the tongue of the dumb shall sing." "The Spirit of the Lord

Isa. 61:1 Lu. 7:22 God is upon me; because the Lord hath anointed me to preach good tidings unto the poor (meek)." "Go your way and tell John," said Jesus, "what things ye have seen and heard; the blind receive their sight, the lame walk, the lepers are cleansed, the deaf hear, the dead are raised up, the poor have good tidings preached to them." That is, John was to see that, although Jesus seemed in some particulars so un-Messiah-like, these actions were really the beginning of that banishment of physical ailment, of death, and of disregard of the poor, which Isaiah had prophesied as part of the glorious Messianic reign. The reference to prophecy was reenforced by a kindly personal exhortation to John to put away his

v. 23 doubts,—"and blessed is he, whosoever shall find none occasion of stumbling in me." It was an assurance that Jesus knew what he was about, and an appeal to John simply to trust him.

When John had listened eagerly and thoughtfully to the report of his messengers, he doubtless turned again to the well-thumbed parchment roll of his favorite prophet, and read the portions suggested to him by Jesus' reply. Perhaps he saw a secret significance in the words that prefaced one of the passages, "Say to them that

Isa. 35:4-5 are of a fearful heart, Be strong, fear not: behold, your God will come with vengeance, with the recompense of God; he will come and save you. Then the eyes of the blind shall be opened." He trusted once more in the reliability of the sign of the descending _{Jo.} dove, which he had learned in the wilderness to expect, and which _{1:32-34} he had seen at Jesus' baptism.

THE DOUBT OF THE GALILEANS

We have next to consider the situation of a large class of the common people. As has already been said, Jesus' conduct was such as to attract the attention of the nation to himself as a personage of great distinction. Candid men like Nicodemus admitted that he must be a teacher from God, because of the mighty works he did, but there was no agreement as to who he was. As time went on there were many to suggest that perhaps he was the Messiah.

This last opinion nearly came to an open expression among the common people in Galilee. His fame as a prophet was so great that the sight of him, starting across the head of the Lake of Galilee in a boat with his disciples, was sufficient to set the crowds hurrying around the head of the lake on foot; so that, when he reached his destination, there was awaiting him upon the shore a crowd of ten or fifteen thousand people,—"five thousand men, be- _{Mt.} side women and children." As the day drew near its close, some _{14:13-21} provision had to be made for feeding them, and this need Jesus met by miraculously increasing the five loaves and two fishes that happened to be at hand. When the crowds became aware of the miracle that was being performed, they went wild.

There is one note that is never absent from the world's composite voice. Sometimes it is the pitiful wail of children, and sometimes the hoarse voice of desperate men. It is the age-long cry of the hungry for bread. For them, he who can make bread cheap may be king. Men's conceptions of the coming kingdom doubtless varied, then as now, with their various ideals. It was to each man the time when that which he most ardently hoped for would be attained. Just as to the Pharisee the Kingdom of God was a state in which every man in his daily life would be a punctilious law-keeper, so to these people on the lake shore it was a state in which the bitter struggle for the common necessities of life would cease, when bread would be plenty and cheap. They had emphasized such passages in the prophets as described prodigious fertility, even the deserts blooming in luxuriant vegetation, "The des-

Isa.
35:1–2 ert shall rejoice, and blossom as the rose. It shall blossom abundantly."

This action of Jesus, making bread to abound for the poor, seemed to them the sure beginning of Messianic plenty, and a sure indication of Jesus' Messiahship. These free-spirited, daring Galileans began to gather here and there in groups. Word was passed rapidly about among them that they would seize Jesus by force, carry him back to Capernaum, throw off allegiance to Herod and Tiberius, and make Jesus Messianic Emperor. Then they would sweep through the country in triumphant procession to the approaching passover in Jerusalem, carrying everything before them. But when the leaders of the crowd looked for Jesus, he was gone! He had slipped quietly up the mountain side.

The next day they found him in Capernaum. At once, with the simple directness of perfect insight, he proceeded to describe them to themselves. He told them that their interest in him was chiefly due, not to their desire for the higher phases of life to be realized in the Messianic kingdom, not even to their desire to see miraculous exhibitions of power like that of the previous day, but simply Jo.
6:26 to their desire for easier physical conditions, for cheap bread. "Ye seek me, not because ye saw signs, but because ye ate of the loaves, and were filled." The people tried to tempt him into a repetition of the miracle of the preceding day by slyly hinting, that, as Ex.
16:4–5, 21 Moses had given *daily free* manna in the wilderness, so he might cause a daily multiplication of free loaves. When this hint did not suffice, they plainly requested him to begin the plenty of the Mes- Jo.
6:31–34 sianic reign,—"Lord, evermore give us this bread." Jesus then proceeded to deliver a characteristic address, presenting to them the spiritual character of his Messianic ideal in a form that we now recognize as profoundly suggestive to the spiritually minded, but so weirdly enigmatical and unpractical in the judgment of the Jo.
6:51–53 multitude as to alienate effectively the element that had desired to crown him Messianic king. He seemed to them to be talking in a senseless way about some cannibalistic eating of his flesh and blood.

This alienated not simply the people that, the day before, would have forced upon him the role of a political Messiah, but others who had been inclined to the theory of his Messiahship and even

called "disciples." "Many of his disciples went back, and walked   v. 66
no more with him." His failure to utilize the opportunity for a
declaration of Messiahship or to take conciliatory attitude toward
the crowd, argued in their minds a fatal lack of the practical
political force and sagacity requisite for the establishment and administration of a great world-empire. Moreover, this obscure,
sentimental style of speech convinced them that, although he did
possess certain strange, miraculous powers, he was a visionary,
a half-daft dreamer. This we know to have been the view held at
one time by his own family. They are on record as having thought
him "beside himself," and in need of their care. Jesus himself,   Mk.
when in Nazareth, significantly confessed that a prophet was not   3:20-21
without honor, except "in his own country, and among his own   Mk.
kin, and in his own *house*."   6:4

THE DOUBT OF THE TWELVE

This doubt among the people and outer circle of his own disciples, Jesus was not able at the time to overcome. He let them go,
and turned his attention to holding his immediate friends, the
twelve men of his choice and those connected with them. There
was sore need that he should concentrate attention upon them,
for it was a critical time in the history of their connection with
him.

It is natural to suppose that the considerations that had tended
to produce doubt in the minds of John the Baptist, the outer circle
of Galilean disciples, and the Galilean common people, must
have been to some extent operative in the minds of the Twelve.
They must have felt very painfully Jesus' failure month after
month to make formal proclamation of his Messiahship, and to
proceed to do the things they had expected soon to see him do,
when they first attached themselves to him. They doubtless were
concerned about his failure to utilize the readiness of the Galileans for a popular movement in his favor, and the unpractical,
enigmatical character of the address in the Capernaum synagogue
must have been a trial to them.

It remains now to cite the evidence of their doubt, and to show
how Jesus overcame it.

The first distinct hint of their danger is found in the solemn warning with which Jesus surprised them as they were sailing away from the Galilean shore after an ominously short interview with some of the principal Galilean Pharisees: "Take heed," said he impressively, "beware of the leaven of the Pharisees and of the leaven of Herod." The disciples at first failed to see the force of the remark. They noticed that they had neglected to replenish their store of provisions with a fresh supply of bread, and dully interpreted Jesus' remark as a playful rebuke of their carelessness,—"You seem to be afraid of the leavened loaves that are to be bought in the Galilean domain of Herod and the Pharisees!"

Mk.
8:15

The real meaning of Jesus' remark is to be sought in the interview with the Pharisees that had just occurred. In that interview the Pharisees had hypocritically desired a sign from heaven, as if ready to accept evidence of his Messiahship, while really plotting for his arrest and execution. In another context Jesus is represented as saying distinctly, that the leaven of the Pharisees is hypocrisy. The fact that Herod is mentioned with the Pharisees indicates that he, too, was in some way leagued with the Pharisees against Jesus, although manifesting no open opposition to him. The Pharisees and Herodians had at an earlier period been in collusion. In Luke 13: 31, 32, when certain Pharisees warned Jesus to get out of Galilee because Herod was going to kill him, Jesus is said to have called him a "fox," which seems to imply that Jesus regarded him as sly and hypocritical.

Mk.
8:11–13

Lu.
12:1

Mk.
3:6

The Twelve, then, at this period were in danger of a kind of hypocrisy in appearing to have more confidence in Jesus than they really felt. The doubts that John the Baptist so frankly confessed to Jesus, they felt, but feared to express. It may be that the apostate spirit in Judas was beginning to develop. Such a state of mind was entirely distasteful to the transparent honesty of Jesus. He, therefore, not long after, took measures to bring out into open statement their real feeling with reference to him. The account of his attempt is given in close connection with this warning against hypocrisy. In the vicinity of Cæsarea Philippi he asked them one day an unusual question. After inquiring what the current opinion regarding himself was, he turned directly upon them with the searching question, "Who do you think that I am?" "If you have doubts, out with them," he seemed to say. Peter an-

Mk
8:29

swered that they believed him to be the Christ. It is hardly probable that all of them could have given this reply as promptly
and sincerely as did Peter. The confession was exceedingly gratifying to Jesus, and drew from him the appreciative exclamation,
"Blessed art thou, Simon, son of John."

The source of Peter's conviction could not be sought in the con-
flicting opinions current among the people, and, as we have seen,
Jesus himself had in all probability refrained from any explicit
assertion of Messiahship even in the inner circle of his disciples.
The peculiar conduct that had recently alienated so large a part
of his following was a distinct obstacle to such confidence as
Peter here expressed. It was an evidence of spiritual enlighten-
ment that Peter, under such circumstances, should still persist in
the conviction that had led him at the first to attach himself to
Jesus, and Jesus seemed to recognize this in saying to him,
"Blessed art thou, Simon, Bar-Jonah: for flesh and blood hath not Mt.
revealed it unto thee, but my Father which is in heaven." 16:17

After encouraging them by the virtual avowal of Messiahship
implied in his reply to Peter, Jesus proceeded to subject their
confidence in the theory of his Messiahship to a severe strain. He
told them that the hatred of the Scribes and Pharisees would succeed in accomplishing his death. The death of the Messiah was a
thought entirely foreign both to learned Jewish theology and to
the popular conception of Messiahship. "We have heard out of the Jo.
law that the Christ abideth forever," the multitude said to Jesus 12:34
when, at a later period, in Jerusalem, he predicted his death. The
Twelve themselves do not seem to have taken Jesus' predictions of
death and resurrection after three days literally. Had they done so,
they would not have given up in despair when he did die, and
would not have regarded the first report of a resurrection as "idle Lu. 24:11
talk."

They probably regarded this prediction as one of the many enigmatical utterances of Jesus that they could not understand. Perhaps they thought it likely that he was figuratively describing
some sort of temporary disappearance to be followed by a triumphant reappearance; for at the time of his famous discourse
upon the destruction of Jerusalem, they seem to have made up
their minds that he was to disappear for a time, and simply asked

Mt. 24:3   him what would be the sign of his *parousia*. That they did not in that question have in mind a death and resurrection is evident from the fact, just noted, that the actual death seemed to them the end of all their hope. It is true that the words of protest ascribed to Peter in Matthew's Gospel indicate that, when Peter for the first time heard Jesus' prediction, he was inclined to take it literally, and regarded it as the expression of a gloomy and somewhat despondent frame of mind, which he sought to remove by

Mt. 16:22   saying, "Be it far from thee, Lord: this shall never be unto thee."

According to Mark's Gospel, which often throws light upon the words of Jesus by preserving the significant circumstances of their historical setting, the disciples were disturbed because Jesus made this prediction in the presence of the people in his *public* teaching. This seemed to them a serious blunder, the repetition of

Mk. 8:32   which Peter vigorously sought to prevent. "He spake the saying openly. And Peter took him, and began to rebuke him." The danger, so Peter seems to have argued, was that the multitude would think Jesus meant what he said, and he thus be entirely discredited in their eyes; for no one could be expected to follow a Messiah who anticipated death. To Peter's thought this was another instance of an unwise use of figurative language, like that which in the Capernaum address had already cost him so large a part of his following.

Jesus, however, would not retract, nor abate the force of his statement. Neither would he avoid publicity, but "called unto him the multitude with his disciples," and told them that not simply did he anticipate death himself, but that no one could keep a

Mk. 8:33-34   place in his following who was not ready to die with him. "If any man would come after me, let him deny himself, and take up his cross, and follow me." This recklessly impolitic statement produced consternation among the disciples, and introduced them into a period of doubt that constituted the most critical stage in the history of their connection with Jesus. It lasted, according to the statement of all three Synoptic Gospels, for one week. During this week of suspense they doubtless debated long and seriously among themselves the pros and cons of Jesus' Messiahship. Should they cut loose from him as so many among the people had done? Back of this unpractical disappointing conduct was there in his personality the real force and sagacity requisite for the founding and administering of a great Jewish world-empire? Would he ever take a decisive forward step? On the other hand, how could a Messiah do works more wonderful than those done by him? Had there not been manifested in his life attractive personal qualities that would make it hard to leave him?

It seems probable that, as the week drew near its close, Jesus, watching his disciples closely, saw how evenly the issue hung in the balance, and proceeded to turn the scale by employing a unique measure for the recovery of their confidence. It is a significant fact that in all three Synoptic Gospels this measure is dated with reference to Jesus' disturbing statements about his death and the possible death of some of his disciples. Matthew and Mark introduce their account of the measure with the expression "after six days," and Luke, employing a different method of reckoning, begins his narrative with the statement, "It came to pass about eight days after these sayings." Jesus invited the three leading spirits of the apostolic company to spend a night with him on the mountain. There, in their presence, he came down from the plane of spiritual demonstration, and, as a concession to their need, condescended to make for them an impressive physical demonstration of Messianic glory. "He was transfigured before them; and his garments became glistering, exceeding white; so as no fuller on earth can whiten them. And there appeared unto him Elijah with Moses: and they were talking with Jesus." The three disciples became sore afraid; for "there came a cloud overshadowing them: and there came a voice out of the cloud," applying to Jesus the Messianic title, and bidding them have confidence in him, "This is my beloved Son: hear ye him."

Mt. 17:1
Mk. 9:2
Lu. 9:28

Evidently this unique demonstration thoroughly convinced the three men, for Jesus felt it necessary to pledge them to secrecy, qualifying his injunction this time by giving them permission to reveal their experience after he had risen from the dead. They obeyed his injunction, but were greatly puzzled as to what the rising again from the dead meant. The other nine apostles, therefore, probably did not know what had happened on the mountain, but they did know that their three companions were now perfectly certain that Jesus was the Messiah, and the confidence

Mk.
9:9

vv. 33–34

Mt.
20:20–21

of these three influenced the rest. Thenceforth they all counted confidently upon the speedy establishment of the kingdom, and straightway proceeded to apportion among themselves in imagination the offices of the new state. The ambitious mother of James and John sought to get the advantage of Peter by trying to pledge Jesus beforehand to give her sons the two highest offices in the new state.

CONCLUSION

There is no opportunity in this discussion to consider in detail the reasons for Jesus' strange method of procedure in the announcement of his Messiahship. It is sufficient to say, in general, that this purpose was to replace the popular conception of Messiahship, and of the Kingdom of God, by the larger, truer one that lay in his own mind. In order to do this, it was necessary to attract the attention of the nation to himself as a prophet of God, or as a possible Messiah, and then to keep it in a period of prolonged suspense which he might utilize to illustrate by life and teaching his own conception of the Kingdom of God and Messiahship. Neither is there opportunity in the present discussion to consider what the details of this conception were, what the expression "Kingdom of God" meant to Jesus, and what he conceived to be the chief business of a Messiah.

As we look back upon the period, we see that his conception was definite and profound. He had seen the vision of redeemed humanity that he who sees forgets nevermore, the details of which are being slowly wrought out, and the ultimate realization of which will amply compensate for all the suffering of the centuries. Two things were dominant in his vision—love and life. Hate and death had disappeared from among men. The age-long cursing and sobbing of humanity had died away forever. He saw the Federation of the men of the Loving Heart extending its high civilization among all nations and into the endless ages. His confidence in the ultimate feasibility of his own conception was so perfect that it did not disturb him to go with it directly athwart the conceptions of a majority of his countrymen, and even to disappoint the expectations of his best friends.

The reason he seemed to his contemporaries to have no plan

was because his plan was so vast and so simple that they could not see its outlines.[3] In the midst of the impatience of his friends and the sneering hatred of his enemies, he stood with the calm patience of a soul that had come out of eternity, silently and steadily maturing a plan, not for the quick realization of a single generation, but for the ages.

[3]"No one can afford to be simple but the great," Inglis Fletcher has said through one of her characters, Lady Caroline. Cf. *Raleigh's Eden,* p. 264. (Ed.)

FAITH

XV

FAITH

WHAT is the meaning of this great apostolic word that
voices, vibrant with hope, rang out through the Roman Empire in the first century; this great word
which, in the Reformation period, called men back again to the
truly religious life; this word that is reëmphasized today even by
those who are inclined to discard much of the phraseology of dog-
matic theology? The purpose of this study is to examine the word
from the standpoint of New Testament usage, and give attention
to its appearance in different types of New Testament presentation. In doing this one fact obscured by our English translation
needs steadily to be borne in mind, namely, that in the Greek, the
words translated "faith" and "to believe" are the substantive and
verbal forms of the same root, πίστις and πιστεύω.

I

"Faith" or "Belief" Emphasized by Jesus in the Synoptic Gospels

The word is most frequently used in the Synoptic Gospels to
describe the state of mind in which sick persons or their friends
approached Jesus for healing. It was this state of mind that Jesus
insisted upon in such cases. He said to two blind men who followed him home one day, piteously begging for sight: "Believe ye   Mt. 9:28
that I am able to do this?" When they assured him that they did   v. 29
believe him able, he promptly said: "According to your faith be it
done unto you," and their eyes were opened. When the synagogue
ruler learned that his little daughter was dead, and when he was
consequently about to give up hope, Jesus assured him that if he
would only continue to believe, his little daughter would yet be
restored to him. In his home town it was the lack of this state of
mind called "faith" that so surprised Jesus and made it impossible

for him to heal as he had been accustomed to do in other towns:

Mk.
6:5–6 "He could there do no mighty work, save that he laid his hands on a few sick folk and healed them, and he marveled at their *unbelief.*"

We have now to inquire what this state of mind was and why it was essential to the act of healing. It is first of all evident that in most cases it did not involve the recognition of Jesus as the Messiah. It is evident from Mark 8:27–30 that Jesus kept his consciousness of Messiahship as the strictly guarded secret of the inner circle of his disciples. Therefore the faith which he openly demanded of those who sought healing from him cannot have been a recognition of his Messiahship. The element in the nation that was favorably disposed to him regarded him not as the Messiah, but as a great prophet, and Jesus was content that they should do no more for the time being. Although occasionally, according to Matthew's Gospel, an individual thought to gratify him by addressing him as the Messiah, the most of those who came for healing regarded him as a great prophet-healer. When they saw the cures that he wrought, they did not infer Messiahship, but simply "glorified God who had given such authority unto men."

Mk.
8:28

Mt. 15:22
also 9:27

Mt. 9:8

The faith of those who recognized him as a prophet involved more than the conviction that Jesus had *power* to cure. The Pharisees acknowledged his power, but explained it by the theory that he was in league with Satan. This attitude of the Pharisees is never called faith. Faith had in it evidently *an element of good will wholly absent from the Pharisees' frame of mind.* Those who had faith were those sufficiently well disposed towards Jesus to regard him as a prophet of God. They came to him, therefore, with a confident good-will which recognized in him a great prophet-healer sent from God.

This friendly confidence in him was based on evidence. People heard what he had done, and what they heard produced faith in him as a prophet-healer. Their faith rested on facts. Their faith led them to expect something in excess of their previous experience, but this expectation was rationally based on evidence. It was after "having heard the things concerning Jesus" that the desperate woman took courage and touched Jesus' garment with the faith of which Jesus said: "Thy faith hath made thee whole."

Mk. 5:27

v. 34

What was the connection between this state of confident good-will called faith, and the cure? Did Jesus arbitrarily decide that he would cure no one who was not in this state of mind? Or did he for some moral reason think it desirable that only such should be relieved of their burden of sickness? Or was there some law of psychological therapeutics that made it necessary in the nature of the case that the patient should be in this frame of mind before Jesus' healing power could operate? We know too little of the way in which the personality of Jesus affected the personality of the sick to speak with confidence on this point. There is an increasing tendency, however, to conclude that such receptive good will as is involved in faith was, in the nature of the case, a psychologically necessary condition of the action of Jesus' healing power, and that Mark's Gospel is to be taken literally when it says of Nazareth that "he *could* there do no mighty work."

Mk. 6:5

The fact that Jesus healed some at a distance, or raised the dead, or cured demoniacs is not inconsistent with such an understanding, for in no one of such cases do we know that the person in question had any other disposition towards Jesus than one of receptive good will. The little daughter of the ruler of the synagogue probably knew that her father had sent to Jesus for help, and as she sank into the unconsciousness of death shared her father's expectancy. The same was also very likely true of the afflicted daughter of the woman of Syrophenicia. As to the personal character of the young man of Nain, concerning his attitude towards Jesus in life and after death we have no knowledge whatever. In the disordered consciousness of the demoniacs one element seems generally to have been readiness to appeal to Jesus for help.

Mk. 5:23

Mk. 7:24-25
Lu. 7:11-17

The case of the high priest's servant whose ear Jesus restored at the time of the arrest seems at first thought inconsistent with this viewpoint, but we do not know what may have been the real attitude of his heart towards Jesus. He may not have been bitter towards Jesus, as were his official superiors. John 18:15–16 reads as though Jesus might have had friends in the high priest's household. Their official relation to the high priest, and not personal hostility to Jesus, may have occasioned their presence at the time of the arrest.

Lu. 22:50-51

This trustful recognition of Jesus as a prophet, or a prophet-healer, was doubtless in many cases followed by *results in moral character*. The paralytic whom Jesus assured of forgiveness was doubtless ever after a different man morally as well as physically. The street woman who bathed his feet with penitent tears, though she may have seen in him nothing more than a strangely gracious prophet of God, became a new woman morally. This trustful ex-

Lu. 7:50 pression of her faith saved her: "Thy faith hath saved thee."

But faith, in the synoptic usage, is not applied merely to the sick and their friends who saw in Jesus a prophet-healer and appealed to him with confident good will, or to the morally ailing who turned to him as a great friendly prophet. In the case of the inner circle of Jesus' disciples, faith meant far more than this. It meant confidence in him as the Messiah. Very likely their lack of "faith" during the storm on the lake was a wavering confidence

Mk. 4:40 in him as Messiah: "Have ye not yet faith?" Certainly at a later time the faith of Peter, which Jesus' prayer kept from utterly and

Lu.
22:32 permanently failing, was faith in Jesus as Messiah: "I have made supplication for thee that thy faith fail not." The word is used by

Mt. 6:30 Jesus to describe *the attitude that a man should assume towards his Heavenly Father*. Those who worry are those of "little faith." The great resource of the disciples for bringing to pass the Kingdom of God was not to be such an aggregation of men and women as were present at the triumphal procession that finally brought Jesus into Jerusalem, nor any such display of force as the disciples probably expected to see Jesus make. On the contrary his

Mk.
11:22–25 great injunction to them at this point was: "Have faith in God," and in the exercise of that faith they were to expect great achievements through prayer.

Some times the object of faith is represented to be the gospel:

Mk.
1:15 "The Kingdom of God is at hand; repent ye and believe the gospel." The "gospel" in this early stage of the Galilean preaching, when Jesus was not yet recognized as anything more than a prophet, was the "good news" of the nearness of the Kingdom. A similar use is that in Luke 8:12–13, where the "word" which people "believe" with a view to being "saved" is the message of the imminent Kingdom. Of course the imminence of the Kingdom meant to the Jew of Jesus' day the imminence of the Messiah and the Messianic judgment, so that belief in the gospel involved as its essential element, belief in the expected coming of the Messiah.

If we now try to sum up the contribution made by the Synoptic Gospels to our conception of faith, certain facts appear. In the large majority of cases Jesus is himself the object of faith, but as a prophet-healer and not as Messiah. "Faith," or "belief," in him consists in recognizing him to be whatever he seems to represent himself to be and in *treating him accordingly.* From the start he represented himself to be a messenger from God bringing men good news of the on-coming kingdom, instructing them regarding the righteousness requisite for entrance into the kingdom, and bringing them personal sympathy and help in their sicknesses and sorrows. Faith is the word that describes the response appropriate to such an approach. The essential element in the response was obedient good will. As it became apparent to some that Jesus regarded himself as more than a prophet or prophet-healer, indeed as no other than the Messiah himself, the only appropriate response was *to recognize him as such and to treat him as the Messiah ought to be treated,* namely, with unreserved obedience and love.

This period in which Jesus did not stand out as an avowed Messiah was therefore a period when faith was a varying experience in so far as Jesus was its object. The beginning of any feeling of friendliness for Jesus, especially in the dark times of his unpopularity, was quickly seized upon by Jesus as the beginning of faith. Anyone who was not against him was for him; and the being for him, no matter how vague and unintelligent the feeling was, counted with him as the beginning of faith.[1] A most dramatic illustration of this is offered by the experience of one of the two brigands crucified with Jesus. This man can scarcely have had a suspicion that Jesus was the Messiah, for even Jesus' best friends gave up that idea when once he was on the cross. This brigand had doubtless been deeply impressed by the behavior of Jesus. Jesus had not struggled and raved when the executioners threw him down and nailed him to the cross. When his enemies walked

---

[1]Those of Doctor Bosworth's readers who have found time thoughtfully to go through the preceding Study on "The Period of Doubt Among the Friends of Jesus," will have gained a picture of Jesus' skill in laying foundations for vastly revised conceptions of life and enterprise, and of struggle to win human confidence therein. (Ed.).

about the foot of the cross chuckling and gloating over their success, he had not hurled down curses upon them. When his friends
stole up to the cross he had not complained, but comforted them.
All this impressed the brigand. He probably considered Jesus to
be a harmless fanatic, or perhaps a half-daft enthusiast who suffered under the delusion that he was a king. In the brigand's heart
there began to develop a genuine sympathy and friendliness which
led him to turn his head to Jesus at some time during the slow
hours and say with grim but friendly humor: "Jesus, remember
me when thou comest into thy kingdom." Jesus saw in this sympathy the beginning of faith and seized upon it with eager enthusiasm: "Verily I say unto thee, today shalt thou be with me in
Paradise."

Lu.
23:42-43

Many a Jew may have had the experience which Richard Watson Gilder attributes to the pagan who had met Jesus and who
found himself powerfully attracted to him, though uncertain as
yet who he really was.

> "If Jesus Christ is a man,—
> And only a man,—I say
> That of all mankind I cleave to him,
> And to him will I cleave alway.
>
> If Jesus Christ is a God,—
> And the only God,—I swear,
> I will follow Him through heaven and hell,
> The earth, the sea, and the air."[2]

II

"FAITH" DURING THE EARLY YEARS AFTER THE RESURRECTION

In this period, for which the first part of the book of Acts is our
chief source of information, the situation had decidedly changed.
Jesus had been declared Messiah by an unmistakable resurrection
from the dead, and now the apostles were urging upon all Jews
faith in Jesus as the Messiah. By faith they seem to have meant the
acknowledgment that the crucified and resurrected Jesus was the
Messiah, that he was now with the Father in power in the spirit
world, that he would soon come to execute the long deferred Mes-

[2]Gilder, *The Poems of Richard Watson Gilder*, 1908 Cambridge ed., p. 53.

sianic judgment, and to inaugurate the Messianic Kingdom. Although absent, he was still operating in the lives of believers through the agency of the Holy Spirit whom he had sent from the Father.

To what extent he was thought of as himself spiritually present and accessible to believers is not wholly clear. Peter seemed to feel that his faith or confidence in Jesus' healing power influenced Jesus to cure the cripple at the gate as he had cured cripples before his death: "And by faith in his name hath his name made this man strong, whom ye behold and know; yea, the faith which is through him hath given him this perfect soundness in the presence of you all." The thought of Jesus' spiritual presence, however, seems not to have been as distinctly realized as it later came to be. Acts 3:16

In the Epistle to the Hebrews, which may logically, though not chronologically, be considered here, faith is a bold unwavering confidence that God will keep his promises; especially that he will bring the Messiah's kingdom to perfection. This involves attaching reality to things that are not as yet seen, acting on the conviction that unseen things are real. The object of faith is not directly the person of the Messiah, and in this particular, as will be seen later, Hebrews differs decidedly from the teaching of Paul. Heb. 4:14-16 Heb. 6:11-12 Heb. 12:28 Heb. 11:1

I Peter and James may also properly be introduced here. In I Peter the object of faith is the invisible personality of Jesus: "Jesus Christ, whom not having seen ye love; on whom, though now ye see him not, yet believing, ye rejoice greatly with joy unspeakable." This involves also belief in God, for "through him" we are "believers in God that raised him from the dead and gave him glory; so that your faith and hope might be in God." In James, with its meagre mention of Jesus Christ, faith is the devout attitude towards God rather than an attitude towards Jesus Christ. The famous passage on faith, seems, if we may hold to the early date of James, to be designed to correct a misunderstanding of Paul's preaching in the period when Paul had not yet learned to express himself as carefully as he did later in his epistles. The contention of the paragraph is that the devout attitude towards God must express itself in works of practical benevolence. I Pe. 1:8 v. 21 Ja. 2:14-26

III

PAUL'S PRESENTATION OF FAITH

In the Pauline letters the words "faith" and "believe" are used in several subordinate senses: as the body of Christian doctrine; the *charism,* or special gift, bestowed by the Spirit upon some but not upon others: "To one is given through the Spirit the word of wisdom, to another the word of knowledge according to the same Spirit, to another faith in the same Spirit"; also faith in the sense of faithfulness. The principal use of the word, however, is that in which God or Jesus Christ is the object of the action or state, and it is this use that we have to examine.

I Cor.
12:8–9

Paul's theological views were the outgrowth of his experience, and his conception of faith will therefore be best understood by considering what his own personal experience of faith had been. The place Jesus occupied in Paul's experience is best seen in Paul's description of the tense moments when he found himself compelled to rebuke Peter publicly for action which was inconsistent with this fundamental principle of the Christian life. The significance of this classic passage will be the more evident if it be translated in such a way as to bring out the similarity between the noun πίστις and the verb πιστεύω, and also the fact that "to justify" is to "pronounce righteous." "Knowing that a man is not pronounced righteous as a result of law works, but only through belief in Jesus Christ, even we believed on Jesus Christ in order that we might be pronounced righteous as a result of belief in Jesus and not as a result of law works; for as the result of law works no flesh shall be pronounced righteous. . . . That life which I am now living in the flesh I am living by belief, the belief that is in the Son of God who loved me and gave himself for me."

Gal.
2:16, 20

It is evident from this statement that "belief," or "faith," was *the central feature of Paul's experience* and that *the object of his faith was Jesus Christ.* What, then, was the state of mind regarding Jesus Christ which Paul designated as "faith"? Light is shed on this question by one other significant passage in which Paul describes succinctly what he means by faith: "The word is nigh thee, in thy mouth and in thy heart; that is the word of faith

Ro.
10:8–9

which we preach; that if thou shalt confess with thy mouth Jesus as Lord and shalt believe in thy heart that God raised him from the dead, thou shalt be saved." Faith, then, is that attitude towards Jesus that believes him to be alive and openly surrenders to him as Lord.

In another place, where Paul states the attitude that is common to all Christians and by virtue of which they are constituted Christians, he says that none can say "LORD JESUS" except in the Holy Spirit. This was what took place when Paul himself became a Christian. He faced Jesus in glory and at once yielded to him as Lord. He not only called him Lord, but treated him as Lord and proceeded to take orders from him. ^{Acts 9:5-6}

It may be said here, as earlier in the discussion, that faith in Jesus consists in recognizing Jesus to be what he claims to be and in treating him accordingly, that is, taking him as Lord. Whether or not it will seem worth while to believe *on* him depends upon what is believed *about* him. What Paul believed about him can be very simply stated. First, he believed him to be alive: "If thou shalt believe in thine heart that God raised him from the dead." Believing him to be raised from the dead means not simply believing him to be in existence, but believing him to be alive and *accessible*. He is a living, present personality who can be approached and called Lord. The other thing that Paul believed about him was that he was the Christ of God, that is, the one who had the right to control every man's life for its good. When intellectually convinced of these two points faith as an act of will becomes possible, and expresses itself in loving surrender to Jesus as Lord. ^{Ro. 10:9}

Paul does not discriminate between faith in God and faith in Jesus Christ because to him Jesus is the Christ of God and the very "image of God," that is, the one in whom God presents himself as an object of faith to the soul of the believing man.

We turn now to examine the bearing of faith upon other truths in the Pauline system of thought. First of all, the man who bows in faith before Jesus, calling him Lord, in word and deed is, in Pauline phraseology, "pronounced righteous," or "justified" as our English version translates the word. *To be righteous is to be rightly related to one's personal environment, God and man.* He who in faith calls Jesus Lord, in that act is rightly related to God,

I Cor. 12:3

for it is God who is in Christ; and also to all men, for Jesus Christ is the friend of all men. So far as his present state is concerned the man of faith is "righteous."

However, to "pronounce righteous" in Pauline phraseology means more than to recognize this present rightness of relationship. This much God, as an intellectually honest Being, it would seem, is compelled to admit without any exercise of "grace." To pronounce righteous implies also a certain attitude on God's part towards the believing man's evil past. It means that God treats him as kindly as though he had never sinned in the past. In other words, when a man in penitent faith calls Jesus Lord, God graciously forgives his past. This he does in view of the death of Jesus: "Whom God set forth to be a propitiation through faith by Ro. 3:25-26 his blood, . . . that he (God) might himself be righteous and one that pronounces righteous him that has faith in Jesus." How the death of Jesus serves as a reason in the mind of God for pronouncing the man of faith in Jesus to be righteous it is not in place here to discuss. It is sufficient simply to note in passing, the place which that profoundly significant event occupies in its relation to the subject we are considering.

The relation of faith to character is something that receives emphasis in Paul's teaching. Faith is not simply an act, but *an act that carries on into a kind of life*. It is the beginning of a personal relationship between Jesus Christ, or God in Christ, and the man of faith. When the disciple takes Jesus as his Lord the beneficent consequences of this great personal relationship begin. The most vital thing that one person can do for another person's character is done through personal association. Faith is the word that describes the life of personal association between the disciple and his Lord: Gal. 2:20 "Christ liveth in me, and that life which I now live in the flesh I live in faith, the faith which is in the Son of God who loved me and gave himself for me." Through constant personal association Jesus saves the man of faith from a daily life of increasing selfishness and its ultimate misery to a daily life of increasing unselfishness and consequent blessedness. That is, out of this personal relationship of faith springs the life of love which realizes the ideal of the law. This is what Paul means by saying in Ro. 3:31 that the law is not made of none effect through faith, but is rather "established." The law was never able to realize its ideal in the life of a man because of the "weakness of the flesh." The law could only stand over against the personality with commands and threats and could never secure obedience. Ro. 8:3

In the case of the faith-righteous man an inspiring personal relationship, a faith-union, has been formed between the spirit of the man and the Spirit of Jesus; and as a result of this personal relationship the ideal of the law is now realized. This ideal is the daily life of love: "He that loveth his neighbor hath fulfilled the law. For this, Thou shalt not commit adultery, Thou shalt not kill, Thou shalt not steal, Thou shalt not covet, and if there be any other commandment it is summed up in this word, namely, Thou shalt love thy neighbor as thyself. Love worketh no ill to his neighbor; love therefore is the fulfillment of the law." This life of practical love springs from the life of faith-union with Jesus: "Faith working through love," is Paul's most condensed statement of this truth. Ro. 13:8-10 Gal. 5:6

These truths just outlined, Paul doubtless learned through his own experience. When he believed in Jesus as Lord he found that his adjustment of himself to Jesus was followed by profound peace. As a good Pharisee he knew that such peace could spring only from righteousness. But Paul was least of all directly conscious of righteousness at this time. He had just discovered the horrible fact that he had been the unrighteous murderer of his Messiah's faithful people. Moreover, before this discovery his conscience had been accusing him of covetousness, as we judge from Ro. 7:7, 8.

In what sense, then, could he consider himself to possess the righteousness of which his new found peace was the evidence? In his perplexity he turned again to the case which was the familiar subject of rabbinical discussion, namely, the case of Abraham, and read a sentence which illuminated his experience and was ever after a favorite text: "Abraham believed God, and it was reckoned to him for righteousness." Righteousness, then, sprang from faith! Abraham's faith constituted him righteous. Paul's new faith in the Messiah secured from God the pronouncement of righteousness, or "justification," of which his peace was the evidence. This relationship to Jesus became a permanent state which ab- Ro. 4:3

Phil.
3:8

sorbed the devotion of his intense nature: "I count all things to be loss for the excellency of the knowledge of Christ Jesus, my Lord." In the life of deepening acquaintance with Jesus Christ, Paul's faith strengthened year by year, and worked out increasingly in that ministration of love which makes him the wonder of the Christian church.

IV

The Words "Faith" and "To Believe" in John's Gospel and Epistles

Here the word "to believe" abounds. It occurs in John's Gospel more than twice as many times as in all three of the other gospels together, and almost twice as many times as in all the Pauline Epistles together. The substantive form of the idea, however, namely, "faith," does not occur at all in the gospel and only once in the epistles. Thus the difference between the Johannine literature and the rest of the New Testament in the emphasis of the idea is not so great as it at first appears to be.

The situation in John's Gospel resembles that in the Synoptic Gospels inasmuch as the object of belief is sometimes Jesus as a prophet or messenger from God, and very often, especially in the inner circle of disciples, Jesus as Messiah; sometimes it is statements about Jesus or God, and sometimes God himself. When Jesus is the object of the act, faith consists in acknowledging him to be whatever he represents himself to be and in treating him accordingly. The result of faith is not said to be righteousness as it is in the Pauline letters, but is called "eternal life." Life, however, consists, according to John, in true personal relationships, and these are secured by being truly related to the great central personality, Jesus Christ, the Son of God and the friend of man:

Jo.
17:3

"This is life eternal, that they should know thee, the only true God, and him whom thou didst send, even Jesus Christ." That is, life consists in being rightly related to one's personal environment, and this is what, as we have already seen, righteousness reduces to in the Pauline teaching.

V

Summary. Jesus, then, began the development of Christian faith in an elementary way by arousing interest in his own person along the lines in which interest could most naturally be felt, that is, physical distress and physical cures. This interest in his own person was furthered by obscuring for a time his official position as Messiah. Submissive good will was drawn out by the moral quality, kindness, exercising power to meet physical and moral need.

Jesus' increasing revelation of his unique personal consciousness made an increasing appeal for responsive good will, and in the man of rudimentary faith this response developed until, after the resurrection, Jesus was fully recognized as the spiritual Christ, a present, living Lord Jesus in whom the unseen God draws near to every man with loving assertion of his right to control every life for its good. When this supreme demand is yielded to his Lord, the man's life of faith has begun. This life of faith develops when every increasing revelation of God in Christ is met with a new response of submissive good will.

THE NEW TESTAMENT CONCEPTION OF
THE DISCIPLE AND HIS MONEY

XVI

THE NEW TESTAMENT CONCEPTION
OF THE DISCIPLE AND HIS MONEY

THE disciple of Jesus raises a question of fundamental importance in the religious life, when he asks, "What shall I do with the money I have or hope to have?" When the rich young Jew came to talk with Jesus upon religious topics, Jesus instantly turned the conversation to money matters. _{Mk.} Mk. 10:17-22

One reason why it is a fundamentally important subject is the fact, stated so clearly by Dr. Schauffler, that money is a form of stored-up personal energy. A man works with his hands or his brain for a period of time, and, as one result of that expenditure of personal force, finds in his hands a sum of money. The money represents himself. In his case the question, "What shall I do with my money?" is, therefore, really the question, "What shall I do with myself?"

This question is specially significant in our day, because *the sphere in which a man can use himself is now so enlarged.* If a man has money in the bank, he can cable a draft half way around the world, and so put food into the mouth of a starving man in China within an hour or two. Seventy-five years ago it would have taken many farmers longer to carry food to their nearest neighbors!

Another peculiarity of our age, which bears upon this point, is the ease and rapidity with which large numbers of small givers can combine to do great things. A reliable religious newspaper publishes a call to relieve famine sufferers in India. Fifty thousand persons send a dollar each and the $50,000 is cabled to India, all within a week. There never before was a time in the history of the world when a man with a dollar's worth of stored-up personal energy could exercise it in so large a sphere or in carrying on such important enterprises as at present. As Dr. Dennis has said, "An ordinary contribution box has become an instrument by which the contributor as he sits in his pew can touch every continent, and do a work for Christ where his own footsteps can never tread."

I

Paul's Conception of the Disciple and His Money

In considering the New Testament conception of the disciple and his money, we naturally turn first to Paul's famous appeal to one of the Western churches in behalf of the needy brethren in Jerusalem. It is found in the eighth and ninth chapters of his second letter to the Corinthian church.

First of all appears his statement of the spirit of the ideal giver as he had seen it manifested in Macedonia. The Macedonian Christians were a people *so glad about something that, although* II Cor. *poor and persecuted, they gave liberally.* "Moreover, brethren, we 8:1-2 make known to you the grace of God which hath been given in the churches of Macedonia, how that in much proof of affliction the abundance of their joy and their deep poverty abounded unto the riches of their liberality." They were having "hard times" in Macedonia. He who had been the Philippian jailor and perhaps now had lost his position, Jason with whom Paul boarded when founding the Thessalonian church, and Lydia, the bazaar woman, all felt the hard times, but were all very glad about something. Their gladness was so great that it led them to give more liberally than Paul felt to be really prudent. "For according to their power, vv. 3-4 I bear witness, yea and beyond their power, they gave of their own accord, beseeching us with much intreaty." "Beseeching us with much intreaty!" As if the people should come up to the platform with their subscriptions, and urge their gifts upon the visiting secretary in spite of his protestations!

The point is, their gifts came welling up out of a great gladness II Cor. 9:7 of heart. "God loves a cheerful giver." Dr. A. J. Gordon, it is said, used to call attention to the fact that the Greek word translated "cheerful" is the one from which the word "hilarious" is derived. God loves a "hilarious" giver!

But what were these Macedonian Christians so glad of? For one thing, glad of the situation in which they found themselves as a result of the benevolence of Jesus. Perhaps Paul had heard them saying, as they pressed their gifts upon him, "You know the grace _{II Cor. 8:9} of our Lord Jesus Christ that, though He was rich, yet for our sakes He became poor, that we through His poverty might become rich." There had been a time of great need in Macedonia. The Macedonians had not been conscious of it at the time, but one who saw things as they really were, had signaled to Paul in a vision, "Come over into Macedonia and help us." And now as _{Acts 16:9} these Macedonians look back upon that period, they realize how dire their need had been, and their gratitude for the message of Jesus is so exuberant that they are inclined to be extravagant in their benevolences. Then, too, they were glad to find out that they really had something that their Father could use and needed. With what a sense of importance and satisfaction a little boy bustles about to get something of his own which he discovers that his father needs and asks for!

Attention is sometimes called to a fact which would be more patent if there were no division of these letters into chapters and verses. In the closing paragraph of the fifteenth chapter of Paul's first letter to the Corinthian church he represents himself as standing upon the verge of his own grave. As he looks down into the deep, dark place into which so many of the hopes of men have passed without expectation of ever being renewed, he sings a song of triumph. "O death, where is thy victory? O death where is thy _{I Cor. 15:55} sting?" And then his soul, thanking God for victory through Jesus Christ, springs from the verge of the grave to go winging its way into the quiet glory of God forever and ever. From such a vision of himself Paul turns immediately and naturally to give an injunction which begins, "Now concerning the collection for the _{16:1} saints." That is, the sense of great benefit received awakens in one's heart a deep gladness that can adequately express itself in no other way than by giving.

Paul maintains, further, that *the spirit of money-giving is a fundamental virtue, like faith and love.* "But as ye abound in everything, in faith, and utterance, and knowledge, and in all earnest- _{II Cor. 8:7} ness, and in your love to us, see that ye abound in this grace also."

A man is sometimes solicitous about his lack of "faith." He even speaks of it in the mid-week service, and asks his brethren to pray that he may have more "faith." It is equally proper for him to be solicitous about his lack of generosity, and to pray in prayer meeting, "O Lord, I am inclined to be stingy. Increase my desire to give." A man sometimes studies himself with reference to developing the Christian virtues. He is a teacher in the Church School and finds that he lacks "knowledge" of the Scriptures. He takes definite measures to increase his "knowledge." A man may just as reasonably be called upon to examine himself in regard to his spirit of giving, and, if he does not find it growing stronger and heartier year by year, to take definite measures to secure such growth. The grace of giving is a fundamental virtue, like faith, knowledge, and love.

v. 8 Again, Paul maintains that the *giving of money is a proof of the sincerity of one's Christian profession.* "I speak not by way of commandment, but as proving through the earnestness of others the sincerity also of your love." A man's real interest in a movement can be pretty accurately gauged by his readiness to contribute money to it. If in a political campaign a man is thoroughly wrought up over certain principles for which his party stands, it is right to go to him and say, "You are thoroughly interested in this matter. How much will you contribute to the legitimate expenses of this campaign?" Does a man really love Jesus Christ? Is he thoroughly enthused over the plan of Jesus to introduce the civilization of heaven upon the earth? It is fair to ask him to prove his sincerity by contributing to the necessary expenses of the cam-

Jo. 3:16 paign. God proved the sincerity of his love in this way. "God so
II Cor. loved the world that He gave." So did Jesus Christ. "Ye know the
8:9 grace of our Lord Jesus Christ, that though He was rich yet for your sakes He became poor."

Would the Christian church have greater influence upon the world if it were to make its interest in the Kingdom of God evident by greatly increased gifts? Would the world begin to suspect that Jesus is a real personality, and that his plan to establish the Kingdom of God upon earth is really feasible, if the Church were to prove the sincerity of its creedal professions by an enthusiastic investment of money in the enterprise?

Perhaps there would be fewer non-Christian children in the families of Christian parents, if the parents proved the sincerity of their professed love for Jesus by generous giving to the various phases of his cause. Children are very quick to detect the real spirit of the home; although the parents may never express that spirit in words. One little girl, to the horror of her mother, concluded her evening prayer with an expression of the dominant, though unconfessed, desire of the family: "O Lord, make all our folks stylish." Perhaps the children of parents who do not prove the sincerity of their professed love by generous giving, detect the fact that their parents do not, at the bottom of their hearts, really believe in the desirability and feasibility of Jesus' plan for the establishment of the civilization of heaven upon the earth, and show they do not by their stinted giving.

Paul maintains, also, that *there is no large development of Christian character possible without generous giving.* "But this I say, He that soweth sparingly shall reap also sparingly; and he that soweth bountifully shall reap also bountifully." II Cor. 9:6

It makes a man a better man to give. Here is a man who confesses sorrowfully that he has not made much progress in the Christian life. Let him at once begin to give more generously, if, as is perhaps the case, he has not been giving as generously as he ought. Here is a man who confesses that he has not much love for Jesus Christ. Let him give generously to some phase of Christ's work, making his gift, not for display on the subscription list, but definitely in prayer to Jesus Christ himself. His love for Christ will increase. Another confesses to little interest in missions. Let him invest money in missions and his interest will increase. Fathers and mothers who have no interest in missions, as soon as one of their children away at college becomes a volunteer and goes to a foreign country, become intensely interested in foreign missions. *The problem of improvement in moral character is the problem of the use of proper means,* and one such means is generous giving.

A man says he has little joy in the Christian life. Let him use the means requisite for the production of joy. Let him give. It is to Paul that we are indebted for the elsewhere unrecorded testimony of Jesus that giving produces blessedness, which is one phase of joy. It was stated in the newspapers a while ago that when Mr. George Peabody was once asked by his host at a dinner party Acts 20:35

which he enjoyed most, making his money or giving it away, he made this reply: "Well, I enjoyed making money. I think it is a great pleasure to make money. When the idea was first suggested to me that I should give money away, it didn't please me at all. In fact, it distressed me. But I thought the matter over and concluded I would try it on a small scale. So I built the first model tenement house in London. It was a hard pull, but after it was done, I went around among the poor people and enjoyed it. And then I built some more, and the feeling increased, and now I can say that although I enjoy making money, I enjoy giving it away a great deal better."

The fundamental feature of the character of God, as far as we are able to understand it, seems to be his endless giving. A son of God who begins to give as his Father gives, finds himself introduced into a personal experience of the deep sources of the joy of the heart of God. He becomes a better man as he finds himself rising into sympathy with his Father. A sense of the true dignity of his manhood begins to develop in him, and he rejoices in it.

> "Rejoice we are allied
> To that which doth provide
> And not partake, effect and not receive!
> A spark disturbs our clod;
> Nearer we hold of God
> Who gives, than of His tribes that take, I must believe."[1]

II

JESUS' CONCEPTION OF THE DISCIPLE AND HIS MONEY

The most striking of Jesus' numerous utterances regarding the use of money are found in the first paragraph of the sixteenth chapter of Luke. The paragraph contains the illustration of the "Shrewd Steward," who used power and position to secure friends in anticipation of a time when power and position would fail. At the close of the illustration, Jesus stated the truth which he intended the story to illustrate.

Lu. 16:9

A man ought to make eternal friendships with his money. "I

[1]From "Rabbi Ben Ezra." Cf. *The Complete Poetic and Dramatic Works of Robert Browning*, Cambridge ed., 1895, p. 384[1].

say unto you, make to yourselves friends with your money (mammon of unrighteousness) that when it shall fail they may receive you into eternal tabernacles." Jesus here, as usual, takes a long look ahead. He says that money ought to be used in laying the foundation of eternal friendships in the age to come.

As one looks back over the long history of life on this globe, it is evident that what is highest and best in any lower stage of development is a prophecy of what is to become commonplace and characteristic in the next higher. One of the two best things in the stage of human existence with which we are now familiar is friendship. Blot out all the friendships in any life and it ceases to be life. It degenerates into mere existence. One of the fundamental characteristics of the age to come in the thought of Jesus is its purified, glorified, eternal friendships. The purpose of life here and now is to develop the friend-making power as a preparation Jo. for entering into eternal friendships of the age to come. 13:35

Jesus proposed to make his disciples specialists in friendship. "By this shall all men know that ye are my disciples, if ye have love one to another." Jesus, therefore, is as usual taking a profound view of the matter when he says that money must be so used as to lay the foundation for eternal friendships. *"Make to yourselves friends with your money,* that when it shall fail, they may receive you into eternal tabernacles." How many surprises there will be in the age to come, when all the lines of spiritual influence are revealed that have contributed to the elevation of a man into the eternal life! Men from India, China, and Africa will say to you, "You are my friend. Welcome here! You do not know me, but I have learned that it is due to sacrifice that you made, and money that you gave, that I ever heard the Gospel. We are friends!" Long ago, without knowing this man, you laid the foundation for an eternal friendship. You are storing up great friendships which will constitute the richness of the life to come.

On the other hand, the man who is selfish in the use of himself, and the money which represents himself, cannot form friendships. *Selfishness and friendship are contradictory terms.* He is, therefore, steadily incapacitating himself for the life to come. He must, in the nature of the case, be friendless and alone. He is preparing his own doom. By a law of nature, written deep in his very con-

Jo.
12:24 stitution, he is condemning himself to eternal solitude. "Except a corn of wheat fall into the earth and die, it *abideth alone.*"

Lu.
16:11 *If a man uses the money-power selfishly,* Jesus went on to emphasize, *God will never trust him with any higher form of power.* "If therefore ye have not been faithful in the use of money, who will commit to your trust the true riches?"

It is perfectly evident that God is trying to train his children to use power unselfishly. They are his heirs. They are heirs of a powerful Father. As a conscientious Father, therefore, he must train them to use power unselfishly or else they cannot be his heirs in the age to come. It is evident in the long history of civilization that God has always been trying to train men to use power unselfishly. He has been putting increasing power into the hands of men just as fast as they could learn to use it with some degree of unselfishness. The money-power is a comparatively low form of power. God puts it into the hands of his children, expecting them to use it unselfishly, and so to prepare themselves for the exercise of higher forms of power. If a man does not use the lower form unselfishly, how can he be trusted with the higher? "If therefore, ye have not been faithful in the use of money, who will commit to your trust the true riches?"

Until the Church learns to use the lower money-power unselfishly, how can God trust it with the higher prayer-power? It would be criminal for him to say to a Church that used money Jo.
15:7 selfishly, "Ask what ye will and it shall be done unto you." A Church that pays selfishly will pray selfishly.

Lu.
16:12 This same thought is stated by Jesus in another striking sentence: *"If ye have not been faithful in that which is another's, who will give you that which is your own?"*

In a certain sense money never really becomes permanently one's own. It often comes to us from another. It is perfectly certain that it will all some day go to another. It is "another's." It a man does not learn to use this transient form of power unselfishly, how can God give him spiritual power which will *become a permanent part of himself,* will be his "own," and pass out with him into an eternal career?

The moneyed men of Jesus' day laughed at his ideas about the use of money. In this same connection it is said: "The Pharisees who were lovers of money heard all these things; and they Lu. 16:14 scoffed at Him." But Jesus' view has been vindicated as the more profound. The Church is coming to see that it is evidently a serious matter to have even a little money to use. A man may learn to be unselfish in the use of a little money as well as in the use of great wealth. One's eternal career depends upon the spirit in which he uses whatever money he has.

As was said at the beginning, in our day through the facilities for swift combination and rapid communication, God as never before in the history of the race is tempting, not only the millionaire, but the man with a dollar to use his money unselfishly, and so to prepare himself quickly for some trust of higher power in the on-coming Kingdom of God. "Thou hast been faithful over a Mt. 25:21 few things, I will set thee over many things."

CONDUCT AND DESTINY

XVII

CONDUCT AND DESTINY

"He that soweth unto his own flesh shall of the flesh reap corruption, Gal.
but he that soweth to the Spirit shall of the Spirit reap eternal life." 6:8

PAUL solved the problem of giving glory to commonplace
lives. He solved the problem by bringing each detail of life
under the dominance of a high motive. In the context of
these words from the letter to the Galatians he is hinting that the
Galatian churches ought to pay their pastors or teachers more generously. To warn them against selfishness in this detail of life, he
holds before them two great types of life, and the consequences
of each.

Is it possible to sum up in a few sentences what Paul means by
these four great words—"flesh," "corruption," "Spirit," "life"—
which had come to mean so much in his own personal religious
life?

Flesh.—The flesh is the selfish instinct. Paul does not seem to
consider the flesh itself to be sinful, but that which gives occasion
to sin. Man is not sinful because he possesses the selfish instinct,
but because he yields to it. It is *sowing to* the flesh that brings the
terrible disaster mentioned here.

The flesh, then, is that instinct in a person which rises up to
demand its own gratification regardless of all other interests. It
says, with the savagery of inherited animalism: "What I want I
take." The sin of yielding to the demand of this instinct, may
show itself in ways that are openly brutal and repulsive, or out-
wardly cultured and polite. The savage may appear in his native
nakedness or in evening dress. He may even look longingly upon
the brotherly civilization of unselfish men and turn away from it
regretfully, as did the rich young man who drew near to Jesus'
company for a while with aspiration for the eternal life; but he
turns away from it, nevertheless, and decides to gratify his own
tastes regardless of the interests of others.

Corruption.—The companion word of "flesh" is the word "corruption." The sin of yielding to the "flesh" results in "corruption." As surely as harvest follows seeding so surely does "corruption" follow the cultivation of the "flesh." What, then, is the corruption which necessarily results from gratifying the selfish instinct and developing it through gratifying it? The word "corruption" means "decay," "rottenness." *It is the word by which Paul describes the wreckage of personality.* What he conceived to be the details of this wreckage he has not discussed at length. We are left to ascertain for ourselves what there is in the nature of selfishness that makes its necessary consequence the wreckage of personality. Perhaps there is no subject in our day that needs more earnest attention from all ministers and educators of public sentiment.

We live in an age that is peculiarly insistent in pressing back of phraseology and reaching facts. We must press back of the phraseology of Paul and inquire what actually happens to the personality that insists upon developing the selfish instinct. Although Paul does not discuss the question in detail, he here and there throws out significant hints. The consequence of developing the selfish instinct, and so of disregarding the interests of others, is that the self becomes separated from other personalities. By psychological law, the continued failure to give interested attention to others produces inability to feel an interest in others. The selfish finally become "past feeling" and give themselves up greedily to the unclean work of gratifying the selfish instinct in all the savage forms Eph. in which it exhibits itself. "Who, being past feeling gave them-
4:19 selves up to lasciviousness, to work all uncleanness with greediness." This resulting isolation of themselves from other personalities involves, most of all, the separation of themselves from God. In their dull insensibility to the interests of others they are neces-
v. 18 sarily "alienated from the life of God," for he is steadily giving himself to the interests of others. In the earlier stages of their horrible development, while there is still some sense of God left, it is Ro. 8:7 a hostile sense; "the mind of the flesh is enmity against God."

Such separation of themselves from others results in their being left alone, shut up to themselves. Others may be all about them, but these others make no impression; and the selfish man is consequently much more fatally alone than he would be if far away from others in space, but wanting them in heart. He is condemned by the violated laws of his own being to solitary confinement.

> "Forever round the Mercy-seat
>   The guiding lights of Love shall burn;
> But what if, habit-bound, thy feet
>   Shall lack the will to turn?
>
> What if thine eye refuse to see,
>   Thine ear of Heaven's free welcome fail,
> And thou a willing captive be,
>   Thyself thy own dark jail?
>
> O doom beyond the saddest guess,
>   As the long years of God unroll
> To make thy dreary selfishness
>   The prison of a soul." [1]

Such isolation must involve pain. The fundamental dread of the soul, revealed in the little child's frightened cry in the night, or the mad rush of population to the city, is the dread of being alone. The solitary cell is one of the extreme punishments of modern penology.

Closely related to the pain of loneliness is the pain of idleness, aimless idleness. Idleness is a necessary consequence of isolation; for there is practically nothing that a person can do without the co-operation of others. Jesus, with his keen insight into the nature of life, expressed this when he said: "Of myself I can do nothing." Jo. 5:30 The Johannine description of the man far on in selfishness is: "He walketh in darkness and knoweth not whither he goeth." He is I Jo. 2:11 alone in the dark. He knows no reason for going one way rather than another. All sense of direction, purpose, and destination is gone. The selfish person, by the natural laws of his being, must ultimately be without friends and without work. He putters away painfully and ever more feebly in his little, lonely, self-made hell. The capacity for friendship and work has apparently rotted out of his personality. His personality has become a wreck. "He that soweth unto his own flesh shall of the flesh reap corruption."

Spirit.—The "spirit" is that part of the personality which Paul strongly contrasts with the "flesh." It is the instinct that is inter-

[1] Whittier, *The Complete Poetical Works Of,* Household ed., 1892, p. 337².

ested in others, and cries out for alliance with them. It is that part of the personality with which the "Spirit of God" forms an alliance. Paul teaches that the spirit of the man who has believed in Jesus is received into a close alliance with the "Spirit" of God. When the believer's spirit has been thus reinforced, he is successful for the first time in bringing his life under the dominance of the unselfish principle, in spite of the strong insistence of the selfish flesh.

Much that Paul says about the "spirit" is said when he has in mind the human spirit reinforced by the divine Spirit; and it is not always easy to ascertain which of the two, if either, is more prominent in his thought. This accounts for the perplexity of the translators as to the propriety of writing "Spirit" or "spirit." That Paul really recognizes the human "spirit" as distinct from the divine "Spirit" is evident from the statement: "The Spirit him-

Ro. 8:16 self beareth witness with our spirit that we are children of God."

Eternal life.—The natural consequence of developing the spiritual side of the personality, now energized by the Spirit of God, is "eternal life." What does Paul mean by "eternal life"? He means the restful adjustment of the human self to its personal environ-

Ro. 8:6 ment. "The mind of the Spirit is *life* and *peace*." This adjustment of personal environment is first of all adjustment to God. The mind of the flesh is enmity against God; the mind of the spirit is alliance with God's Spirit. It is the projection of this present relationship with the Holy Spirit into the future that constitutes the eternal life of the future, for the presence of the Spirit is called

v. 23 the "first-fruits" of that for which we wait. This idea of adjustment to God is involved in the frequently recurring phrase "in Christ." In the vital union with Jesus Christ, described by this phrase and involved in "faith," the believer finds God. It is the projection of this present fellowship with Christ into the eternal

I Thess. 4:17 future that constitutes "eternal life." "So shall we ever be with the Lord," is the brief sentence by which Paul describes the life to be.

This adjustment of the personality to God, his Spirit, his Son, in loving friendship, involves also a similar relationship to man, for in Paul's teaching all God's law is summed up in one word:

Ro. 13:8–10 "Thou shalt love thy neighbor as thyself." This Pauline view of life is in accordance with our modern attempt to define life as the adaptation of an organism to its environment. The principal part of a man's environment is made up of the persons that surround him, and that adaptation to them which constitutes "life" is love. Paul is at one here with the teaching of Jesus: "Thou shalt *love* the Lord thy God with all thy heart and thy neighbor as thyself. This do and thou shalt *live."* _{Lu. 10:27–28}

Eternal life, then, consists in the great friendships with God and men which are to ripen in the age to come. The Pauline conception of life involves, not only adjustment to personal environment, which is friendship, but also adjustment to non-personal environment, which involves work. In the Pauline teaching regarding a "spirit- _{I Cor. 15:44} ual body" in the age to come, there is provision for operation upon a so-called physical environment, or for work. These two fundamental aspirations of the human personality—the aspiration for friendship and the aspiration for achievement, or work—are necessarily involved in Paul's conception of life. Just as sowing to the "flesh," or to the selfish instinct was seen necessarily to result in the painful loneliness of friendlessness and idleness, so sowing to the "spirit," or to the unselfish instinct, necessarily results in the increased capacity for, and enjoyment of, friendship and achievement, or work. The civilization of the age to come is a civilization of friendly workmen. Over against such a civilization, throbbing with faith, hope, and love, the eternally abiding centripetal forces of the ultimate civilization, is the anarchy of selfish- _{I Cor. 13:13} ness characterized by the great disruptive opposites of faith, hope, and love—distrust, despair, and hate.

"He that soweth unto his own flesh shall of the flesh reap corruption, but he that soweth to the Spirit shall of the Spirit reap eternal life."

Section III

Interpretative Addresses

THE FINE ART OF GETTING ON
WITH MEN

XVIII

THE FINE ART OF GETTING ON
WITH MEN[1]

OLD Gorgon Graham, the Chicago meat-packer, in a letter to his son told him this great truth: "You can't do the biggest things in the world unless you can handle men."[2] The Christian minister, whose business it is to do the biggest things in this world and the other world as well, more than any one else needs to be able to "handle men." This fact gives me my theme for the opening of another year of work together: "The Fine Art of Getting On with Men."

By "getting on with men" I do not mean merely living in peaceable relations with them. I mean literally getting on—so coöperating with them as to get on in their company to some desirable destination. Fortunately, the minister's office no longer gives him the artificial influence it once afforded. His power to handle men now depends upon his personal character and equipment, and the godly shrewdness with which he can adjust himself to their varieties of peculiarity. Really, therefore, our problem is to ascertain what kind of men we must become in order to "get on with men."

I

The points I shall make are not necessarily brought forward in the order of their importance. But you will expect me first of all on this occasion to emphasize the fact that the minister in order to get on with men, must be able to win their respect for the intellectual equipment that he brings to his life work. Men must see that he knows his business. Lawyers must know law. Physi-

1. Opening Lecture before the Graduate School of Theology, Oberlin.
2. Lorimer, *Letters from a Self-made Merchant to His Son,* by permission Mr. Graeme Lorimer and The Curtis Pub. Co., Philadelphia.

cians must know medical science. Ministers must know theology. A minister cannot depend exclusively upon his social attractiveness nor even upon the deep, true sympathy which he aspires to bring to all men, any more than the lawyer and physician can depend upon these valuable qualities. He must have the respect of men for his intellectual outlook upon his life work. *He must have thought and lived his way into the great problems of life, and must have found a rational way out.* He must have an intelligent, well-grounded philosophy of life. Men who come to him must find help in thinking through to a rational conclusion the problems of personal life that bewilder them. He must be the kind of man that will often hear persons say to him, sometimes with a suppressed tremor of relief in the voice, "I never thought of it that way before!" He must know from experience the truth of Browning's words:

> I say, the acknowledgment of God in Christ
> Accepted by thy reason, solves for thee
> All questions in the earth and out of it,
> And has so far advanced thee to be wise.[3]

This means also that he must be intellectually a hard-working man; men must see in his work evidence of intellectual thrift and strength if he is to win the respect that is accorded to hard work. His processes of thought must show intellectual strength to withstand the criticism of the thoughtful, logical man; he must be sure of his facts and careful in his estimate of evidence. Ministers are at a disadvantage, especially as compared with lawyers, because their statements are seldom contradicted. The lawyer knows that every statement he makes is being listened to by a man who will disprove it if he can; the real validity of every bit of evidence adduced will be questioned by the other man. But no one in the minister's audience ever rises to take exception to what the minister says or to ask how he knows that what he says is so. The natural result is that the minister sometimes becomes careless about his facts and slovenly in his scrutiny of evidence. It would be well for all of us to read some good legal work on "evidence." For the past few years I have been advising college students pre-

3. From "A Death in the Desert." Cf. *The Complete Poetic and Dramatic Works of Robert Browning,* Cambridge ed., 1895, p. 390.

paring for the ministry to include in their curriculum a number of thorough courses in science in order to secure for their intellectual processes some large measure of scientific exactness.

In the theological seminary the student has opportunity to foresee the great problems of life, almost all of which are essentially religious, and to prepare to lead men and women to their solution. It is sometimes forgotten that the main purpose of seminary life is not to secure experience in city mission work or to learn the methods and eccentricities of "great preachers," *but quietly to think one's way through for himself to a philosophy of life that shall be his own and that shall be a real evangel to hundreds of men and women afterward.* Such a philosophy of life cannot be lectured into a student by a professor. For that reason the lecture system has been largely abandoned in this seminary and replaced by a system of research that necessitates at least a considerable degree of independent thought by the student.

There is a goodly number of ex-ministers who are now in the real estate and insurance business because they began to preach without adequate training. Some of them consequently wandered cheerfully and innocently off into theological by-ways full of pitfalls that any middler in the seminary, especially after his course in history of dogma, would have already learned enough to keep out of. Others were mere desultory sermon-makers, with no carefully considered philosophy of life, preaching at random, grasping at miscellaneous thoughts and subjects for next Sunday's sermon as drowning men grasp at straws, until finally the waters closed over them and only little bubbles of air showed where they had been.

II

If the minister would get on with men, he must be recognized by them, in the next place, as a man of strict honesty, fairness, sincerity. I mean by this, first of all, honesty in the narrow sense of commercial honesty. He must be a man of sensitive commercial conscience; if he has given his note he will never let the day when the interest is due pass unrecognized. Every man is quick to resent in another any dereliction at a point prominent in his own code of honor. In the business man's code of honor any failure to meet a business obligation, to pay a debt when it is due, or at least to recognize that it is due and arrange for its future payment, is a serious blow to confidence. Some ministers, who are so unfortunate as to have had no experience in business life, seem to have only a rudimentary conscience in business obligations.

But, to speak now more broadly, I mean by honesty a true sincerity that shall show itself in all the relations of life. It must mark the minister's bearing in social life. The demand for much small talk necessarily incident to the minister's large social life is a menace to his sincerity. He is called upon to say pleasant things to many persons; the danger is that he will not mean what he says, will not even think what he is saying. I rode one afternoon in a buggy with a minister and watched him meet casually a score or more of his parishioners. He asked them all the same question. It was a most earnest and solicitous inquiry regarding the health of the "folks," but in most cases he did not notice what the answer was, and sometimes did not wait for it. Such conduct made one suspect that his intercourse in prayer with the Lord was equally professional, and that he may have fallen into the habit of also asking the Lord questions without expecting an answer.

It is often necessary for the minister to conceal his thoughts. He must necessarily know things about persons that he must keep strictly to himself. This subjects him to the danger of insincerity. He must watch himself carefully to see that while he does not say all he thinks, *he does really think all he says.* He must not feel gratified to see his caller go away thinking he has learned a great deal when he has learned nothing, or thinking the facts are other than they are. He may wish his caller to go away in ignorance, but not with a misconception of the facts. That is, *he must not use language to obscure thought;* if he does he will pay a double penalty. In the first place, he will impair his ability to think clearly, for the habit of clear thought is inextricably knit up with the habit of clear speech. In the second place, there will some day pop unexpectedly out what even his degenerating sense of truth will have to recognize as a *lie.*

III

There is particular need just now that the minister keep a vigilant eye upon himself in regard to sincerity in conversation and preaching, for the present is a troublous time. Within a single generation great changes have taken place in theological thought and statement. Positions that seem to some conscientious people to be absolutely essential to Christian faith and character are being openly abandoned by other conscientious people. The air is full of "new theology." Men are "liberals" and "conservatives." How shall a minister, somewhat influenced by what is called more advanced theological thought, get on to some desirable goal with the conservative element in his congregation, and yet be absolutely sincere? This is probably the most serious problem that confronts many young ministers.

The fear that absolute sincerity in the expression of one's theological views will not be tolerated by the church serves to keep some earnest men out of the ministry. I wish to stop for a little to consider the situation.

The first thing I care to say is that most—not all—of the questions raised by the so-called higher criticism and new theology, while important, are comparatively superficial and do not vitally affect the fundamental experiences of the religious life. Some of the newer modes of conceiving religious truth certainly seem to clear the way for a better religious experience, but they are not essential to it. The most of your preaching ought to be in the realm of the fundamental truths of religious experience. Your main convictions, those which really lie deeply rooted in your own soul are presumably in this sphere. Keep these main convictions steadily at the front. Do not let yourself be forced into the discussion of subordinate questions, regarding which many of your people differ from you, before you have had a chance to show them the fundamental convictions of your religious life, which will probably be the same as their own.

In due time you will wish to state clearly for them your views regarding any less important points of significance and general interest, but you have the right to choose the time when, and the connection in which you will make such statement. If a young minister should begin his pastorate in a strongly conservative church with a series of sermons on the nature of the inspiration of the Scriptures or on recent advances in theological thought, he would probably antagonize a large portion of his people. If these subjects loomed up in his thought as the great themes regarding which a man would naturally wish to speak his mind out to a new people, then he would deserve their antagonism. He would have shown them that his main interest was in the academic phases of theology rather than in religion. *But if the great message that cried out in his soul for immediate utterance* concerned the many phases of the relation of God to the daily life of troubled and tempted men, the significance of Jesus Christ the living Lord and Savior of selfish men, or some other phase of profound religious experience, he would establish a relationship with his people that would make them in due time ready to listen with reasonably tolerant respect to his views of less important subjects, even though they might not be able to agree with him.

Furthermore, when the time comes for the discussion of these less important questions, there are several things that may be said regarding the method of approach. Be sure that you approach them in a constructive rather than a destructive spirit, from the positive rather than the negative side. Do not spend most of your time showing how absurdly men have misused the Old Testament, but show wherein the real religious value of the Old Testament consists, and leave this positive view gradually to work out the displacement of what seems to you to be the less reasonable one. Refrain also from applying offensive epithets to the other man's view. Do not describe it as the "old" view. Do not call your view the "advanced" or the "progressive" or the "liberal" position, all of which adjectives cast reflections upon those who do not agree with you. Do not say that all scholars of any reputation, or all thoughtful people now hold the view you advocate.

Yet more urgent, always state *fully* and *fairly the other man's view*. Look at the subject from his viewpoint. State the reasons for his view. State them more clearly and convincingly than he can state them himself. It will be a great comfort to him to hear his side put so well, and will do much to prepare his mind to listen hospitably to the other side of the case. What angers men is to find, or fear that their views are not being fairly treated. When once they are relieved of apprehension at this point their minds cease to be antagonistic. It is said that whenever Abraham Lincoln was attorney for the plaintiff he always, in the course of his own argument, presented the other side of the case so fully and fairly that there was nothing left for the defendant's counsel to say when his turn came. If you cannot state the side of the question you do not hold more clearly than can the average man in your congregation who does hold it, you are seriously at fault. I cannot emphasize too strongly the importance of developing the *habit of fairmindedness,* the habit of seeing both sides. It will prevent that angry flaring up into controversy with the man who holds the other view which is so certain to ruin your chance of usefulness with him and with those who think as he does. It will ensure your being in a frame of mind to search out and make the most of everything you and he hold in common. And when this has been done, the points of disagreement will often be found to be inconsiderable.

IV

It is not in the sphere of theological discussion alone that the absolutely sincere minister will often be perplexed. Lines are sharply drawn between the working-man and his employer, and between both workmen and employers on one side, and on the other side the great public not included in either labor unions or the employing class. Standards of business honor are changing. Things that have been tolerated in business life are rapidly becoming morally offensive to the developing public conscience. There are men prominent in church life who are law-breakers in the business world. Church-members are doing things in the business world which their sons and successors of the next generation will reprobate. The present situation is in some respects like that which existed during the last decades of American slavery. Christian men owned slaves, but the sons of these slave-holding Christians would not now think of defending slavery. The minister in this generation of economic transition needs to remember, as in the case of theological transition, that the important economic questions are nevertheless of subordinate importance and do not constitute the most prominent feature of his message. He cannot and would not escape discussing them at the proper time. When he does come to their discussion it must be *with a thorough intellectual preparation that shall insure him against superficial or doctrinnaire economic theories and with such sincere fair-mindedness as will enable him to appreciate the offending business-man's view-point,* and if possible, *secure the business-man's acceptance of the higher standards of commercial ethics with which the church of Christ must unmistakably, sincerely and quickly identify itself.*

Perhaps it is worth while, before leaving this general point, to mention a minor matter. The poisonous gossip-fly which buzzes up and down country roads and village streets and destroys or blights the fruit of many a man's ministry with its sting, can be largely driven out by the exercise of this quality of which I am speaking. The minister's fairness will prevent his believing or being influenced by any piece of gossip until he has heard the other side of the case. When the other side of the story is told the case will frequently seem quite different. His spirit of fairness will prove contagious. Others will begin to withhold judgment until all the facts are known. It is worth while to insist upon this, for in some communities there has been developed through long years of diligent exercise a disposition to believe without evidence anything discreditable to another. Such a disposition in a community makes it extremely difficult for a minister to get on with men, and he must give his attention to its cure.

V

The minister who is given sufficient time to establish a well-deserved reputation for honesty, sincerity, fairness, will with rare exceptions be able to speak his mind freely on all subjects that are worth discussing without failing to get on with his people, provided another thing is true. I have almost mentioned it in what I have just been saying, for it is closely related to fair-mindedness. The minister who would get on with men must be *conspicuous for his respectful sympathy.* It is, of course, respectful sympathy with the other man that leads you to see his side of every question and to state it fairly. But I wish now to follow out this characteristic into broader applications than that of theological discussion.

The man who has thought his way through to an intellectually respectable viewpoint, and who is honest enough to look fairly at both sides of every question and express himself sincerely, needs also deep, broad, respectful sympathy with men. I say *respectful* sympathy, for much that is called sympathy has no foundation in adequate respect for the other man, and is really disrespectful sympathy such as men naturally resent. There is need that all of one's intellectual equipment be thoroughly and continually warmed by a deepening sympathy with men. *It is interest in men that transforms truth into message.* If this interest be lacking, it is impossible to get on with men. Let me quote an additional clause from Gorgon Graham's sentence: "You can't do the biggest things in this world unless you can handle men, and you can't handle men unless you are in sympathy with them." The minister who gets on with people, and who gets people on, will have steadily in view the bearing of all that he says and does on the *life of men*. We ministers do not always impress people as being profoundly interested in the *life of men*. A distinguished college president is reported to have said that the most searching criticism ever passed upon his preaching was that of a man who said to him after the sermon: "You seem to be more interested in truth than in men." The same idea was in the mind of a man who said to me regarding a certain preacher: "He talks to his subject and not to his audience."

The same thought is more amply expressed in the following extract from a letter written to me some months ago by a thoughtful teacher: "I must confess that I miss the tone of life and inspiration, the sound thought and the modern interest in so much that I hear in the churches where we have been recently. All that is said from the pulpit seems cast in one mold. Sermon: 'Cast thy bread upon the waters' follows hackneyed, third-class historical reference to some supposed custom of the Egyptians; then other possible interpretations of the text; a few illustrations, commonplace, lifeless; and then an appeal for a collection for some stated church contribution. And all the time the people keep getting farther and farther from any present local realization of what is good in the Word. Down the street the sixty saloons are wide open; the night clubs are crowded, and there is no lasting life in things. Pray don't think me bitter and pessimistic; but when I work hard for six days trying to bring life to the young folks in the school, doing what my strength permits to build up the state, I begin to feel anarchistic, like challenging the right of any and every man to take up even an hour of time unless he has something to say."

In the nature of the case, the minister's only valid reason for being a minister is his interest in the *life of men*. A great value has entered into his own *life*. This value he wishes to introduce into the life of other men. He has placed himself under the spiritual control of Jesus Christ, and finds himself through the contagion of personal association being lifted up by Jesus Christ into an increasing share of Jesus Christ's own fellowship with his Heavenly Father and his brother men. This great experience reaching up into the spiritual world where life is eternal, the minister of Jesus Christ now wishes to share with his brother men. This he can hope to do only as he has a profound regard for, and brotherly sympathy with the other man. He does not talk down to, or preach at, the other man. He has learned to feel that this man is his brother. He is ready to make respectfully sympathetic recognition of whatever there is in the other man's life that seems to the other man to have religious value, whether that other man be a Buddhist in India or an agnostic in Ohio. He simply draws near to the other man's life, and in a spirit of respectful sympathy wishes to share with him a religious experience that he himself firmly believes to possess supreme religious value.

His success will depend upon the genuineness and respectfulness of his sympathy with the other man. I have found two types of missionary. One type is ready to speak of the people as "natives" or "heathen,"—in a superior manner to ridicule their peculiarities, jest about their queer social customs, sneer at their religion, to make it perfectly evident that he considers himself superior to the people among whom he lives. The other type of missionary, far more numerous, *has cast his lot in with the new people*. He resents any thoughtless criticism of them. He is sensitive to any jests at their expense, appreciates everything that has value in their religion, is quick to explain at all points where they are likely to suffer disadvantage by being misunderstood, is quick to see and make the most of all desirable features in their civilization. It is needless to point out which of these two types is doing the good work of a true missionary.

VI

This sympathy with men will keep the minister in constant readiness for the individual in need. A good deal is to be said about the necessity of protecting a minister's time from interruption. Some city ministers keep themselves so shut away behind secretaries and ante-rooms that it is next to impossible to gain audience with them. There is some reason in this. There are plenty of thoughtless persons who prey unscrupulously upon the minister's time. They are unmitigated bores. But in avoiding bores the minister runs great risk of missing the man in need. Graham told his son that it was better to see ten bores than to miss one buyer! When Doctor Bradley was pastor in Grand Rapids his study in the church opened directly without ante-room, upon the main corridor of the building, and the study door stood always open. Callers might come in at any hour, and come they did from all quarters of the city and from all classes of society, sure of finding good measure of sympathy and cheer in their large-hearted, broad-minded pastor. How he kept his work up to the intellectually respectable point always characteristic of it, I do not know. You and I in his place probably could not have done it, and I recommend you to follow his example only in spirit and not in detail of method.

The danger that a busy pastor will be shut away from the individual in need is very great. He must guard against getting the reputation of being a phenomenally busy man, for the reputation will keep some of the modest individuals who need him most from venturing to find him. A public speaker is apt to fall into the sad delusion that it is worth while to talk to audiences only, that it is not worth while to spend time upon an individual. But it is only the man whose heart has been trained by constant exercise into the habit of quick response to individual need who can be what he ought to be to an audience. The audience is merely a collection of individual needs, and the public address is a success only as each individual feels himself singled out by the speaker for personal touch.

The minister that gets on with men must carry this sense of genuine brotherliness into all his daily contact with men. It must not characterize his preaching merely. It will not be obtrusive. The last thing he will do will be to talk about his feeling. What we really feel and accept as unquestioned matter-of-fact appears to us too common-place to talk about. I have seen ministers who mingled freely with men, who used the vernacular of common life with a fair degree of accuracy; but they were conscious that they were doing so, and hoped others noticed that they were doing it and were duly impressed by it.

Wherever the minister possessed by genuinely respectful sympathy goes, men feel themselves more manly and more capable of becoming what they know they ought to be. James Lane Allen says of one of his characters: "She walking ever broadminded through the narrowness of the little town . . . and from every life which touches hers, however crippled and confined, extracting its significance instead of its insignificance, shy harmonies instead of easy discords which can so palpably be struck by any passing hand."

G. K. Chesterton, in his recent "Critical Study of Charles Dickens," says:

There is a great man who makes every man feel small. But the real great man is the man who makes every man feel great.[4]

In Julian Hawthorne's account of his father's friends as he, a boy of twelve years, saw them, occurs a most interesting picture of Emerson, in the village of Concord. It illustrates so well the important characteristic I am trying to describe that I shall quote an entire paragraph. "Mr. Emerson was, and he always remained, the hub round which the wheel of Concord's fortunes slowly and contentedly revolved. He was at this time between forty-five and fifty years old, in the prime of his beneficent powers. . . . Upon his modestly deprecating brows was already set the wreath of a world-wide fame, and yet every village farmer and store-keeper,

[4]Chesterton, *Charles Dickens, A Critical Study,* p. 8.

and every child found in his conversation the wisdom and companionship suited to his needs, and was made to feel that his own companionship was a valued gift. . . And so selflessly and insensibly were the riches of his mind and nature communicated to the community that innocent little Concord could not quite help believing that its wealth and renown were somehow a creation of its own. The loafers in Walcott and Holden's grocery store were, in their own estimation, of heroic stature because of the unegoistic citizen who dwelt over yonder among the pines. Emerson was a great man, no doubt; but then, he was no more than their own confessed equal, or inferior! This will and power to secularize himself is perhaps Emerson's unique attribute. It is comparatively easy to stand on mountain-tops and to ride Pegasus; but how many of those competent to such feats could at the same time sit cheek by jowl with hucksters and teamsters without a trace of condescension, and, while rubbing shoulders with the rabble of the street in town-meeting, speak without arrogance the illuminating and deciding word? This, at last, is the true democracy that levels up instead of down. An Emerson who can make common men feel more like Emerson than he himself did is the kind of man we need to bring America up to her ideals."[5]

Of course you will not be too quick to assume that you are the Emerson of the village, or if you find yourself suspecting it, you are probably sufficiently Emersonian to forget it instantly! This broad respectful sympathy is *really elemental in character* and is essential to any success which, like that of the minister, involves moral issues. It is absolutely essential that one should have enough of brotherly sympathy with other men to be interested in everything that seems to them to have vital connection with their lives. The minister must come to a conversation not full of his own concerns and ready to consider any one who will not listen to him a bore, but ready to listen with genuine interest to the other man. *The successful conversationalist is not the fluent talker, but the appreciative listener.* Emerson said of himself; "Though I am fond of writing and of public speaking, I am a very poor talker."[6]

To revert to Julian Hawthorne's account, he admits that Emerson was better in listening than in speech, and adds: "His look,

[5]Hawthorne, *Hawthorne and His Circle*, pp. 62–65.   [6]*Ibid.*, p. 63.

averted but attentive, with a smile which seemed to postpone full development to the moment when his companion should have uttered the expected apple of gold in the picture of silver, was subtly stimulating to the latter's intellect and prompted him to outdo himself."[7] It is worth while to emphasize this point, for many ministers, who ought on other grounds to succeed, have large measure of failure because they are undeveloped socially. Or, to use a term that appears in letters from church committees constantly received in my office inquiring for ministers, they are not "good mixers." To be a good mixer means, in many cases, the ability to be an appreciative listener in conversation with anybody, and this ability is simply an expression of a quality that is essential to character; namely, the readiness to take genuine, genial satisfaction in another man's success.

VII

In close connection with this, mention ought to be made of another reason why the minister's sympathy with other men is essential to getting on with them. It will deliver him from the lust for recognized leadership and the consuming desire to receive public credit for what has been done. The minister whose interest in other men is deep and true will so do his work as to bring other men forward into places of recognized responsibility and usefulness. He will generally be the real leader. He has been appointed to bear the responsibility of real leadership; but his best work will often consist in developing men and women in his church by bringing them forward into positions of recognized responsibility. One reason for the remarkable success of the missions of the American Board in Japan has been the readiness of the missionaries to stand in the background and to place upon Japanese pastors the responsibility of recognized leadership. The number of its self-supporting churches is surprisingly large. Among the Japanese the missionaries get scant credit for this. But that fact does not trouble the missionaries. Their profound sympathy with the people among whom they live makes the prominence of Japanese leaders a source of joy to most of them, and their own comparative lack of recognition a matter of indifference.

[7]*Ibid.*, p. 64.

Not only must the minister, who would really get on with men, have such sympathy with them as will make him take satisfaction in seeing them brought forward, but his own general itch for notice must be allayed. He will not be trying to get his name in the paper and his sermon reported in the public print. He will be glad of a chance to *cast his lot in with the great mass of the unobserved* and quietly do there in deep sympathy with them the work that God gives him to do. The pastor who would really get on with men and do them good must not always be trying to get into the public eye. He is almost certain, as Mr. Dooley says, to find that he is a "cinder in the public eye." If his church expects him to push forward into an artificial prominence for the sake of advertising the church, let him seek some church where a man can be left to do the work of God quietly and faithfully without teasing some reporter to describe it in the "Daily Advertiser." If publicity comes to him unsought, let him pay no attention to it lest it come to be essential to his happiness. Let him regard it as a wholly evanescent thing that will soon pass away.

VIII

Again, it is only this strong unfailing sympathy with other men that will enable the minister to meet criticism as a broadminded man ought to meet it. Two things are responsible for many failures in the ministry: laziness in intellectual and pastoral work, and unchristian resentment of criticism. No one will have a full fund of sympathy with the faulty men all about him, unless he is keenly alive to his own faults. Once more, and for the last time, let me return to Gorgon Graham's sentence, and this time quote it in full: "You can't do the biggest things in this world unless you can handle men: and you can't handle men unless you are in sympathy with them, and sympathy begins in humility. I don't mean the humility that crawls for a nickel in the street or cringes for a thousand in the office, but the humility that a man finds when he goes gunning in the woods for the truth about himself."

I have said in the hearing of some of you, and I wish to repeat it often: there is one sure way of getting on with the person who comes to criticise you. To adopt this way may mean success; to reject it will certainly mean a large measure of failure. No matter how unjust the criticism may seem to you to be, no matter how much it may anger you at the instant, never fail to utter these two sentences: "Thank you for your suggestion. I will give it careful consideration." After you have given it careful consideration and tried sympathetically to look at yourself as the other man seems to see you, it may be proper to explain your conduct to him in self-defense against his criticism. There is always a large chance that his criticism is just, or at least that there is something slightly wrong in your conduct which served as pretext for a criticism on the whole unjust. It is hard for us to realize our own faults. Zangwill somewhere says, "It is very hard for saints to see through their own halos." A wise saint will give careful heed to any dark object, however vague, that does succeed in penetrating his halo. The readiness to give careful and sympathetic attention to criticism not only results in the correction of one's faults, but it also does much to assuage the bitterness of an unjust critic. The captious critic finds no satisfaction in offering criticisms that are not resented!

IX

The minister who would get on with men must have this feeling of respectful, sympathetic relationship on the basis of a common humanity, with the so-called bad as well as the good. He stands at the threshold of his personality looking out for sinners as well as for saints. No man is wholly good or wholly bad. You are to be on the lookout for *that in every man which shall constitute his natural point of departure for a higher life.* To quote Chesterton again: "The error of Diogenes lay in the fact that he omitted to notice that every man is both an honest and a dishonest man. Diogenes looked for his honest man inside every crypt and cavern, but he never thought of looking inside the thief. And that is where the Founder of Christianity found the honest man. He found him on a gibbet and promised him Paradise." You will find many men in the community, especially in these days, who never enter the church, who are not reckoned among the moral resources of the community by church people. They are oftentimes not so bad as they seem. Certain unfortunate features of the local church life may have repelled them from the church.

They may have simply drifted away or never had any natural connection with it. Take pains to draw up to them. Find out in due time what their religious view-point is. This friendly outreach to the so-called bad man must not be with any ostentatious purpose of doing him good. It must be simply a normal overflow of that sympathy of man with man which springs out of a clear recognition of what it means to be fellow-men. We shall not too often repeat the honest words:

> Let me live in a house by the side of the road
>   Where the race of men go by—
> The men who are good and the men who are bad,
>   As good and as bad as I.
> I would not sit in the scorner's seat
>   Or hurl the cynic's ban—
> Let me live in a house by the side of the road
>   And be a friend to man.[8]

The minister who is to get on with men must do so in spite of much friction and many things that go wrong. He must therefore be a man who *sees all things in true spiritual perspective.* These many small things that go wrong must *seem* small to him. But all things are measured by comparison, and *if they seem small* to him it will be because *something else seems much larger.* The great realities of religion must rise in your spiritual landscape like mountains and cast upon you the spell of their perpetual peace. You must be able to lift your eyes at any moment and perceive the majestic reality of the spiritual world. The present moment must seem to you a throbbing segment of a continuous eternity. The living Christ, in his hourly fellowship, must ever freshly bear you up to God, begetting in you his own sense of the presence of the Heavenly Father, his own vision of the redeemed race, the full consummation of the developing civilization of friendly workmen.

The fine art of getting on with men, as I said at the beginning, is the prerogative of character, and character is growth. One must *grow* into *habits* of intellectual thrift and thoroughness. One must grow into the habit of honesty, fairness, sincerity so that in a

---

[8]Foss, Sam Walter, "The House by the Side of the Road" Cf. *The Home Book of Verse*, 6th. ed., Vol. II, p. 3040, or *Dreams In Homespun*, p. 11.

startled moment it shall be the truth that instinctively springs to his lips. One must grow into the habit of putting himself with respectful sympathy into the other man's place. One must grow into an habitual sense of the reality of the eternal spiritual world, with its presence of God and its dawning vision of the race to be. The strength of God must daily rise within him like a tide that comes up out of the great mysterious depths of eternal being.

THE DISCOVERY OF GOD

XIX

THE DISCOVERY OF GOD[1]

JESUS said: "Go unto my brothers and say to them, I ascend unto my Father and your Father, and my God and your God."

The most precious possession of the human race is Jesus Christ, with his sure sense of the Heavenly Father and his power to develop this sense in any man of any age who without reserve yields himself to the ever-present influence of Jesus Christ. This statement is true because the deepest need of the soul of man is its need of God, and yet God is not at all the most conspicuous fact in personal experience. *The deepest need of the soul of man is its need of God.* The soul may for a time disguise this need with self-indulgence; it may not be immediately apparent to coarse natures; but it is a need that persists through generation after generation of human history, and it is a need that finally reveals itself in the soul of every man. When a man comes to his real self he finds himself needing God. When the prodigal son came to himself he found himself saying, "I will arise and go to my father."

And yet the presence of God is by no means at first the most evident fact of personal experience. This is nothing against the reality of the presence of God. The air that we breathe is of vital importance to us, and yet it is by no means the most conspicuous feature of our personal environment. In these last days of scientific discovery it becomes more and more evident that the most potent unseen physical forces are those least conspicuous at first in the experience of men. It is a good thing that the presence of the Almighty God is not too conspicuous a feature of personal experience, because there is always a great danger when a strong personality associates with a weak, frail personality. A strong, forceful father may so overpower the frail personality of his child and so force upon it his own strong convictions that he will leave no

[1]Published in *Young Men of Madras* (India).

chance for initiative in the child, and, therefore, produce a result which has no special value as character.

But because God is not at first the most conspicuous feature of personal experience, we may find it difficult to form a distinct conception of him. We say that he is a personal God, but we are obliged to confess that we scarcely know what we mean by saying that he is a personal God. We do not think of him as an infinitely enlarged human personality. We think rather of human personality as personality in the embryo and the Infinite God as being perfectly developed personality, but how to picture perfectly developed personality to ourselves we scarcely know. Indeed, we scarcely see how to define personality even in the embryonic form in which we find it in ourselves, because we realize that even in our rudimentary personalities there are unexplored subconscious depths which we do not understand; and so if we were to be honest with ourselves we should confess to one another that many times our instinctive cry after God is an undefined, somewhat vague longing for something vast and stable that shall be able to respond to us with unfailing sympathy and sure guidance. I sometimes am awakened in the night by a little voice by my bedside that says, "Hand, hand!" It is the voice of my baby girl, and it means that she wishes me to reach over into her little bed and take her little hand in mine and let her know that she is not alone in the darkness of the night time. Sometimes when our infantile souls put up their cry to God, they have not even the meager vocabulary of a little child. What am I?

> An infant crying in the night:
> An infant crying for the light:
> And with no language but a cry.[2]

And so I say it is true that the most precious possession of the human race is Jesus Christ, with his sure sense of the Heavenly Father and with his power to develop this sense in the soul of any man in any age who without reserve yields himself to the ever-present influence of Jesus Christ as Lord.

The presence of God is all about us. We dream sometimes of an age to come when he will be nearer to us than he is now. You

[2]Tennyson, "In Memoriam." Cf. *The Poetical Works of Alfred Tennyson*. Household ed., p. 300[2].

remember the experience of Richard Watson Gilder, who has so recently passed over into the other form of existence, when he and his friends were camping among the pine trees one summer and talked late into the night about the future of humanity, the way to know God, and the time to come when men should see face to face the loving Father; and then as they turned to sleep, with his poet's imagination, he conceived the pine branches above their tents to be whispering among themselves about what they had heard these men talking of, and saying to each other:

> Heard'st thou these wanderers reasoning of a time
> When men more near the Eternal One shall climb?
> How like the new-born child, who cannot tell
> A mother's arm that wraps it warm and well.[3]

Jesus Christ felt sure that he could gather all men about himself and give them sense of the presence of the Heavenly Father. In the words of Jesus which we read at the beginning, it is as though he put his arm around a brother man and said, "I ascend unto my Father and your Father, unto my God and your God. No man knoweth the Father save the Son and he to whom the Son willeth to reveal him. Come unto me, come unto me all ye that are weary and heavy laden, and I will give you rest"—the only rest that the soul can call peaceful rest, the rest of Jesus Christ in the fatherhood of God.

Jesus gave one fundamental direction for the discovery of God. Out of his own experience and with the authority of his own unique experience he said, "Have faith in God." This is not an appeal to lay aside reason. The small boy in Sunday School was wrong when he told his teacher that faith consisted in believing something you know is not true. It is, rather, an appeal to reason.[4] There are certain reasons for believing that there is a God. They do not prove that there is a God, but they create such a probability as lays upon every man an absolute obligation to accept the theory of the evidence of God as the working hypothesis of his life and to begin to act as if there were a God. *Faith is the scientific venture in action* by which a man seeks to transform a reasonable

---

[3]Gilder, "The Voice of the Pine." Cf. *The Poems of Richard Watson Gilder,* 1908 ed., p. 60.
[4]Cf. Dean Bosworth's study of "Faith," pp. 171f.

probability, or something reported as fact by another person, into a practical certainty of his own personal experience.

My pastor is fond of saying that if a man would become conscious of the presence of any unseen physical force in his environment he must adjust himself to the nature of that unseen force and it will answer him. The air about us is full of electricity, but we do not sense its presence; but if there should come into this room a man able to adjust himself to the nature of this unseen physical force, it would soon answer him, and he would have in his own personal experience some convincing proof of the truth of his theory.

What is the nature of God and how shall a man adjust himself to the nature of God in such a way as to secure an answer, to find something in his own personal experience that he may reasonably accept as corroboration of the working hypothesis of his life? Jesus' teaching at this point is explicit. Jesus says that God is a father, and if a man will adjust himself to the nature of an unseen father he *must simply act like a son.*

Specifically, if he would act like a son, first of all he must obey him. Years ago, in London, I heard Doctor Fairbairn say that there is in all fatherhood an element of sovereignty, and that the fatherhood which has not as one of its elements sovereignty is no true fatherhood. A son ought to obey his father. That means that a man shall be ready to do anything, at any cost, which he believes to be the will of God. This was the path along which Jesus walked when he found God. He obeyed him in the region of daily life. "I do always those things which please him." He obeyed him in the great emergency of Gethsemane and Calvary. "Not my will, but thy will be done." He prescribed this to his brother men as the way in which they must walk if they would find God. He said, "If any man willeth to do his will, he shall know of my teaching about the fatherhood of God, whether I speak of myself or whether it be a true message from the depths of the heart of God."

Is your sense of God growing dim? If it is, question yourself at this point. Is there any duty rising before you in the wakeful hour of the night which you find yourself unready to do? Is there any subject you shrink from investigating for fear that such investigation might reveal a duty that would at first seem to you unwelcome? Is there in your life any selfish habit to which you cling? If so, that must make in your experience an ever more dimming sense of the presence of the Heavenly Father.

In process of acting like a son it is necessary that a man should speak to his father. A son ought to speak to his father. That is, he ought to pray. So Jesus found God. He came out of eternity, as Bishop Lloyd said yesterday, a great praying soul. He prayed as he came up out of the baptismal waters. He prayed sometimes all night. He prayed in the garden of Gethsemane. He prayed on the cross. In the last glimpse that his disciples had of him, as a cloud received him out of their sight, he was praying with outstretched hands of blessing over them, and he disappeared into eternity, where he ever lives to make intercession for us. The great praying soul that came out of eternity and passed before our vision disappeared into eternity again praying, praying, praying evermore. It is this that he prescribes to his brother men as the way of finding God. "Enter into thine inner chamber, and when thou hast shut the door *pray to thy Father.*"

> Speak to Him thou for He hears, and Spirit with Spirit can meet—
> Closer is He than breathing, and nearer than hands and feet.[5]

Is our sense of God growing dim? Then we need to question ourselves at this point. How about the prayer life? Are there a few moments at least of spiritual high tide—even two or three within the day—when you find yourself, with large sense of the reality of the transaction, reaching out in spirit to touch the Spirit of the living God? Do doubts about the availability of prayer sometimes paralyze your prayer life? Do you fail sometimes to find yourself convinced of the fact that the mind of God is so related to the mind of a man that God can put a thought into the mind of a man, and by means of putting a thought into the mind of a man make provision for the answer of almost all the prayers that we shall ever have occasion to present before our Heavenly Father?

When I was a senior in college I roomed in old North College, on the Yale campus. There was one room in that building of historic spiritual significance, to which we conducted our visitors as one of the points of interest on the campus. It was a room in

[5]Tennyson, "The Higher Pantheism." Cf. *op. cit.,* p. 123[2]

which a man had discovered God. When Horace Bushnell was a tutor in Yale and a great revival passed over the students, he and his body of students were untouched by it, until finally in that room he made the discovery of God; and years afterwards he came back to the Yale College chapel and described the experience to the students in the chapel in a sermon which all of us would do well to read—his sermon on "The Dissolving of Doubts." He describes the situation into which he had come,—a situation in which it seemed to him finally that he believed almost nothing, and then he uses these words: "Finally, pacing my chamber, there arose suddenly the question, Is there, then, no truth that I do believe? Yes, there is this one, now that I think of it: there is a distinction of right and wrong, that I never doubted, and I see not how I can; I am even quite sure of it." "Then, forthwith, starts the question,"—the first point that I made a moment ago—"then forthwith starts the question, 'Have I, then, ever taken the principle of right for my law? I have done right things as men speak. Have I ever thrown my life out on the principle to become all it requires of me? No, I have not; consciously I have not. Ah, then, here is something for me to do! No matter what becomes of my questions,—nothing ought to become of them, if I cannot take a first principle so inevitably true and live in it.' The very suggestion seems to be a kind of revelation; it is even a relief to feel the conviction it brings. 'Here, then, will I begin. If there is a God, as I rather hope there is, and very dimly believe, he is a right God. If I have lost him in wrong, perhaps I shall find him in right. Will he not help me, or perchance, even be discovered to me?' Now the decisive moment is come. He drops on his knees, and there he prays to the dim God, dimly felt, confessing the dimness for honesty's sake, and asking for help that he may begin a right life. He bows himself on it as he prays, choosing it to be henceforth his unalterable, eternal endeavor. It is an awfully dark prayer in the look of it, but the truest and best he can make,—the better and more true that he puts no orthodox colors on it. The prayer and the vow are so profoundly meant that his soul is borne up into God's presence, as it were, by some unseen chariot, and permitted to see the opening of heaven even sooner than he opens his eyes. It is the morning, as it were, of a new eternity. All troublesome doubt of God's reality is gone, for he has found him. A being so profoundly felt must inevitably be." He made this discovery of God through obedience and prayer.

If a man would act like a son and so adjust himself to the nature of the Heavenly Father, he must act like a son by treating all men as his brothers. He must agree with God in God's feeling about his other children. The best way to get at a father's heart is to be good to his children. So Jesus found God. He was the most brotherly man that ever walked the earth. He prescribed this method to his brother men, if they would find God. He means that they shall adopt, as the fundamental policy of their lives, the unalterable endeavor to secure for all men such a fair chance at all good things as a man would wish his brother to have. It means that he shall come, in the concrete, to the individuals near him and *share with them something that he values and that they need;* that he shall look out upon all the circle of his human relationships, high and low, in the spirit of Jesus Christ's brotherly soul. It means that he shall share his religion with another man. It means that he shall forgive the man who has done him the bitterest wrong. It means that he shall ask forgiveness from the man whom he himself has wronged. Is our sense of God growing dim at these points? Then let a man look at his life, share something with some other man, do it soon, something that you value and that he needs. Share your religion with some other man, and do it quick. Pray for some other man. Stop right here now and pray for the person at your side. All over this vast audience, stop for a moment and pray for the person at your side. Do you think now of some person who has sorely wronged you? Pray for him. Do you think now of some person whom you have wronged? Write a letter to him or to her to-day and make the wrong right. You will find, it may be, at some one of these points the sense of God welling up out of the depths of your subconscious self to the surface of consciousness in a way in which you have not before known him.

Jesus not only points out the way of finding God, but he helps men into the way of finding God. He helps men now. The great message of the Christian Church is that Jesus Christ is alive. The message that the women brought as they flew in the morning twilight through the city gates to some house in Jerusalem saying, "Jesus is alive! Jesus is alive!" has never ceased to be the message of the Christian Church. Jesus Christ comes now to stand by the side of men and help them into the way of finding God.

He helps men to obey. Some years ago, at Lake Geneva, when men, on paper, reported to me in one of my conferences their attitude towards the Christian ministry, one man sent in this slip, which I have kept ever since: "The ministry used to be unattractive to me, because being raised in a Methodist parsonage, I knew all the hard knocks that the minister must take—criticism, indifference, etc. But now, having been shown by Christ that he wishes me to enter it, it has become attractive, more so than any other work."

Jesus helps men to pray. "Where two or three are gathered together, lifting up prayer to the Heavenly Father, there," he says, "will I be in their midst, their partner in prayer, lifting up their petitions to the Heavenly Father with them, nursing their prayerful souls into strength."

Jesus Christ is with men to-day helping them in all departments of life into the spirit of brotherliness.

> That the dear Christ dwells not afar,
> The king of some remoter star,
> Listening, at times, with flattered ear
> To homage wrung from selfish fear,
> But here, amidst the poor and blind,
> The bound and suffering of our kind,
> In works we do, in prayers we pray,
> Life of our life, He lives to-day.[6]

> Wherever are tears and sighs,
> Wherever are children's eyes,
> Where man calls man his brother,
> And loves as himself another,
> Christ lives.[7]

And it is not only the poets that have seen this. A business man in Minneapolis, a little while ago, gave me this clipping from an

[6]Whittier, "The Meeting," Cf. *American Poetry and Prose,* edited by Foerster, p. 629[2] or *The Complete Poetical Works Of John Greenleaf Whittier,* Household ed., 1892, p. 337[1].
[7]Gilder, "Easter," Cf. *op. cit.,* p. 51.

editorial in a great Minneapolis daily, *The Journal*. The editor said: "There is some force abroad that is new. It may be no more than the spirit of Christ, which, under new names and in many disguises, is prompting men, all men, men everywhere, to mutual forbearance, to brotherly co-operation. This spirit once reserved to religion, may have entered economy and politics to a greater extent than we quite realize as yet."

What sort of experience shall a man identify as satisfying his sense of what it ought to be to find God? How shall a man find in feeling the discovery of God? Not a physical sensation. One of my little boys, when he was young, just tumbling about and learning to walk, said to me one day, "How do you know there is a God? I never bumped up against him."

It must also be an imperfect and developing experience. It must be like the progressive experience involved in finding a friend. Man's career is, at its longest, only an era of beginnings, a beginning of discoveries, particularly in the sphere of personal life. But this gradual and progressive discovery of a great Friend may be marked in its beginnings or it may be obscure in its beginnings. You take two persons out of a room filled with poisonous gas, and one of them becomes conscious of revived life the moment he reaches the fresh air; the other lies still unconscious for half an hour after the revivifying process has actually begun. But whether the beginnings of this progressive discovery of a great Friend be clearly marked or obscure, this must be the certain evidence that the process is taking place: *a growing likeness in character to the invisible Friend.* Your metaphysics of God may not much clear up, but your character will become like his in its fundamental features. Your metaphysical description of your friend does not much clear up as you more and more discover the value of his friendship, but you become more and more like your friend if the friendship is a true one. You become more and more like the character of God in these three fundamental particulars—a growing sincerity, a strengthening sympathy, a deepening peace—more honest, more kindly, more profoundly peaceful. And this will be your great contribution to any community on any side of any ocean to which you go. The greatest contribution you can make will be yourself being led into a deepening acquaintance with

God through fellowship with Jesus Christ, a man or a woman learning to be more and more intolerable with the insincerities of his life, more and more sympathetic, more and more deeply and profoundly at peace, able

> To hear at times a sentinel
> Who moves about from place to place,
> And whispers to the worlds of space,
> In the deep night, that all is well.[8]

And so, as you here and now endeavor to make the discovery of God, you may find here and now, with some degree of consciousness, the great, infinite life of the ever-present Father welling up through the unexplored depths of your subconscious personality and coming in some measure even to the surface. The energy of God will bear you out for lives of work—glad, joyous work—and, it may be, to brave, unostentatious dying in the face of human hate on some continent or other of this old world; and then the victorious energy of God will lift you up and over into the great mystery, and carry you on, strong and steady and peaceful, into the endless ages of enlarging achievement in fellowship with Jesus Christ and in the never-ending discovery of the Heavenly Father.

[8]Tennyson, "In Memoriam." Cf. *op. cit.*, p. 320.[2]

THE ETERNAL YET CHANGING GOSPEL

XX

THE ETERNAL YET CHANGING GOSPEL[1]

IN the fierce heat of war much that has been traditional in political and social life has been melted down. World civilization has, to a certain extent, become suddenly plastic, ready to receive and retain impression. What gospel should a Church, alive to God, try to impress upon this plastic situation? At first glance this seems to be a superfluous question. Has not the Church an eternal gospel, one that has long been in her possession and one that knows no change? Upon second thought, the question is not so simple. The Church's gospel is an eternal gospel *because it is capable of eternally changing without losing its identity.* At the end of his life, Jesus, as he looked forward to his spiritual career, said to his disciples: "I have yet many things to say unto you." He bequeathed to them a growing gospel. The gospel is not simply unchangeable words in a book. It is the living God acting through the living Christ upon a changing world order. In so far as "the gospel" is a literary statement it is a description of this activity of the living God, operating through the living Christ, to make the life of all nations develop according to his good will.

I

The writings which record the beginnings of this activity in the historical career of Jesus of Nazareth and in the experience of his first disciples possess a value that lifts them above all other literature. In them appears at the very beginning the germ of the age-long gospel—that which through all the centuries has given the growing gospel its identity. We rightly call them "the gospels." But if there were no growing gospel as a present-day experience in the growing life of the world, *"the gospels"* would never

[1]Published in *The North American Student.*

have reached the unique place they now have in the world's esteem.

Our question then is this: In what form would God have his Church put her eternal gospel in order to make it profoundly influence the life of man in the present plastic world situation? One great fact stands out with startling clearness. If the gospel is to be made clear to men it must be so lived and so described as evidently to have some vital connection with what is most real to the mass of men—some vital connection with what they spend most of their time doing, namely, the day's work. This is not a new idea in theory but it is one that the war has made to be practical and insistent. Certainly one great cause of the present world upheaval and probably *the* great cause was an economic one. In 1908, the German Kaiser said: "Our country is a young and growing empire. She has a world-wide commerce which is rapidly expanding and to which the legitimate ambition of patriotic citizens refuses to assign any bounds. She must protect that commerce." At the beginning of the war the minds of the diplomats on all sides were influenced by the more or less legitimate desire to secure commercial advantage. One country wanted access to the sea for the sake of its commerce. Another wished more colonies or spheres of influence for its trade. As the war has gone on, the vital importance of economic conditions has become more and more evident. Success depends on the successful administration of farms, mines and factories; on the efficiency of railroad management, on good banking, on the proper conduct of all the work and business of the nation. When penalties are thought of in connection with the end of the war, it is chiefly economic disadvantage that one nation proposes to inflict on another.

In the United States progressive democracy or liberty has almost always asserted itself in terms of economic or commercial advantage. "No taxation without representation" was our slogan in the Revolutionary period. The famous tea party in Boston harbor was an incident in the wholesale grocery business. The economic aspects of the slavery question were necessarily of fundamental importance in the Civil War period. Economic considerations bulk large in the present trouble between Negroes and whites.

The peril of our traditional friendly relation to Japan lies largely in possible economic jealousies or business competition for the trade of China. Every one knows that the economic relationship between capital and labor in this country more and more has a bearing on almost every great question that arises in national politics or in Supreme Court decisions.

In Africa the impact of race on race is constantly raising economic questions. A Christian missionary in Johannesburg finds them facing him at every turn. The introduction of labor-saving machinery among China's millions, who live from hand to mouth, will raise insistent economic questions with which the Christian missionary must grapple. All the world is in a state of upheaval over economic questions. These questions will be more insistent after the war is over. Everywhere men will be asking: To what extent ought economic measures, necessary and effective in war, to be made permanent in times of peace? I do not mean that the Church will identify itself with any particular economic program. But in penetrating to the heart of the world's life, as it certainly will, *instead of being content to have its gospel a veneer on the surface of the world's civilization,* it must make its gospel effective in the economic sphere. World peace depends upon right international relations. International relations are largely economic. If, therefore, the Christian gospel is to contribute to world peace, it must become dominant in the economic sphere. This does not mean that the gospel must be pulled down to a materialistic level, but that the gospel must show itself *able to lift up all the work of the world into the dignity and beauty of a religious experience.* And it must be so preached as to spiritualize fundamental economic relationships.

II

Take this idea up in detail. This means, in the first place, that men must learn to find God and be true sons to him in the day's work. Some men can find God in the private rapture; but many more cannot. They have not the requisite mystic temperament. Few can find him in the life of a recluse. They have not the time for it. They must look for the presence of God in the midst of the day's work.

We need not underestimate the importance of what goes on in

the study of the philosopher or the theologian. These oft-slandered men do much in the sphere of thought leadership to clear the way for human experiment and experience in finding God. But the mass of men must have the experience in factories and mines, on the farm, in the bank, in the store and the office, in the home.

The central fact in the nature of God is his *loving will*. He is personal energy working out in love a great world purpose that has place in it for every individual. Men directly touch this loving energy and share its activity in doing the world's work. The farmer in the field has a right to realize that he is working with the loving, personal energy of God embodied in soil and seed, sunshine and rain. The motorman, when he turns on the electric current, is working with the energy of God. When the directors of a great business corporation plan a campaign in accordance with the principles of a just and true economic development, they are working with the God whose directive energy is itself the vitalizing force in all true social and economic development.

III

Again, this presentation of the gospel in terms of spiritualized economics means that men will learn to build up human brotherhood by doing the day's work together for the common good. The great Christian ideal of human brotherhood which is so central in the gospel must be wrought out in terms of the day's work. Everybody must be taking his part in the day's work. Every one must continue to do his "bit" after the war is over in the great reconstructive peace campaign for a world, Christian in spirit.

And what shall this spirit be like? A thousand men will pour out of the factory gates at night, not afraid of being shot by other workmen who want their job—not with a sullen sense of being overworked and underpaid, but eager to meet again the next morning for another day of work for the common good. It will be a sense of brotherhood that does not simply extend laterally to other workmen in a labor union, but a sense of perpendicular brotherhood that goes up and down from the head manager to the lowest position on the working force—everybody, from the bank president to the scrub-woman, possessed by a contented sense of working together for the common good. It means stockholders not interested solely in dividends, but regarding their shares of stock as a device by which they unite with others in making contribution of capital to the common good.

All those who have been connected in any way with the manufacture of a useful article might gather in the shipping department to send that article out with God's blessing upon it to the brothers who need it. They turn the manufactured article over to the great distributing agencies. All the railroad men—the president, the office force, train crews, telegraphers, track repair gangs—all have a Christian sense of working together for the common good. The inventor is a man who gets something from God, discovers some new item in the unfolding will of God, which may be made useful to the common good.

IV

The gospel for the present economic world crisis must also connect the day's work with the immortality of the soul. The war has certainly made the immortality of the soul a practical question. As the world looks out over the five, six, seven million graves of her strongest and best young men, she cannot help asking, "If a man die—shall he live again?" This is no time to assert with a doubtful or apologetic voice the great Christian expectation of immortality. If the economic life of the world is to be lifted up by the gospel into the dignity and beauty of a religious experience, the radiant light of the larger, unseen, immortal world must be let in upon it. This means that the future life must be conceived in terms that shall connect it with the glorified day's work. The future life will be thought of as a life in which men live and work together, as they have begun to do here, in obedience to the gospel. A desire for immortality will be the natural result of working here and now with God and men for the common good. Men who have learned the joy of working together with God and each other in the gospel way, will resent the idea that their chance to work for the common good ends with death. They will look forward to immortality not as compensation for suffering, but as a *continuance of opportunity* to do and dare for the common good in a glorified fellowship with God and right-minded men. A vital connection between the day's work here and the day's work there will appear. A man's chance for good work there will be seen to depend upon the way in which he has done the day's work here. The day's work well done here, with strong sense of a Heavenly Father and human brothers, leads the workman naturally to a place in the great industries of eternity, where men work together on the unfinished universe of God.

The reason why many men have no interest in the future life is because it has never been put before them as an *interesting* life. This life they cling to because it is so interesting. There is so much going on. Huxley said it filled him with a sort of horror to think that in the year 1900 he should probably know no more of what was going on than he had known in 1800—before he was born. But when men conceive the future life in terms of the day's work, they will conceive of something "going on" in it which will fill them with a sort of horror to think of missing. They will feel that they must be there to see what is going on. It will be too interesting to miss. When the human mind once conceives a really good thing, it has no difficulty in believing that this good thing can in some way be had. All doubt about the fact of the future life quietly disappears.

V

The last feature of the eternal gospel which must be emphasized in the present world crisis is the *leadership of Jesus Christ* in the world's busy work-a-day life. It is the leadership of Jesus Christ that has always given peculiar character to the gospel. It is this that has distinguished the Christian gospel from the gospels of other religions. Jesus Christ, his character, his purpose, his power, his sacrifice, reaching forward into the endless ages, has always been the great asset of the Christian church. Just now there is peculiar significance in the fact that he lived his life in the midst of the day's work. He was not a philosopher, although he furnished data which must be central in all philosophy. He found God to be a Heavenly Father in the day's work. His beautiful vision of human brotherhood took shape while he was building houses and making agricultural implements. Much of his teaching is in the phraseology of the business world. He began to gather men about himself in a great working brotherhood, and bound them to God. He gave to the brotherhood victorious conviction of an immortal career, and felt himself destined by God to an immortal leadership. *The great message of the gospel today is that the immortal spirit of Jesus has not left the world, has not withdrawn from the affairs of men.* He is present in the world, laying hold of individual men to redeem their lives from selfishness and connect them with his great unselfish world enterprise. God is working through the living Christ to shape the economic development of the world.

Jesus is the great international leader. He was born a Jew, but no one thinks of him today as a Jew. He is claimed by Russian, German, Englishman, Asiatic, European, American, African. It has come to pass, as a certain scholar has said, that Jesus and Buddha are the two saviors who compete today for the souls of men. No other way has yet been found. How this competition will end is not doubtful. Jesus, with his emphasis on personality, with his gospel of action, with his immortal brotherhood of friendly workmen, will win the day—not Buddha, with his gospel of impersonality, inaction, Nirvana. It is the love of Jesus constraining men that will be able to furnish the tremendous motive necessary to drive the great Christian economic program through to success in all the civilization of the world.

VI

This conception of the gospel for the times which has more and more been possessing the minds of men in recent decades may, perhaps, be summed up in this statement. The gospel promises the establishment of a world civilization in which all men, regardless of race or social condition, shall together find God to be their Father, do the day's work happily with him and with each other as brothers forever more, under the redeeming leadership of Jesus Christ.

Such a gospel can be effectively preached only by a Church ready for great sacrifice. No long step forward in the redemption of the world is ever taken without great sacrifice. The crucified Lord himself led the way and assured his disciples that they must follow him in sacrifice. This whole gospel program is baptized in the spirit of redemptive sacrifice. This world war is a part of it.

What form the sacrifice will take in the future, especially in America, we cannot tell. This gospel is certain to meet with violent opposition. It will be opposed by fierce economic greed, racial hate, man's primeval love of fighting. It will find enemies among all classes. Drunken mobs of working men rioting through the streets will be against it. Hard, unsympathetic manipulators of capital will be against it. Luxurious women will be against it. Small stockholders, whose chief desire is for large dividends, will be against it. But the Church of Christ will be for it. The Church of Christ will not lack the spirit of self-sacrifice and devotion necessary to overcome this opposition. The Church will live this gospel and preach it until it prevails in all the earth. After the long, terrible strain of the war is over, multitudes of men will be ready to look to the high heaven, eager for the eternal gospel. But it must be such a gospel as can be stated in terms of the experience out from which they will come and the day's work renewed before them,—a day's work so done as to preclude the possibility of another great world war, springing out of pagan economics.

We may all join in Richard Watson Gilder's prayer:

Increase Thy prophets, Lord!
Give strength to smite shame to the heart of luxury and sloth!
Give them the yearning after human souls that burned in Wesley's breast!
Let kindle, as before, Oh Heavenly Light,
New messengers of righteousness and hope, and courage for our day!
So shall the world that ever surely climbs to Thy desire
Grow swifter toward Thy purpose and intent.[2]

[2]From poem written in commemoration of the two hundredth anniversary of John Wesley's birth. Cf. *op. cit.*, p. 360.

THE GOSPEL OF FORGIVENESS

XXI

THE GOSPEL OF FORGIVENESS[1]

"That repentance and remission of sins should be preached in his name unto all the nations."

OUR theme bears us into the very heart of God. It speaks of sin and love and mysterious tragedy, of peace after pain, and of home after loneliness. It is a theme of which one must speak softly in a spirit of reverent inquiry and personal gratitude, rather than with loud and controversial dogmatism.

It is the central thought of God's age-long message to men. The Hebrew prophets and psalmists were at their best when, with swelling hearts, they testified to Jehovah's forgiveness of their sins. That which dominated the consciousness of our Lord when he brought God into the daily lives of troubled men was the glad conviction that he had authority on earth to forgive sins. The message which he has pledged you and me, my brothers, to carry to the earth's remotest end is that *sins may be forgiven*—"That repentance and forgiveness of sins should be preached in his name unto all the nations."

And yet it must be said that a deep sense of guilt and the penitent's joy of forgiveness are not characteristic of the typical Christian experience of our day. We begin the Christian life from prudential considerations, driven to it perhaps as our only resource in the battle with evil habit; or from rational considerations, because it seems reasonable to do so. We do not possess a guilty sense of having done something personally offensive to God for which we need to ask and receive his forgiveness. We do not often find ourselves in what Dr. Edwin Hatch called "the half-tearful heaven of forgiven sin."

Doubtless this phase of the Christian life, which has been so prominent in the history of Christian experience, will in time re-

[1]Baccalaureate sermon delivered before the Graduate School of Theology, Oberlin.

sume its normal place. It must be our aim to secure this result in the experiences of those to whom we bring the Great Message.

We are to raise four questions to-night: What is forgiveness? What is the need of forgiveness? What are the conditions of forgiveness? What are the consequences of forgiveness?

What Is Forgiveness?

Forgiveness is wholly a personal matter. One cannot think religious truth at all except in terms of personal relationships. Two persons are concerned in forgiveness. One of them is God, and the other an individual man. God has in some way suffered wrong at the hands of the man. He is a God of love, and so feels no bitter ill will towards the man. *But he who, with an infinite honesty sees all things as they are, and in infinite purity all things as they ought to be, looks upon this evil doer with disapproving love.* It is the disapproval that turns daylight into darkness and heaven into hell. The man who did the great wrong repents, realizes the wrong he has done, regrets it, and ceases it. Then the changeless love of God passes from disapproval to approval, and the night becomes light as the day. Since forgiveness is the exercise of God's approving love, there can be no forgiveness, where there is no repentance, for God cannot approve of unrepented evil. In the far more effective picture language of Jesus, forgiveness is the sinner coming home from the far country, the father with eager hand and hungry eye hurrying out to meet him, folding him in the arms of an infinite love, and putting the kiss of an infinite tenderness upon his cheek.

The heartiness with which God forgives sin is the great theme of his messengers. He "forgets" sin with a glad and jubilant forgetfulness. "He casts it triumphantly behind his back" to be seen no more. He takes it far out from continents and men, and sinks it "in the depths of the sea" where neither man nor devil shall dredge it up. No man shall speak to him again of his child's wayward days. In forgiveness the father gains a son: "This my son was lost and is found." Jesus said of the man who succeeded in inducing his fellow man to repent and be forgiven, that he had gained a brother; so the angels might gather about the Heavenly Father and say, "Thou hast gained a son."

THE NEED OF FORGIVENESS

What real wrong can a little man of a few days have done to the great God? What have you ever done for which you owe the infinite God a personal apology?

The need of forgiveness rests upon two assumptions, fundamental in the teaching of Jesus,—the fatherhood of God and the nearness of the fatherly God to the soul of the man. Jesus, out of his own sense of the nearness of the fatherly God, used strong language to describe it. As he saw the dead sparrow lying in the path at his feet, a sudden throb within him told him that his Heavenly Father had been near to note the little bird's last heartbeat. His own consciousness bore instant and convincing testimony to the fact that much more was God near to the heart of a man, his son.

Stolid men seem not to recognize the nearness of the Heavenly Father at all; less stolid men talk of a time yet to come when God shall be near to men as he seems to them not now to be. But God is round about us, holding us in the subtle yet powerful embrace of an unremitting presence. "In him we live and move and have our being."

What is, then, the wrong that is made possible by the closeness of the relationship between the Heavenly Father and his human child?

Failure to Love a Father

A good father suffers a fundamental wrong if his child does not love him. A father can bear carelessness, stupidity, outbursts of temper, and acts of disobedience soon repented, if only his wild, wayward child loves him. Sometimes we see a father or mother doing everything for a boy growing up into young manhood, and yet the boy is wrapped up in selfish unconcern. There is a dead insensibility to love. Perhaps the son is roused from his selfish stupor by the death of the parent. Then follow painful remorse and the wild longing to call back the one that is gone and ask forgiveness. *There is no deeper sense of guilt, no more bitter sorrow than that which arises from finally realizing that one has been close to a great love and has made no response.* One who has passed through this experience feels that he needs to ask forgiveness for the long nights of painful sleeplessness and the days of unrelieved monotonous sorrow that he has occasioned. Such is the case of the man who does not love his Heavenly Father. "Thou shalt love the Lord thy God with all thy heart" may no longer seem to be the words of arbitrary command resounding with Sinaitic thunder in the hearts of frightened men. As the words come to us on the lips of Jesus they are an appeal of a father's heart, an infinite love asking for a human response.

> So, through the thunder comes a human voice
> Saying, "O heart I made, a heart beats here."[2]

When God sees his human children growing up to the point where they are capable of beginning to love him, and finds them ignoring him, he suffers a grievous wrong. Otherwise there is no real thought behind the expression "our Heavenly Father." The conduct of multitudes of thoughtless men and women whom we pass daily in the busy street, we may say reverently, hurts God. We must not reduce God to a philosophical abstraction or a theological dogma without feeling. Doubtless there is a balance of feeling due to his comprehensive view of all things, but in the composite of feelings that make up the consciousness of God *there must be an element of sorrow*. The man who does not love his Heavenly Father hurts God and owes his Father a penitent heartbroken apology.

Neglect of a Father's Children

The need of forgiveness may be stated in another way, resting still upon this fundamental assumption of Jesus that God is a Father infinitely near to the spirits of men: We need to ask God's forgiveness for having abused or neglected his other children. A father's tenderest point is his solicitude for his child. Men who are not greatly disturbed by attacks upon themselves are roused to the utmost by attacks upon their children. If a man should find one of my little boys on a wintry day lost on a country road, hungry and crying, stumbling along, almost overborne by the freezing cold, and should do him harm, or should simply pass him by un-

---

[2]Browning, "An Epistle," Cf. *Browning's Shorter Poems*, edited by Franklin T. Baker, p. 190; also Browning, *Op. cit.*, p. 341[1].

helped and so let him come to harm, that man would have to reckon with me. He would have hurt me. He would need to make his apology to me because I am the little boy's father.

In God's great family of human children there are many lost and overborne by the wayside of life.

> I hear around me sighs of pain
>   And the cry of fear,
> And a sound like the slow, sad dropping of rain,
>   Each drop a tear.[3]

Many who do not seem at first glance to be in need, from whom you do not hear the sigh of pain or the cry of fear, nevertheless upon close observation are seen to be putting up certain mute signals of distress that the absorbed and unobserving pass easily by. All these people are dear to God. He is their Father. This is the meaning of that other part of the great summary of human duty. "Thou shalt love thy neighbor as thyself" is the message of a Father, pleading with the sovereign authority of an infinite love the cause of his needy children. When they are struck he is hurt; when they are neglected, he is sore at heart. This is the significance of Jesus' great transforming word to the Hebrew rabbi, "Saul, Saul, why persecutest thou me?" When the helpless Nazarenes were being dragged by the fierce young rabbi along the stony streets of Jerusalem to the synagogue, their unseen Lord felt each bruise. This is the significance of the judgment scene; when hungry people went unfed and the sick lay without sympathy and the imprisoned without friends, the Lord's heart was hurt. "Ye did it not unto me" said the awful voice of judgment. It was with him that the selfish had to reckon in the judgment day. *"God's poor" is no idle phrase with which to ornament a well-turned sentence. They are his; he carries them on his heart.* If the miseries of the poor in the great city make no appeal to us, if our hearts feel no sympathy for them, it is to their Heavenly Father that we must make our stammering explanations, and it is his heavy judgment that will fall upon us. If the little children who play unblessed in the streets of Delhi and Peking make no impression upon us, it is to their Heavenly Father that we must make our apologies.

---

[3]Whittier, "My Soul and I", Cf. *The Early Poems of John Greenleaf Whittier,* p. 275, and *The Complete Poetical Works Of John Greenleaf Whittier,* Cambridge ed., 1892, p. 94[1].

Failure to Do Our Father's Business

Again, we need God's forgiveness for the personal wrong we have done him in failing to be about our Father's business. There is authority in the highest type of fatherhood. It is our glory that our Heavenly Father is a sovereign. We need once more to clothe our idea of God with the majestic garments of sovereignty. We need to recognize the authoritative will of God. It seems no longer, as it perhaps once did, the arbitrary will of an inscrutable Sovereign, but the infinitely loving will of a sovereign Father.

If a son wastes his time in college, ruins himself by a life of dissipation, and comes home unfit for the business his father took pains to prepare him for, he has done his father a personal wrong. So also if he does paltry things instead of great things. A boy with inventive genius, who is sent to college by his father to prepare himself for responsibilities in a great industrial enterprise, may not become dissipated; but if he refuses to attend classes and insists on running a peanut stand on the corner of the campus, he owes his father an apology for failing to fit himself for the high career his father planned. The need of apology for ruining himself, or for allowing petty activities to prevent him from fitting himself for a high career, is all the more evident when his failure to become what he ought to be makes him a positive hindrance in his father's business. If the Crown Prince Frederick had failed to co-operate with his father in the days of German unification, if he had been a positive hindrance to his father in that great enterprise, he would have owed the old emperor a personal apology. God is a Father who trusts his children and gives them large place in the great enterprises that occupy his mind. The long history of civilization shows that he has chosen to do many things in such a way as to give to his children the largest practicable share in the achievement. It is the glory of the children that they are workers together with God. If they unfit themselves by lives of dissipation for the high business that is theirs by inheritance, or if they putter with paltry things when their Father calls them to great responsibilities, they do their Father a personal wrong which calls for repentance. If they so live as to become a positive hindrance to their Father in the accomplishment of the great thing on which he has set his heart there is still sorer need of apology. If the trend of a man's life is against the coming of an era of universal good will, he is opposing himself to the greatest purpose that God has revealed to men. A man must apologize to God if he so lives as to hinder the introduction of that age when "all men's good shall be each man's rule"

> And universal Peace
> Lie like a shaft of light across the land,
> And like a lane of beams athwart the sea,
> Through all the circle of the golden year.[4]

Who is there of us that has not need to ask the forgiveness of the sovereign Heavenly Father who is so infinitely near to our human spirits this day?

WHAT ARE THE CONDITIONS OF FORGIVENESS?

There are two: that the father shall do his utmost to show the son the character of his wrong doing, and that the son shall repent. These conditions appear more and more with each passing generation to be the central event of human history, namely, the mysterious suffering death of Jesus. It is so represented in the context. "Thus it is written that the Christ should suffer and rise again from the dead on the third day and that repentance and forgiveness of sin should be preached in his name unto all the nations."

In the death of Jesus every one of us may see the true nature of his own selfishness,—and all sin is some form of selfishness.

In this death the real nature of human selfishness stands exposed. It was human selfishness that put Jesus upon the cross. He and his ideas stood between the Pharisaic rabbis and the attainment of their selfish ambition for social prestige and religious leadership. Their selfishness rose in a blind fury that refused to consider who Jesus was and that determined relentlessly to put him out of the way. He stood between the priests and their selfish political and financial ambitions. They therefore cut him down with a hard unwillingness to consider who he was. It is the nature of far developed human selfishness to kill whatever opposes it even though the opposition happens to be such a manifestation of God himself

[4]Tennyson, "The Golden Year." Cf. *Op. cit.,* p. 83[1].

as was Jesus. *In this conspicuous case of highly developed selfishness each man may see what his own selfishness will surely lead to.* The selfishness of these rabbis and priests was no different in kind from our own. A man may look with indifference at a spot upon his skin until he learns that it is cancerous. If he would see what the word "cancerous" means, let him go to the bedside of some man in whom the disease is well developed, and see there what sort of disease it is that has fastened itself upon him. So every selfish man may stand by the cross of Jesus and see in that black, selfish deed of priest and rabbi what the real nature of his own sinful selfishness is. He may say to himself, "If my selfishness is not checked I too shall some day be ready to do a deed like this."

The horribleness of human selfishness, for which we need to be forgiven, becomes still more evident when its effect upon Jesus is more closely scrutinized. *The death of Jesus shows how he felt about human selfishness.*

It becomes more and more clear, as the narrative of Jesus' death is examined, that the death is not accounted for by the wounds of the crucifixion. The palm of the hand is not a vital part of the body. A nail driven through the palm of the hand cannot produce speedy death. Jesus' death was a speedy death. The procurator could not believe that he was dead. The other two men were pounded to death by the executioners. The crucified sometimes lived for days, and finally starved to death. That which occasioned the death of Jesus, as one looks more narrowly into the circumstances of the narrative, is seen to be some mysterious, awful mental agony, a mental agony so intense as to produce physical effects and finally stop the life currents of the physical heart.

To one who understands the spirit of the life of Jesus, it is not hard to see, in part at least, what the occasion of this mental distress was. Connected it must have been with the wrong-doing of men whom he so loved. These men just about the cross, he loved with the infinite tenderness of God. These four soldiers with the pot of sour wine, gambling with brutal indifference over his garments, he loved with infinite tenderness. These priests and rabbis, gathered about the foot of the cross, gloating over their success in nailing their enemy to the cross, were men of power whom he had longed to enlist in his great enterprise of renovating the world. The jeering crowd going by were lost sons of the Heavenly Father to whom Jesus could have called out in infinite love. As he turned his head and looked at the housetops of the city and thought of the men, women and children that they covered, he could have cried out with sorrowing love, "O Jerusalem, Jerusalem! how often would I have gathered thy children together, as a hen gathers her chickens under her wings, and ye would not." Those are the words of One who loved. The selfishness of these men, and of other generations like them, caused a mental suffering that finally terminated his life. It is not so much the force of the blow delivered in the old man's face that kills him, but it is the fact that the blow is struck by the fist of his son which shocks the life currents of his heart into the stillness of death.

Still further, in this marvelous death of Jesus, the true nature of our selfishness is seen by us, because *the death of Jesus shows how God himself feels about human selfishness.* The great message of Jesus' life was that he was himself the revelation of the unseen Father. He had said the evening before the crucifixion, that whoever saw him, saw the Father. It was true of him the next morning as he hung on the cross, suffering to the death with intense mental distress over the wrong-doing of the men that he loved. There an everlasting revelation of the heart of God was made. There welled up out of the infinite heart of the Father all that composite of emotions that we cannot understand,—love, sorrow, indignation— and in gaining expression for itself in the heart of Jesus, killed him. We need not hesitate to say that God suffers; else fatherhood has no meaning. Doubtless there are other elements in the consciousness of God for he is the God of peace and the God of hope. But one element in the composite consciousness of God is his suffering over the wrong-doing of his children.

Jesus was a true man, and so his feelings doubtless varied. He was tempted for a while, and then the tempter "departed from him for a season." He "rejoiced in the Holy Spirit," and again he was "sore troubled." Doubtless the main facts always lay before him. He had seen, long before, that he must die. But in Gethsemane there *began an experience which he had up to that time been spared. There he began to share in some special way the great pain that exists in the heart of God over the wrong-doing of his children.* As this began to be borne in upon him it filled him with terror and depression of spirit that sent him in an agony of prayer to his Heavenly Father. "He began to be greatly amazed and sore troubled, and saith unto them, My soul is exceeding sorrowful, even unto death: abide ye here and watch. And he went forward a little and fell on the ground, and prayed, that if it were possible, the hour might pass away from him." But it was not possible. The hour might not pass from him, and the great pain in the heart of the Heavenly Father over the wrong-doing of his children arose in the heart of Jesus, the revelation of the unseen God, and killed him.

Now we know in some measure what sort of thing human selfishness is, as we see the effect it produces in the heart of our Heavenly Father. A father can do nothing more vital to reform the wrong-doing of his child than simply to show him how in the depths of his heart he really feels about the wrong-doing. The utmost has now been done to show humanity the real nature of our selfishness. *God for a moment exposed his heart, and in this moment something was seen from which men have never been able since to take their eyes away.* There has been made a revelation of the way in which the wrong-doing of his children affects the Father's heart. There will never be another able to express it more fully than Jesus has expressed it. There will never be another event in all human history, in which God will be able to show more clearly and vitally how he feels about the wrong-doing of his children, than appears in the death of the matchless personality of Jesus Christ—killed in giving expression to the heart of God.

And here it is that men repent. Age after age men have had an experience in view of the cross of Jesus Christ that they express best in this simple sentence: "Christ died for me." You and I go back in thought to the cross of Jesus Christ; we stand there and say, "It is my kind of wrong-doing that causes him the pain that is killing him. It is my kind of wrong-doing that affects the Father's heart in the way he manifests it. I ought to feel about my sin as he does. I ought to be hanging there with him. I ought to be experiencing this pain that he experiences. I would like to climb to his side, feel as he feels, and be crucified with him." Then, when the heart of the penitent man has come to an agreement with his Heavenly Father in the heart of Jesus Christ and he shares the feeling and purpose of God about his own sin, there is atonement, there is at-one-ment. Father and son are brought together in sacred forgiveness. The nations meet in penitence around the cross of Jesus Christ.

> When I survey the wondrous cross
>   On which the Prince of Glory died,
> My richest gain I count but loss,
>   And pour contempt on all my pride.
>
> See, from his head, his hands, his feet,
>   Sorrow and love flow mingled down!
> Did e'er such love and sorrow meet,
>   Or thorns compose so rich a crown?
>
> Were the whole realm of nature mine,
>   That were an offering far too small,
> Love so amazing, so divine,
>   Demands my soul, my life, my all![5]

There may be other meanings in this great event. It may be that the feasibility of making such a revelation of the heart of God, determined his method of approach to the human race from eternity. It may be that the great law of self-revelation, that requires all personality to reveal itself, demanded such an event. It may have been a necessity of God's personality that he should so reveal himself. Doubtless we have much yet to learn about it. A child sometimes stands dumbly by, solemnized by his father's suffering, but not understanding it. So it may be that we little children of the eternal life stand dumbly by this great manifestation of our Father's heart, solemnized by it, and broken into penitence by it, but only to understand it fully in some far age when we shall have grown up and shall be better able to enter into sympathy with the Father's heart.

> We may not know, we cannot tell
>   What pains he had to bear,
> But we believe it was for us
>   He hung and suffered there.
> He died that we might be forgiven,
> He died to make us good.[6]

[5] Isaac Watts.   [6] Cecil F. Alexander, from hymn, "There is a Green Hill Far Away."

The Consequences of Forgiveness

Do we not live in a world where effect follows cause with unwavering certainty? If a man has sinned, must he not also experience the natural consequences of sinning, even though he be forgiven?

We shall be helped at this point if we continue to think of the relation between father and child. When a child disobeys a father, the most serious consequence of the act is the estrangement that arises between himself and his father. The interchange of affection which makes home a blessed place ceases. There may be also certain subordinate consequences that follow necessarily from the act. A little child is forbidden to go out into the storm, but disobeys. The subordinate consequence is that he catches cold. When the disobedience is repented and forgiveness follows, instantly the chief consequence of wrong-doing is removed, the estrangement between father and child is at an end. The child is in his father's arms. The subordinate consequence is not instantaneously removed; the cold is not instantaneously cured. When the prodigal son came back to his father's home, and was forgiven, the estrangement between father and son ceased instantly. His father folded him in his arms, clothed him richly, and gave him his place in the family. But the effects of the life of dissipation upon his constitution may have been long continued. It may have been months before he could do a full day's work in his father's fields.

But even regarding these subordinate consequences of sin that continue after forgiveness, there is this to say: certain recuperative forces are set in action which tend ultimately to remove even these. The life of the penitent son in his father's house was in a healthful environment. His constitution had recuperative power. The forgiven man is not forevermore a scarred soul. *There is a transforming power in forgiveness.* Paul saw this in the case of those who had been converted from the slums of the great cities in which he preached repentance and the forgiveness of sins with such royal courage. When he wrote to the Corinthian Christians he enumerated a list of sins which we shrink from reading in a miscellaneous audience. At its close he said, "Such were some of you, but ye were washed, ye were made holy, ye were declared righteous in the name of the Lord Jesus Christ and in the spirit of our God." He could even picture these men of Corinth who had been sunk up to the very lips in the mire of that infamous city's ancient filth, walking in strength and beauty on the hills of the blessed, a holy brotherhood, fit companions of the radiant figure that walked in their midst. It was in this foul city, with its iniquitous sights assaulting his vision on every side, and with these forgiven Corinthian wrecks in his mind that he could write these words: "fore-ordained to be conformed to the image of his Son, that he might be a first-born among many brethren."

The glad years that passed after the prodigal son had come back to his father brought the two into an ever-closer fellowship. The son who had thought to be only a hired servant, shared more and more in all the highest occupations of his father. As Jesus contemplated the possibilities of this great relationship between the forgiven man and his Heavenly Father, he experienced flights of thought that we scarcely dare to follow. He saw the very peace of God deepening in the forgiven man's soul. He saw developing in his heart a love that was destined to be as perfect as his Heavenly Father's. He even seemed to see the forgiven children of God finally joining their Father in the high prerogative of forgiving sin. The rabbis held up hands of holy horror as they said "Who can forgive sin but God only?" Yet Jesus, speaking out of his own consciousness of power, dared to turn to a group of forgiven fellowmen and say to them, "Receive ye the Holy Spirit; whose soever sins ye forgive, they are forgiven unto them."

My Brothers of the Graduating Class:—It remains to add a single personal word, after these months and years of happy research together in the class-rooms of your teachers, and my word is suggested by the sentence which follows the text: "Ye are witnesses of these things."

The purpose of your Seminary course has been to lead you to speak of these things from experience. We have not tried to fasten upon you any iron-clad creeds. The simple creeds that you have been making for yourselves in the class-room, we believe will best serve you. For every real creed is simply the *effort of a life to explain itself with reference to propagating itself*. We believe that you will be able, out of your own experience, to bear witness to these things.

We believe that you are *forgiven* men, and that you have in your hearts the beginnings of the deep peace of forgiveness. There can be no peace except that which is grounded on self-respect, and there can be no self-respect for any son of Adam, except as he sees his sin, confesses it and receives the peace-giving forgiveness of God. You will have to speak to restless, feverish men. Our age cries out for peace. Wherever a man rises up to offer men peace, there they will flock. We believe that you will be able to go among these feverish, restless spirits of men, having in your own hearts the deep peace of forgiven sin.

We believe that you are *forgiving* men. No one will be able so to smite you in the face as to stop the outflow of forgiving good-will from your heart. Men will criticize you, men will slander you, as they do lawyers and physicians—why should ministers escape more than other men?—but we know that you will be able so to treat all men as to suggest to them by your own lives the forgiveness of God. The gospel of forgiveness shrinks and shrivels on the lips of an unforgiving man, but from the lips of a man who has in his heart what we believe to be in your hearts, the gospel leaps out into the hearts of men and finds them.

We covet for you a gospel of life and word that will lead *multitudes of other men into God's forgiveness*. The age calls for it. The fascination of the ministry lies in what the minister sees of the mysterious, unseen influence of God, transforming the hearts of sinful men; and he who does not feel this fascination, fails to experience the minister's greatest joy.

For you, my brothers, as you go away from us, there will often be heard in the class-room the prayer of your teachers. Their thought will follow you far. Across the ocean and into dark continents, it may be that some of you will go, and everywhere you will preach the Gospel of Forgiveness.

CAN PRAYER ACCOMPLISH ANYTHING APART FROM THE MAN WHO PRAYS?

Its Practical Consideration

XXII

CAN PRAYER ACCOMPLISH ANYTHING APART FROM THE MAN WHO PRAYS?

Its Practical Consideration[1]

WHEN a man prays, what actually happens? If some kind of spiritual photography could catch the soul in the act of prayer, what would be revealed? *What is the environment of the soul at prayer?* Is the soul alone, or is Another there, vast and enfolding? If Another is there, what goes on in that Other when a man prays? Is there any change in the enfolding Other when the soul of the man prays?

These are questions suggested by our theme. In answering them we must of necessity make one great assumption and proceed to reason from it. In a previous address we have seen the reasons for making this assumption.[2] We assume that there is Another, a vast and enfolding personality, a parent personality of which the human soul is an offshoot. There is a personal environment about the soul which is always saying to it:

"Oh, heart I made, a heart beats here."

That is, we assume the truthfulness of the great teaching which came to its fullness in the personal religious life of Jesus—the nearness and the Fatherhood of God.

I

What does the soul of a man do when it prays to the Heavenly Father? It rises up in love to make conscious gift of itself to the Heavenly Father and to take in return whatever the Heavenly Father may give. When the soul prays thus does anything happen

[1]Delivered before the World's Student Conference at Constantinople.
[2]Ch. XIX, "The Discovery of God."

apart from the praying soul? Is there movement in the Heavenly Father? If there is the slightest propriety in calling God our Father, it is necessary to say that the heart of the Father goes out in love to the soul of his praying child and makes itself felt there; the soul of the child touches the soul of the Father in some special way, and the soul of the Father touches the soul of the child in some special way in response to the prayer. This conception may seem to represent God as changeable in a certain sense. God's unchangeableness is *an unchangeableness of love,*—not an absolute inertia. To ascribe absolute inertia to God would involve a denial of personality, for *an essential element of personality is varied activity.*

In prayer, then, something does happen apart from the man who prays. The soul of the Heavenly Father is stirred and sends something back to the praying child. There is an interplay of feeling between the human child and his Heavenly Father. We shall not easily over-estimate the value of prayer so conceived. Such interplay of feeling purifies the human soul and must give satisfaction to the Heavenly Father. A human father is pleased when his children come to him wanting nothing except to be with him for a little time. As the relation between a son and his father develops, the son cares less and less for the things that he may receive from his father and more and more for his father for his own sake.

Can anything besides feeling pass from the heart of the Heavenly Father to the heart of his human child? All that we know about the relation of persons to each other gives us reason to say that not simply feeling but thought also can pass from the mind of God to the mind of a man. Persons are able to put thoughts into each other's minds by the use of words, by gestures, by the glance of an eye. It seems probable that by telepathic action they may even think thoughts directly into each other's minds without the use of word, gesture, or look. We have seen reason for calling God in some vital sense a personal being. It is necessary, therefore, to conclude that God can do what other persons can do—namely, *put a thought into the mind of a man.* The Heavenly Father can produce not only a feeling in the heart, but also an idea in the mind of his human child.

This opens a wide door for answer to prayer, for it involves not only the power of God to put a thought into the mind of the man who prays, but also into the mind of some third person, or into the minds of many persons. Have you need of guidance in some emergency? In answer to your prayer God may put a thought into your mind that will give you the needed guidance. He may so influence your mental processes that you shall rightly reason out your course of action. Do you need money for some good purpose? God, by putting a thought into your mind, may show you how to get it, or by putting a thought into the mind of some other person he may lead him to send you what you need. Here seems to be wide scope for answer to prayer, because almost all of the petitions we ever have occasion to make to God are such as can be answered by his producing feeling and thought in the mind of some man. The power to do this, as has been said, is inherent in the very nature of personality. We may, therefore, without hesitation attribute this power to God, since the assumption with which we started is that God is, in some real sense, a personal being.

II

There are, however, certain objections to prayer felt by many earnest men which are not fully met by the position just taken. The chief of these objections should be considered here.

First of all, it is often thought that since we live in a world of law and order, where an unvarying cause produces an unvarying effect, there is no place left for God to make things happen in answer to prayer. The first word of reply to this objection *should be one of appreciation*. We have reason for gratitude that we live in a world of law and not in a world of caprice or chance. We must be able to count upon the steadfastness of the so-called forces of Nature if we are to forecast results in a civilized way. There is, however, one thing that becomes more and more evident with every advance in human experience—namely, that the so-called forces of Nature which surround us are extremely susceptible to the influence of a personal will. The more we learn about the forces of Nature and the laws of their action, the more we are able to do, not in spite of them, but by means of them.

Every advance in acquaintance with these forces increases our power to answer the appeals of our fellow men for help. Three thousand people are in imminent peril in mid-ocean. Once there would have been no hope for them, but since the personal will of men has learned to manipulate natural forces the wireless sends its radiating appeal, great ships change their courses and hurry thither from all points of the compass to answer the cry for help. The air is increasingly full of aeroplanes flying swiftly to every point of need. The forces of Nature do not keep persons apart; they facilitate intercourse. They are mighty devices for enabling men to answer each other's calls for help. *The unvarying regularity of their action is what makes them serviceable under the manipulation of a personal will.* Since men can so use them, much more can God answer the prayers of his children by means of them.

It seems evident, however, that God does not intend frequently to answer prayer by co-ordinating natural forces in unusual ways. If we were near to death for lack of water in a desert, where it never rains, we should not have faith to ask God so to co-ordinate natural forces as to produce rain. We should rather ask him to put into the mind of some man the thought of going out into the desert on some errand that would incidentally result in relief to the sufferers. God has evidently purposed to leave the sphere of natural forces to man for his investigation and conquest. He has let men freeze to death with undiscovered beds of coal beneath their feet; he has let the generations suffer pain for centuries with the elements of undiscovered anæsthetics about them. We would not have it otherwise. The zest of life is in overcoming difficulties under the spur of fearful necessity. A wise father leaves his children to find out many things for themselves. He does not intervene to make life easy for them at every point. The independence and self-respect essential to character result from difficulties met and overcome.

A difficulty of a different sort is sometimes raised by earnest minds wishing to pray; God is supposed to have planned all things, great and small, from the beginning. If the occurrence of the thing prayed for is in his plan, it will certainly occur and there is no need to pray for it; if its occurrence is not in God's plan, it will not occur and it is useless to pray for it. So runs the objection.

The futility of this objection to prayer appears sufficiently for practical purposes when it is noted that if it proves anything it proves too much, for it proves that it is useless to ask anyone for anything. I may not ask the simplest favor of my friend because if God has planned that my friend shall grant the favor, grant it he will without my asking. If God has not planned it, grant it my friend will not, no matter how much I ask him. Such reasoning is recognized at once to be foolishness, for we know perfectly well that we constantly get things from each other by asking each other for them. Even so we may get things from God by asking him, for he also is a person.

Another and more serious objection to prayer that arises in many earnest minds is this: since God is a good Father, he will surely give good gifts to his children without waiting to be asked. Certainly a good father does give many good gifts to his children without waiting to be asked. Does God always wait for the prayer of his child before giving a good gift? Can he not always be left to do what is best without any presentation of a human petition? Regarding this several things may be said. First of all, it is abnormal for a child to suppress all petition. In a free, spontaneous family life children ought to make all their wants known without restraint.

Child life is largely made up of asking many, many trustful questions, and among them requests for things the child believes he wants. One important mark of true development is the gradual decrease in the *number* of questions and requests, and increase in their thoughtful *quality*. Furthermore, a father often waits before doing a good thing for a child until the child cares enough about it to ask for it. It might be unwise to give it before the child cared enough for it to ask for it. Still further, it is often the policy of a father to do things in such a way as to give the largest feasible share in the achievement to his children. Character is developed by giving them large and responsible part in the enterprise. Prayer is a way of working together with God. Genuine prayer is not mere words. *It involves as real an output of vital energy as is involved in an act of the will of God.* It is a normal, wholesome way of working together with God, and for such co-operation God might sometimes wait before proceeding to action.

This objection assumes a more difficult form when the prayer is in another's behalf. Would God wait before doing a good thing for one of his children until another child asked him to do it? Certainly, God would do many things for his child in need without waiting for another child to ask him. But is it even proper for a child to suggest to his Heavenly Father the doing of a good thing for one of the other children? Is so-called intercessory prayer ever anything except impertinence? The answer to this question appears clear when we stop to consider the moral purpose that the institution of the family serves. At least a large part of the moral purpose of the family is accomplished *when the children become unselfishly interested in each other*. The family is an ethical success when each one of the children comes to his father and says regarding some good gift: "I wish you would give this to my brother." Therefore, it is not at all strange that a father, for the sake of securing this great ethical success, should sometimes wait before doing a good thing for one of the children until another child has time to realize his brother's need and to say: "I wish you would do this for my brother." It is not inconceivable that God should sometimes wait before doing a good thing for some of his children in one country until some of their brothers in another country *should have time to see what brotherhood means and to pray for their brothers in a foreign land*. Such waiting may sometimes contribute to the accomplishment of God's great purpose to fill the earth with a race of brotherly men, profoundly interested in each other.

Prayer, then, is never an effort to bend the will of God. It is never an effort to persuade God to do something he would rather not do. It is, instead, the normal, reverent rising up of a son of God to inquire whether there may not be some good thing which the Heavenly Father wishes to do so soon as he can have the co-operation of this son through prayer.

III

There are three classes of things in an ideal human family. First, the things that the father does for his children without waiting to be asked. They are many and of fundamental importance. So God pours the great gifts of his love lavishly into the lives of his children without waiting to be asked to do so. No one asked him to send his Son into the world. In the second place, there are the things that the children ask for and are refused. In the spontaneous life of a happy family all requests, wise and foolish, may be freely made. Many of the requests of little children are certain to be foolish. In God's great family the oldest of us are but little children in the eternal life and certain to make many foolish prayers that God is too good to grant. Because God does so many things without waiting to be asked and refuses to do so many things that he is asked to do we are sometimes inclined to think that there is no place for the prayer of specific petition. But in God's great family, as in any other, there is a third class of things— namely, those that are given by the Father only when and because the children ask for them.

Something does happen, then, in prayer apart from the man who prays. Prayer is not a deluded soul rising to make conscious gift of itself to an imaginary Father. Prayer is not lifting up pitiful hands to brazen, unanswering skies. There is a living God, a Heavenly Father. He is near at hand, waiting to listen to his child's voice and ready to answer. His heart is stirred by prayer. The heart of him who prays is stirred by the answer. The minds of men receive thoughts from God in answer to their prayer. All the mechanism of the world is so arranged as to enable the living God to act freely upon the lives of men.

Speak to Him thou for He hears, and Spirit with Spirit can meet—
Closer is He than breathing, and nearer than hands and feet.[3]

Jesus was no false guide when he spoke with full conviction out of the experience of his own life of answered prayer and said: "Ask and it shall be given you; seek and ye shall find; knock, and it shall be opened unto you: for everyone that asketh receiveth; and he that seeketh findeth; and to him that knocketh it shall be opened."

[3]For ref. cf. p. 205.

CAN PRAYER ACCOMPLISH ANYTHING APART FROM THE MAN WHO PRAYS?

Its Philosophical Approach

XXIII

CAN PRAYER ACCOMPLISH ANYTHING APART FROM THE MAN WHO PRAYS?

Its Philosophical Approach

WHEN men find themselves facing disaster or danger they are instinctively moved to pray. Thoughtful men necessarily inquire whether they ought to yield to this instinct, or, instead, to repress it as the incidental survival of a primitive fear characteristic of a lower stage of development. The present great world pain is moving men everywhere to instinctive prayer and therefore to thoughtful questioning regarding the rationality of prayer.

From the Christian standpoint the instinct to pray is a central permanent function of human life the exercise of which leads to a higher stage of human development. The present war may teach the whole race certain important lessons regarding the causes of war and the necessity of their removal, but if it is to be followed by any great and permanent improvement in the race it must introduce men into a better understanding of the theory and practice of prayer. Christian men and women must let the present crisis drive them to prayer—to prayer of a superior quality, expressing a new fineness of spirit and springing out of a growing appreciation of the rationality and centrality of prayer in its relation to the whole of life.

The most frequent and perhaps the most vital inquiry regarding prayer is expressed in the question: Can prayer accomplish anything apart from the man who prays?

Does prayer consist in anything more than a devout soliloquy? Is it anything more than a kind of spiritual exercise, healthful for the one who practices it, but without direct effect upon any other person, God or man?

The answer to these questions depends upon what we mean by God and what we mean by prayer. There are two propositions regarding the nature of God and the nature of prayer which, if valid, give to prayer more than a merely subjective value. The first is this: *There is all about us a friendly vital energy called the Living God steadily working upon human life to make friendship, brotherhood, universal and secure throughout the human race.* The second is this: *Prayer is a process by which a friendly man gets something from the Friendly God for the common good or to share with a fellow man in need. This process binds men in fast friendship to one another, brings them together into conscious friendship with the Living God, and so contributes vitally to making friendship universal and secure throughout the human race.*

These two propositions furnish the foundation for the nearest approach to a philosophy of prayer to be found anywhere in the teaching of Jesus. In the illustration by which he presents this philosophy a man had an unexpected guest appear at his door at midnight, tired and hungry. The man, who had no food to set before his guest, hurried through the darkness to the house of a well-to-do neighbor, asked from him, and received, what he needed for the purpose. "And it came to pass, as he was praying in a certain place, that when he ceased, one of his disciples said unto him, Lord, teach us to pray. . . . And he said unto them, which of you shall have a friend and shall go unto him at midnight and say to him, Friend, lend me three loaves; for a friend of mine is come to me from a journey, and I have nothing to set before him? . . . He will arise and give him as many as he needeth. And I say unto you, ask and it shall be given you." That is, the man who prays is *a friendly man standing between two persons,* getting something from one to share with the other. He looks out to the gracious Living God and says: *"Friend,* lend me three loaves, for a *friend* of mine is come to me from a journey, and I have nothing to set before him."

The two propositions stated above constitute a challenge to action, and may be put to the test of experience, even though the following attempt to make them seem antecedently reasonable should not succeed to the reader's satisfaction.

I

There is a friendly Living God whose purpose it is to make friendship universal and secure throughout the human race. The scope of this article does not permit any thorough discussion of this first proposition, although what it means may be made clear in a few words.

We know that we are living in the midst of vast unseen energy. Since beginning to read this article the reader has silently and without jar been carried some hundreds of miles in the earth's swift, unhurried journey around the sun. Immense vital energy is easily lifting countless tons of matter from below the surface of the earth to leaf and flower in the air above the earth. Through a long evolutionary process vast energy, beginning with low forms of life, brought personal human beings into existence. When once the human race was well established, this energy, in spite of elemental human greed, racial hate, and man's primeval love of war, introduced the life of Jesus Christ into the race. Since Jesus' day, in spite of these same adverse influences, the race has moved on, increasingly influenced by the ideals and power of his life.

More and more it becomes a demand of thought that the unseen energy which finds expression in all the various phenomena that confront the mind of man be recognized as one. The nature of this one energy is to be inferred from the highest phenomenon in which it has expressed itself. This highest phenomenon is human personality, and in the sphere of human personality that which is highest and best is Jesus and the men who adopt his ideals of life.

It might be argued that "bad" men, as well as "good" men of the Jesus type, are the phenomena that must furnish us our clue to the nature of the one force behind all phenomena. But when "bad" men are closely scrutinized they are seen to be acting contrary to the laws of normal growth written in the very constitution of their being. Their very natures show that they were meant to be "good" men, men of the Jesus type. Or it might be argued that the sum total of all phenomena, impersonal as well as personal, ought to give us our idea of the one energy behind all phenomena. But when we look at the sum total of all phenomena we find that these phenomena are not miscellaneous and unrelated, but are all gathered up in an evolutionary process which culminates in man at his highest and best. So we may for this reason, to say nothing of others that might be stated in a discussion of larger scope, assume the existence of one energy behind all phenomena which has most clearly expressed itself in the personality of Jesus Christ, and in the character and institutions of men vitally affected by his ideals.

What would this Living God—this power near enough to us to give us being and keep it going, but distinct enough from us to give us a chance to be ourselves—have the human race to be? There are two sources to which we may look for the answer to this question. One is the trend revealed in the history of human development. The other is the ideal of human life presented in the teaching of Jesus Christ. Both sources yield the same reply, namely, the Living God is working toward the secure establishment of a world civilization, in which every man shall wish for every other man of every nation and social condition such a fair chance at all good things as a man should wish his brother to have.

In this civilization all the legitimate activities of human life are to find free productive expression. It is to be a civilization in which all men will together find God in the day's work, and do the day's work happily with him and with each other forevermore under the leadership of Jesus Christ. All of man's physical environment is to be mastered and utilized for the accomplishment of friendly purposes and all the latent powers of personality are to be developed. Men will work creatively with God and with each other on the unfinished universe. In a sense both high and broad we are to be "workers together with God." In this far-reaching purpose of the Living God friendship will be universal and secure throughout the human race; men will be consciously sons of God, brothers to each other, and all the institutions of human civilization will be in accord with this consciousness.

II

Prayer is the process by which a friendly man gets something from the friendly Living God for the common good or to share with a fellow man in need. This means first of all that Christian prayer is never selfish. It may be for one's self, but it is never an effort to get something for one's self alone. *Selfish prayer is pagan prayer,* not Christian prayer. Christian prayer is "in the name of Christ," that is, in the spirit for which the name of Christ stands, the spirit of Christ's unselfish love. It is "for Jesus' sake," that is, for the sake of the civilization of brotherly men which Jesus purposes to make secure on the earth. It is such prayer as Jesus himself can share with us—the prayer that rises from the little group of disciples with Jesus in the midst.

The question naturally arises: Why should it be necessary to appeal to the Gracious God in behalf of a fellow man in need? Does not God see the belated traveler, hurrying on through the darkness tired and hungry, and is not God more truly the man's friend than any fellow man can be? Would the Benevolent God delay relief until some man urged him to bring it?

Certainly he would not always wait for man's prayer. Jesus taught that the ceaseless providence of God sends rain and sunshine on both the just and the unjust. But in the light of God's great purpose to make friendship universal and secure, it is apparent that God would sometimes wait for the intermediary friendly prayer. He will sometimes wait until one man's need has had time to appeal to a fellow man and arouse within him the friendly desire to get something from God with which to meet the need. This procedure binds the two men together in lasting friendship and brings them together into a sympathetic relation with the Friendly God. The process therefore directly contributes to the development of a sense of brotherhood among men and of sonship to God. It is a vital, elemental way of making friendship with God and men universal and secure throughout the human race, of realizing the fundamental ambition of God for the life of man.

Next comes the question: How does God operate in answering prayer? How does the enfolding, vitalizing energy of the

Living God *give* to a man anything to share with a fellow man in need? Of course the answer to this question can be only partial because we have only very incomplete knowledge of the nature of God and man. The physicist, the psychologist, and all other investigators of the nature of being and life have much to learn and to teach regarding the method by which many things that are common-place in human experience occur.

Two things already stand out with reasonable clearness. God could give something to a man by affecting the man's profoundest feeling in accordance with psychic law. By "feeling" is meant not mere superficial emotion or fancy, but that deep-seated element in personality which seems to underlie all acts of will, all appreciation of the beautiful, and to furnish the intellect with warm material for thought processes. Success and failure in life seem often to depend on the feeling, on the presence or absence of the feeling involved in faith, hope, courage, enthusiasm. If, in answer to prayer, something passes from the enfolding energy of God into the feeling of a man, a result of vital importance has been secured. An effect has been produced that can be shared with a fellow man in need. A man comes to you weary with life's journey, in midnight darkness, with a great hunger for things that he lacks. What can you do for him? Turn to the Living God, and say, "Friend, lend me three loaves; for a friend of mine has come to me from a journey, and I have nothing to set before him." Then there will flow into your soul from God the feeling involved in faith, hope, love, courage, and you will be able to pass these on to your friend in need. Nothing is more satisfying or more vital in the dark hour than to sit by a friend and to receive from him the fresh hope, courage, and comfort that God gives him to share with you,—a friend in need. The experience binds the two together in the love of God.

In another way something passes from God into the personality of the praying man to be shared by him with his fellow man in need. In accordance with psychic law thought passes from the mind of God to the mind of man. Your friend suddenly appears before you in great perplexity, perhaps in desperate need. He has come to a point in the life journey where it is night and he does not see which way to turn. What can you do to help him? Turn to the Friendly God and ask for some idea, for some suggestion that may be passed on to the advantage of your friend. As you and he counsel together prayerfully you will be bound together in friendship, with each other and with the Living God, and so the great purpose of God for the life of the race will be somewhat advanced.

Suppose that the man in need is far away so that he cannot sit by the side of his praying friend. Could he yet receive something from God through his praying friend? Experience seems to indicate that he could. In the sphere of psychic relationship distance seems to be, to some extent at least, a negligible factor. We may yet learn how to explain the philosophy of the fact that,

> Away in foreign lands they wondered how
> Their simple word had power;
> At home the Christians, two or three,
> Had met to pray an hour.[1]

It is not necessary to suppose that the answer to prayer must always consist in God's giving something to the one who prays which he may pass on to the person for whom he prays. It would seem that God, in accordance with psychic law, might directly affect the feeling or thought of a man in answer to the prayer of some one who had no direct connection with the man so affected. One might ask for his distant friend something that God would grant by directly affecting the feeling or thought of the man prayed for, or of some third person who would bring the desired aid without knowing why he felt himself moved to do so. The sensitive network of personal relations furnishes a variety of opportunities for God to answer prayer in accordance with psychic law.

> More things are wrought by prayer
> Than this world dreams of. Wherefore, let thy voice
> Rise like a fountain for me night and day.
> For what are men better than sheep or goats
> That nourish a blind life within the brain,
> If, knowing God, they lift not hands of prayer
> Both for themselves and those who call them friend?
> For so the whole round earth is every way
> Bound by gold chains about the feet of God.[2]

[1] Horton, R. F., London, in *The Intercollegian*, 1910.
[2] Tennyson, "Morte d'Arthur," Cf. *Op. cit.*, p. 61[1].

The rationality of such prayer from the standpoint of world friendship is seen in the fact that the man who prays is, in his praying, brought into active friendly cooperation with God and made to feel a keener sympathy with the friend for whom he prays. The gathering of others also into the friendly process, though they may not dream that answer to prayer is being wrought out through them, helps to increase the sum total of friendly feeling in the world and so to accomplish the great ambition of the Living God.

Does "natural law," the law of "cause and effect" in the "natural world," prevent answer to prayer? Evidently in the sphere of psychic force, as we have just seen, law does not prevent but instead facilitates the answer to prayer. The "law" of psychic action is such as to make the transfer of feeling and thought from mind to mind possible.

Accepting for a moment the distinction generally made between psychic and physical force, without inquiring into its legitimacy, it is evident that physical forces are so coordinated as to be extremely susceptible to the manipulation of a personal will. The more men know about these forces and the laws of their action, the more they are able to do in answer to each other's requests for help. It would seem theoretically probable, therefore, that the will of God should be able so to manipulate physical forces as to answer prayer. It is an evident fact of experience, however, that God does not to any considerable extent answer prayer in this sphere. We do not pray for rain in the Sahara, sudden transportation through the air, or direct vision through a solid. Fortunately God has left this field for the glory of human achievement. Men must through invention and discovery learn how to subdue and utilize their physical environment. In so doing they will learn how to use power in a friendly way, *which is an essential qualification for the inheritance of larger trusts of power in an immortal career.*

Does the theological doctrine called predestination or the philosophical theory called determinism forbid the expectation that God will, in answer to prayer, act as he would not act if there were no prayer?

It is sometimes said that since God must be conceived to have a plan that includes all happenings small as well as great, it follows that the thing prayed for either is or is not in God's plan. If it is in God's plan, it will occur without prayer for it. If it is not in God's plan, it will not occur no matter how much one may pray for it.

It is enough to say here that the objection is not logically sufficient to stop prayer. One who really felt that this objection ought to stop prayer would be logically bound to stop asking anyone for anything. If the objection proves the futility of making requests of God, it proves equally well the futility of all requests made by men of each other. Such a conclusion is of course contrary to daily human experience. If I wish to ask my friend to dine with me this objection would lead me to say to myself: "My friend's dining with me either is or is not a feature of God's unchangeable plan. If his visit to me at this time is a part of God's plan he will appear at my table without having been asked by me. If his visit is not in God's plan, he will not appear no matter how urgently I invite him." What we call "common sense" teaches us that we constantly get by asking. Certain things happen only when and because we ask each other that they may. God has no plan that prevents this. Therefore, so far as this particular objection is concerned, we see no reason why certain things may not happen when and because we ask God that they may. Prayer is a result of that same "common sense" that we constantly exercise in human personal relationship carried into the sphere of the great personal relationship to God. "If ye then, being evil, know how to give good gifts unto your children, how much more shall your Father who is in heaven give good things to them that ask him?"

When this objection to prayer is stated in the form of philosophical determinism, it represents all being as necessitated to proceed in a way absolutely determined by its own nature. Therefore appeal to God in prayer, it is said, could not move him; or if it could conceivably move him, he could produce no effect on the fixed order of events. Regarding this form of objection it may be said, as was just said about predestination, that the objection cannot logically stop prayer any more than it stops the appeals we are constantly making to each other. We are certain from constant experience that the highest form of energy visibly known to us, namely human personality, often acts when and because we ask it to do so. It is not therefore unreasonable to suppose that the unseen energy behind all human personality and manifesting itself in human personality may often do the same.

III

What is the condition of growing success in prayer? Evidently that a man shall be a truly friendly man at both ends of the prayer process. He must be able to look Godward and say with growing genuineness, "Friend," glad to do all the will of the Great Friend, with no controversy over any point of duty. He must be able to look manward on every side and say with growing unselfishness to everyone about him, of every race and class, "Friend." This is why Jesus laid such emphasis on the absolute necessity of forgiveness if one would pray: "When ye stand praying, forgive, if ye have aught against any." We must hope eagerly *for a chance to forgive,* not only the individual enemy but also the national enemy, or else prayer will become obsolete.

Men who would pray well must look out with friendly sympathy on all of life, upon those oppressed by unfortunate industrial conditions, or living in parts of the world where the name of the Friendly Christ has not yet been heard. Perhaps one reason why the Church has never been able to realize at all adequately in experience the possibilities that Jesus saw in prayer, is the fact that it has not yet thoroughly done this. We can individually look thoughtfully over our circle of acquaintances in order to realize the various forms of need existing among them, so that there may spring up within us the strong friendly sympathy essential to successful prayer.

It is essential also that we begin at once to *act* in the expression of friendly feeling. If there is nothing given out at the outlet, there will be no sense of anything coming in at the intake. If nothing is passing out from us in the friendly meeting of human need all about us, there will be no sense of anything coming in to us from the Friendly God.

Men who would pray well must, in Sam Foss' interpretation of the Homeric line, keep an open "house by the side of the road" where travelers, by day or in midnight darkness, may easily turn in and find "a friend to man." When men discover that the house is no cheap, gossipy tavern, but that it has wireless connections with the unseen world, it will be to them a "house of God."

As was said in the beginning the present great world pain, which we hope may be followed by the birth of a new age, summons all Christians to a better understanding and use of our Lord's great resource, Christian prayer. The Christian men and women of all nations by rising in prayer for others above racial hate, bitter sense of injury, humiliating greed of gain, may yet make what seems to be a world catastrophe the occasion of a forward movement in the growing Kingdom of God. They may test in experience the truthfulness of the propositions we have been considering:

There is all about us a friendly, vital energy called the Living God, steadily working upon human life to make friendship, brotherhood, universal and secure throughout the human race.

Prayer is a process by which a friendly man gets something from the Friendly God for the common good or to share with a fellow man in need. This process binds men in fast friendship, to one another, brings them together into conscious friendship with the Living God, and so contributes vitally to making friendship universal and secure throughout the human race.

THE MEANING OF LIFE

XXIV

THE MEANING OF LIFE

THERE is one story that never fails to interest men. It is the story of the real experiences of a human life. If an old man should rise in any audience and describe with absolute frankness the most vitally important experiences of his life, he would hold the attention of his audience to the end. In his account he would describe his earliest recollections of home, parents, brothers and sisters. He would tell of his first boy friend. He would describe the way in which he earned his first dollar. He would tell how he first met, learned to love and asked in marriage her who afterward became his wife. He would speak of the holy sensation of fatherhood that welled up in his heart as he held his first-born in his arms. He would speak of the dumb outcry of his heart as he held the same child in his arms and watched its breathing slowly cease. He would tell the story of the great loves and hates of his life. He would speak of the timid wonder or eager anticipation with which now, in his old age, he looks out upon a near eternity.

God is the supreme inventive genius of the universe. Men are possessed of wonderful inventive genius that has expressed itself in all the countless devices of modern civilization. We may say of them in homely phrase that in this particular they simply "take after their Father, who is himself the supreme inventive genius." So far as we know, the supreme product of his infinite inventive genius is the situation which we call plain, common place daily life. Nothing else is more wonderful than the continuous relation of a man to his personal and physical environment, which we call plain daily life.

I

What Is Life For?

What is the meaning of this experience, the story of which never fails to interest men? What is the purpose of this situation

293

devised by the infinite ingenuity of God? What is life for? The answer is to be sought in six brief words dropped by a man who lived and wrought and thought not far from the vivid time of Jesus. The phrase speaks from the standpoint of the Fatherhood of God: "If a son, then an heir." God appears as a Father of sons whom he wishes to be his heirs. *Human life is a situation devised by the infinite ingenuity of God, in which to train sons for an inheritance of power by teaching them to use power in a friendly spirit.*

There are certain things implied in this statement of the purpose of life. It is implied that God is a Father who *has vast power to bequeath.* The evidences of it are on every side. It is said that if one of the fiery whirlstorms on the sun should occur on the surface of the earth, it would be in the Gulf of Mexico thirty seconds after it had left the St. Lawrence and everything in its track would be a hot vapor. The words that God left ringing in the ears of men, when he launched the race upon its career, were calculated to arouse expectation of power: "Subdue the earth," "Have dominion." The words which Jesus spoke to his fellowmen at the close of his life of marvelous manifestation of power were also calculated to make them expect to exercise power. "He that believeth on me, the works that I do shall he do also, and greater works than these shall he do."

It is implied that God is an *ambitious* Father, ambitious to see his sons make the most of themselves. We sometimes think of God as a Sovereign whose plans are good for the world as a whole, but involve so much of hardship and limitation for the individual that a man may well wish to have the least possible personal connection with them. Such is not Paul's thought. To him God is indeed a Sovereign, but a Sovereign Father, ambitious to see his sons become his heirs.

It is implied also that God is a *conscientious* Father, too conscientious to allow his sons to become his heirs unless they are fit to possess that which he would bequeath. Heirship was once synonymous with license. The heir to the throne was allowed certain exemptions from ordinary obligations. He would gratify his appetites with a disregard of consequences unpardonable in the case of other men. But with increasing conceptions of the responsibilities inseparable from the possession of power, this idea is largely passing away. He who would inherit must be trained into fitness for the inheritance. It is said that one of the present European sovereigns gave little promise as a child of ever being fit for the inheritance that would naturally come to him. His father, however, was a conscientious man and systematically set about the process of making his son fit for heirship. He provided for his physical development, gave him military training, educated him in the branches of learning most essential to statesmanship, and in every way so devoted himself to the preparation of his son for the responsibilities of heirship that, finally, when the prince inherited the kingdom few rulers were better fitted than he for the responsibilities of power.

II

LEARNING TO USE POWER IN A FRIENDLY WAY

That human life is a situation devised by the infinite ingenuity of God in which to teach his sons to use power in a friendly spirit is evident from several considerations.

The nature of life as revealed in its two most characteristic features shows that it is intended to serve this purpose. It may seem difficult to determine what features of life ought to be selected as characteristic. We naturally look for something very generally present in life and of fundamental significance. Perhaps nothing more exactly meets this requirement than the phenomenon of human suffering, and the family.

Suffering is a universal and vitally significant feature of human life. Who escapes it? It begins with the physical pains of infancy. How many thousands lie today suffering in hospitals! How many millions suffer pain outside the merciful ministrations of the hospital! But who is there who lives long without knowing something of the suffering that is keener than bodily pain, the suffering of the soul, in all the violent passion or steady, relentless oppression of sorrow in its manifold forms? We may be unable to form a complete philosophy of suffering, but this much is at once evident: It makes a compelling appeal for the friendly use of power. Especially is this seen to be the case in our day when

easy combination and swift transmission of power make it possible for a large number of men, each of whom has a little power,
quickly to apply that power in a friendly way to any remote
point of need. It is possible for thousands of persons, each with
a small amount of personal power represented in his single dollar, to accumulate a sum of money within a few hours in the
hands of a reliable central agency that will cable it to the other
side of the world and release it there in some form of personal
activity that shall be the friendly relief of suffering.

By the side of the phenomenon of suffering stands the family
as a great characteristic feature of human life. A large part of the
significance of the family consists in the training it affords its
members in the friendly use of power. A little child is born into
the world, "an appetite and a cry." Very soon an appeal is made
to the little soul for love. It is the appeal of the mother's eyes.
The appeal of the father is soon made and felt to be different from
that of the mother. In time a third appeal is made by the baby
brother, and a fourth, different from the other three, by the baby
sister. The child becomes a man and loves a woman. The appeal
of the wife for love, that is, for the friendly use of power, differs
from any that has preceded it. When a baby boy lies in the father's
arms a new appeal is made; and the appeal of the baby girl touches
a new chord in the father's heart. The seven-fold appeal of father,
mother, brother, sister, wife, son, daughter which is experienced
in the fully developed family relationship constitutes an appeal
for the friendly use of power that can be matched by no creation
of the imagination. When one looks therefore into the nature of
human life as expressed in its two characteristic features, human
suffering and the family, he is constrained to regard it as a situation devised by the infinite ingenuity of God in which to teach
his children to use power in a friendly spirit, and presumably
with reference to giving them larger bequests of power.

The truth of this proposition becomes evident when we recognize that *this conception underlay Jesus' theory of life.* When the
rich young senator came to him as to an expert, professional
prophet, asking him to specify something, the doing of which
would guarantee him the advantages of "eternal life," Jesus simply
directed him to begin at once to use the power he already pos-

sessed in a friendly spirit. He pointed out to him the suffering on every side and told him to begin to use his possessions in relieving it.

Jesus' general teaching regarding the proper use of money is based on this theory of life. "Make to yourselves friends," he said, "by means of the mammon of unrighteousness, so that when it shall fail they may receive you into eternal tabernacles." That is, a man's money power is to be used in a friendly spirit that will lay the foundations for eternal friendships. When two men meet for the first time in the age to come, it may very possibly be discovered that one is there because of the friendly spirit in which the other once used his money to meet the great needs of those whom he did not then know personally, and who perhaps lived in other lands.

Jesus regarded money as a *comparatively low form* of power put into a man's hands for a little time in order that he might learn to use it in a friendly way and so prepare himself to be trusted with higher forms of power. "If therefore ye have not been faithful in the use of unrighteous mammon, who will commit to your trust the true riches?" How can the Church expect God to trust it with any such large degree of prayer power as is described in the great promises of achievement through prayer, until it.has first learned to use the lower money power in a friendly spirit? Jesus regarded money as something that really belongs to another. It often comes to us by inheritance from another, and is certain at death to pass from us to another. It remains in our hands a little while in order that by using it in a friendly way we may be prepared to inherit some higher form of power that we can carry out into the eternal future as our permanent possession. "And if ye have not been faithful in that which is another's who will give you that which is your own?"

Jesus not only held this view of life as a theory, but he actually used human life as a situation in which to prepare men for an inheritance of power by teaching them to use power in a friendly way. The salvation which he brings to men is one which saves them to this kind of life. *There is no more striking evidence of the seriousness of sin than the fact that the powerful appeal made by life itself is not sufficient to induce men to use power in a friendly way*. There is still need that a great Saviour should enter the situation and bring the persuasive power of his own friendly personality to bear upon men.

But human life, as we have conceived it, is a situation big enough for, and suitable to the operations of a great Saviour. It affords him the opportunity he needs to link men's lives with his own ever present life, and to train them through personal association with himself in the friendly use of power. He not only pointed out the suffering poor to the rich young man who came inquiring about eternal life and directed him to use money in their relief, but he said also, "Come, follow me." He proposed to attach the man permanently to himself and to the friendly enterprise into which he was leading his disciples. The disciples of Jesus were a company of men being personally trained by him in the friendly use of power. They were to be specialists in friendship: "By this shall all men know that ye are my disciples, if ye have love one to another." The Church of Jesus Christ is not a club which men and women join for what they can get out of it. It is a company of men and women banded together to be trained by the Living Lord in the friendly use of power. They keep the search-light of their investigation playing all round the world's horizon, and when it falls upon some point of special need, to that point some members of this Christly company prepare to go with power for its relief.

It is further evident that human life is a situation devised by the infinite ingenuity of God in which to prepare sons for an inheritance of power by teaching them to use power in a friendly spirit, because *human life has actually been serving this purpose*. When we look back over the long history of human life in the world, it is evident that God has fairly been crowding more power into the hands of men, as fast as they have learned to use what they already possessed with even an imperfect degree of friendliness. This is seen, for instance, in the case of explosives. Men in the brutal first century of our era could not be trusted to use the power of modern explosives. We see evidence enough of brutality still but, if some new explosive should be discovered that would destroy the lives of a million men in an instant, there is now a friendly sentiment in the hearts of men that would instantly demand the elimination of this explosive from modern warfare, as is already being done in the case of poison gas.

In the industrial development of our day, increasing power is being put into the hands of employer and employed, as men are able to use it with increasing though imperfect friendliness. Once neither employers nor employed could have been safely trusted with the power that organization has given to both parties, but now the growing sense of responsibility for the general welfare makes it safe to give larger power to both. It seems probable that vast industrial enterprises conducive to human welfare lie just ahead of us, which can be undertaken only when men have been trained to use power with a friendliness that will make it safe to trust them with the great increase of power that these enterprises will demand.

Human life, then, by its very nature, by Jesus' theory and use of it, by what it has already accomplished through the centuries is seen to be a situation devised by the infinite ingenuity of God in which to train sons for an inheritance of power by teaching them to use power in a friendly spirit.

III

THE PERIL OF LIVING

It is in the light of this conception of the meaning of life that the peril of living appears. The danger is that men will *refuse to learn the friendly use of power and therefore be unable to inherit the bequests of power* that would naturally await them. Such failure means unspeakable loss. He who throws himself athwart the deep trend of the long evolution of life inevitably suffers indescribable disaster. It is of him that the most ominous words of Jesus are spoken. The power that he has will be taken from him and be given to him that has shown himself fit to be trusted with large and growing grants of power.—"Take away the talent from him and give it to him that hath ten talents." From the farmer who refuses to sow his seed, the seed shall be taken and given to him who has it in abundance and is willing to sow it, for seed must be sown that God's children may have bread. "He will be cast out into the outer darkness," eliminated from Jesus'

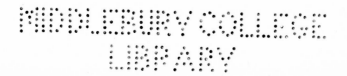

civilization of friendly workmen. Over against these busy friendly workmen to whom, as they work together God gives growing grants of power, the persistently selfish man putters away ever more feebly and painfully in his little lonely self-made hell.

The peril is that men will not see the significance of plain daily life, with its commonplace and constantly recurring opportunity to learn to use power in a friendly spirit. The men that stood for judgment before the Son of Man cried out in surprised chagrin, "When saw we thee hungry and thirsty?" They had not noticed the significance of daily life. It is those with least power, one-talent people, who are in greatest danger. They are too proud to do the little they can do because it will appear to others to be so little,— "Others can do it so much better than I." Or the little power they possess is not sufficiently impressive to overcome the wicked lethargy of their anaemic good will,—"It is too much trouble." So they merit the descriptive words of Jesus, "wicked and slothful," proud and lazy, and pass out into the sphere of self-wrecked personalities.

IV

The Great Hope

But, on the other hand, this view of the meaning of life gives birth to a great hope. The man who has only a little power and who faithfully uses it in the friendly spirit of a son of God, is certain to inherit vastly increased power. He lives in a generous economy in which he who is "faithful over a few things" will surely be "set over many things." It is *this conception of the future life as one of achievement* that appeals to the strong men of our age. We do not like to think of the future life as one of endless rest. Tennyson struck the chord to which our age responds, when he said of his departed friend:

> And, doubtless, unto thee is given
> A life that bears immortal fruit
> In such great offices as suit
> The full-grown energies of heaven.[1]

The thought of "the full-grown energies of heaven" and the opportunity for their exercise that heaven must afford, makes im-

[1]Tennyson, "In Memoriam." Cf. *Op. cit.,* p. 297[2].

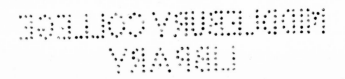

mortality seem worth while. *The sons of God are to inherit a career.* Men may walk the shores of the "silent sea" not shivering and cowering with fear of death, but feeling rather as Columbus did when he finally got his three ships, and sailed away expecting to find opportunity for great achievements beyond. They may walk the shore like spiritual Vikings, ready to start out on a beneficent career of high adventure. They may feel an enthusiasm for eternity which will

> Greet the unseen with a cheer.[2]

But this future outlook is best grasped by him who has present insight into the meaning of life and who puts himself under the daily discipline of Jesus. Browning's Aged Apostle in the desert expresses the same great conception in stately phrase.

> For life, with all it yields of joy and woe,
> And hope and fear,—believe the aged friend—
> Is just our chance o' the prize of learning love.[3]

Human life, then, comes into its full meaning through experience. It is a situation devised by the infinite ingenuity of God in which to prepare sons for an inheritance of power by teaching them to use power in a friendly spirit. "If a son, then an heir."

[2]Browning, "Epilogue to Asolando." Cf. *Op. cit.,* p. 1007[2].
[3]*Ibid.,* "A Death in the Desert," p. 387[2].

VITAL ELEMENTS IN THE DEVELOPMENT OF PERSONAL POWER

XXV

VITAL ELEMENTS IN THE
DEVELOPMENT OF PERSONAL POWER[1]

BY personal power is meant the ability to kindle character
in another man. Under this definition character is conceived to be a growing good will expressing itself in appropriate action. The good will includes both God and men as its
objects. It approaches God in the spirit of obedience. It approaches
men with the desire to secure for each man a fair chance at all
good things. Such good will necessarily expresses itself in some appropriate action. A man's good will is not genuine unless there is a
readiness to express it in some efficient way.

The same thought is expressed by saying that friendship and
work are the fundamental and inseparable elements of character.
It is upon these two elements of character that Jesus laid supreme
emphasis. He required that his disciples should become specialists
in friendship, men of invincible good will: "By this shall all men
know that ye are my disciples, if you have love one to another."
He also always aimed to fit men to contribute to the life and welfare of the community through some form of useful work; that is,
through some form of efficient action. Almost all of his miracles
were designed to give men the health requisite for efficient work.
If his conception of the Kingdom of God be carefully analyzed it
is found to demand a world-wide civilization of friendly workmen.

I

POWER ROOTS IN CHARACTER

It is evident, then, that any improvement in character must show
itself in heartier friendliness and more efficient work. When the

---

[1]Delivered before the Conference of Employed Officers (Y. M. C. A.) at Omaha;
later published in *Association Men*.

lawyer improves in character he becomes a man of heartier good will and determines to give more effective expression to that good will by being a more competent lawyer. When the manufacturer improves in character he becomes a more friendly man and also endeavors to be a more competent manufacturer. He strives to make a better product more economically so as better to serve the interests of the men and women whose welfare is affected by the production of his manufacturing plant. The man of increasing good will cannot content himself by expressing his good will simply in the casual services that he does for his neighbors now and then, but he must show it also in the increased efficiency with which he does the main work of his life. The trade or profession that he adopts as his life work constitutes the chief means by which he has chosen to express his good will to the community. This close and necessary connection between *the good will of the friendly heart and its expression in some form of useful work* accounts for Jesus' strong reprobation of laziness. Laziness is a moral fault because it shows an anaemic good will. Therefore Jesus banished the "slothful" servant from the civilization of friendly workmen and consigned him to the outer darkness.

Personal power, then, which is power to kindle character in another man, is power to rouse within him the purpose to be a truer friend and a better workman, to be his best and to do his utmost. There is special need that this character kindling power be cultivated. It is possible for men to have less and less of this character kindling power as they grow older. Men may even gain in prominence and attain to places of leadership in religious organizations, and yet possess less and less of character kindling power. Religious organizations, in our day, are in many of their features necessarily like other organizations. A man may achieve a certain sort of success in perfecting a religious organization by virtue of the same executive ability that would yield him success in industrial or political organization, and yet have little more character kindling power than the foreman of a factory or a ward boss. His very success in running the machinery of an organization may blind him to the fact that his character kindling power is becoming less instead of greater. He is able to secure conspicuous and impressive results of a certain type, while at the same time departing farther and farther from Jesus' type of character. This may be what Jesus had in mind when he said that he had never been personally acquainted with certain persons who had prophesied in his name, cast out devils, and done many mighty works.

On the other hand, there are great numbers of men who, with increasing executive responsibilities, find themselves also constantly increasing in power to kindle character in other men. Such men possess a more vitally redemptive influence over others when they are fifty than they were able to exercise when they were forty, and will doubtless go on increasing in influence until the failing physical powers of old age withdraw them from contact with life about them. Such men, even in old age when they sit in blindness with the weight of many years upon them, still unconsciously exercise personal power to kindle character in all who know them.

There are three vital elements in the development of personal power: a growing sense of the presence of God; a growing sense of human brotherhood; a growing sense of immortality.

II

A Growing Sense of the Presence of God

Why should a growing sense of the presence of God give to him who possesses it increasing power to kindle character in others, increasing power to make other men true friends and efficient workmen? It is because the sense of the presence of God makes the man himself a truer friend and a better workman, and his power over others will depend upon *his being himself what he would like others to become*. What a man honestly is when he is not trying to be anything unusual determines his personal power over another. When one comes upon him in some moment of relaxation, when he is his simple self, what the other man then reads in his face is his life message and the measure of his personal power.

Now it is the sense of connection with God that makes the man himself a truer friend and more faithful workman because God himself is the Infinite Friend and the Perfect Workman. It is the presence of the Great Friend and Perfect Workman operating upon him that gives him in turn the personal power of a true friend and faithful workman over others. We realize that God is the Great Friend. We do not always so distinctly apprehend the fact that God is also the Great Worker. It was Jesus, the carpenter, who said, "My Father works and I work." God is at work in the heart of the earth, in the growth of the grain, in the winds of the sea. The reverent miner, the devout farmer and sailor are working together with God. God is at work in the expanding steam and the electric current. The factory hand and the motor man are working together with God. The theory of Christian evolution is the theory of a working God.

When one feels in manifold forms the temptation to abandon the friendly spirit, that which keeps it strong is the sense of the friendliness of God rising within his soul like a tide out of the depths of God's infinite being. When his spirit becomes irritable and his temper grows hot with an unfriendly heat, that which holds him is the sense of the peacefully friendly Spirit of the infinite God within him. When he grows weary of his work, tired of keeping store, tired of practicing law, tired of teaching, tired of the routine of the factory, that which renews his courage is the sense of inner co-operation with God, the Great Workman who, with the unfailing energies of his nature works on night and day. The strength of the great God rises within him and he feels once more equal to his work. Once more he takes his place with good cheer in God's growing civilization of friendly workmen. He finds himself possessed of character kindling power born of the growing sense of the presence of God. The growing sense of the presence of God, the Infinite Friend and Worker, the great working Father, makes his child a better friend and more efficient workman. This, and this alone, gives the son of God character kindling power.

III

THE GROWING SENSE OF HUMAN BROTHERHOOD

Personal power is the power to kindle character in another, that is to stimulate within him a growing good will toward God and men, expressing itself in increasingly efficient action,—to introduce him into the civilization of friendly workmen which Jesus called the Kingdom of God. One element in the development of such personal power is a growing sense of the presence of God, about which we have just been speaking. Another element is a sure, unabating sense of brotherly relationship to other men.

The basis for this growing sense of human brotherhood is the growing conviction that *the world of men is a unit.* Irresistible forces are drawing men together geographically, industrially, socially. They are making it evident that all men are inextricably involved in one great world enterprise. Seemingly insignificant classes of men are having significance thrust upon them. Every new invention gives them power to do evil or good to those whose welfare the rapidly unifying forces of society give them opportunity to affect. We are learning sociologically the great truth that is expressed theologically by saying that since God is the one Father, all men are brothers. Some men who have loved this truth as a doctrine shy off from it as a sociological fact. Some who seem to themselves to care nothing for theological doctrines are really heartily adjusting themselves to this great fact.[2]

What does this growing sense of human brotherhood really involve? It involves, first of all, faith in the other man's *capacity for character.* Since he is your brother he can do what you have done. Since God is his Father he can be what a son of God ought to be. One of Jesus' dominant characteristics was the faith that he had in men because of their relation to God: "Be ye perfect even as your Father which is in heaven is perfect." The sense of human brotherhood involves also a sense of personal loss if the other man fails to develop character. I have lost a brother, just as God has lost a son, if the man fails at this point.

The sense of brotherhood furthermore involves readiness to do what we can to redeem the other man from the disadvantages under which he suffers. We desire to see all men have such a fair chance at all good things as a man would wish his brother to have.

Such a growing sense of human brotherhood is a vital element in the development of power to kindle character in another man.

---

[2]This broadly conceived view, resting as it does upon the basic unity of mankind underlies the human aspect in the missionary outreach of the Church to other peoples,—an emphasis which repeatedly appears in Bosworth. (Ed.)

There is something in the expression of honest sympathy, such as one true brother feels for another that tends to make the other a truer friend and a better workman. He who appears at the threshold of another's life with the sincere, unostentatious consciousness that the other man is his brother and who knows how to give a brother's call, *will rouse into action the best that lives across the threshold.* Such sympathy must be ready for instantaneous, spontaneous expression. As Mr. Charles Williams has pointed out, inventions like the telegraph and telephone make it possible to confront a man suddenly with an emergency calling for instant action. The captain of an ocean liner on the bridge may be observing only clear skies and a smooth sea when suddenly the wireless informs him of an awful disaster below the horizon. He must be ready by previous training to respond instantly to the call for help.

What is the relation of Jesus Christ to the development of this growing sense of human brotherhood? Jesus Christ who has revealed himself in your experience as an Inseparable Friend stands by the other man and draws you also to the other man. Paul felt this when he wrote to a company of his merciless critics. I am "your servant for Jesus' sake." It was this identification of himself with the man in need to which Jesus appealed when he said, "Inasmuch as you have done it unto one of the least of these *my brothers,* you have done it unto me." The other man is *Jesus' brother.* A man once explained his readiness to stand night after night in a great city handing out bread to the desperate wrecks of manhood who walked in the bread line. "I could never do it" he said, "but for the idea that He comes down the steps in every one of them, and what we do to them we do to Him."

IV

THE GROWING SENSE OF IMMORTALITY

It remains to show the relation between a growing sense of immortality and the power to kindle character in another man, that is to make him a true friend and a more efficient workman.

What is meant by immortality? Immortality is personal; it is the continuance of conscious personal existence after death. The mere continuance of the race upon the earth, with the extinction of its individual members at death is, as Tennyson called it, a "faith as vague as all unsweet." Herbert Spencer himself is an eloquent witness to its unsatisfying character. Immortality is a personal existence after death in which the highest forms of life and character, known at present though but rarely it may be, become commonplace and characteristic. The occasional highest forms of life in any stage of development are *a prophecy of what shall become the normal occurrence* in the next higher stage of development. Following this clue, we are led to suppose that perfected friendship and enlarged achievement will be the characteristics of the life that shall be.

How does a growing sense of immortality help to kindle character?[3] In general by making a man to be himself a truer friend and more faithful workman, for he must himself be possessed of the character he would kindle in others. More specifically, it gives a higher estimate of personality. The men we meet in daily life are seen to be doing a bigger thing, to be making a longer journey than we had supposed. They have started on the long journey of Eternity, and because of that fact they stir within us far deeper meanings and respect.

We therefore take more pains with our friendships. Friendship is a relationship between persons, and the importance of the relationship is determined by the significance of the things related. We proceed to make ourselves as fit for such friendships as immortal spirits are capable of being. We cultivate our friendships. We do not take pains to cultivate friendships with the stranger on the street car because we are not to travel far with him, but on a Pullman car between New York and San Francisco, or on a steamer between San Francisco and Hongkong we begin to cultivate friendships with our fellow passengers for we have a long journey to make together. If we see some one on board with whom we have had an uncomfortable disagreement we proceed, if possible, to come to a friendly understanding for we must travel far together. It is in this spirit that the man, engaged in the daily practice of immortality, meets his fellow man day by day.

---

[3]The remainder of this section is a résumé of the argument presented in the next chapter,—"The Daily Practice of Immortality and Its Influence on Character." For the more ample treatment found there, the reader is referred to that Address. (Ed.)

The growing sense of immortality makes us take more pains with our work. The chance for good work in the future depends upon the way in which work is done here and now. A slovenly piece of work is not something that we can pass on and soon leave behind us. Each such piece of work registers itself in the personality of him who does it. He passes on into the future a more slovenly person because of his slovenly work, and therefore less fit for the great opportunities that await him farther on. On the other hand, work faithfully done registers itself in the personality of the workman, and he may anticipate larger things to come. "Thou hast been faithful over a few things, I will set thee over many things."

Matt.
25:21

The daily practice of immortality gives the peace and poise that kindle character in another. The frictions of life have less power to irritate. If small things are really to seem small, there must be some great thing with which they can constantly be contrasted. The pedestrian in the Alps who stands before the Matterhorn thinks little of the blister on his foot. So the man who has come under the spell of Eternity is not much agitated by the small frictions of daily life. He is relieved furthermore, from the irritation incident to enjoying other men. He feels sure that there will be plenty of chance for him finally. He does not wish to elbow aside the man who is entering into the opportunity he would himself like to use. On the contrary, he bids the other man God-speed for he is absolutely sure that he shall sometime have his own chance. In a perfect organization, there are always some men in secondary places capable of stepping instantly forward to fill a sudden vacancy in the front line. They will be contented with such an arrangement if they feel sure that some time and some where each man shall have his chance to do his utmost.

What is the relation of Jesus Christ to the development of the growing sense of immortality? First of all, immortality is demanded as an adequate explanation of Jesus himself. If a soul capable of Jesus' moral attainment, his vision of eternal life, his sure confidence in immortality for himself and his friends could be hopelessly extinguished in such death torture as he suffered, we should lose all confidence in the rationality of the universe. We should be willing at the slightest provocation to put ourselves out of such a universe. It is simply unthinkable that there should be no immortality for such a soul as that of Jesus.

Furthermore, Jesus' love and present fellowship with the spirits of men guarantees them a share in his immortality. "Because I live, ye shall live also" is the constant message of his love. "For I am persuaded, that neither death nor life, nor angels, nor principalities, nor things present, nor things to come, nor powers, nor height, nor depth, nor any other creature shall be able to separate us from the love of God which is in Christ Jesus our Lord."

Jo. 14:19
Ro. 8:38, 39.

THE DAILY PRACTICE OF IMMORTALITY
AND ITS INFLUENCE ON CHARACTER

XXVI

THE DAILY PRACTICE OF
IMMORTALITY AND ITS INFLUENCE
ON CHARACTER[1]

BY the daily practice of immortality I mean the practice of thinking of one's self and all other persons about him as immortal spirits.

I

WHAT IS IMMORTALITY?

By immortality I mean the *continuance of personal existence after the mysterious experience we call death.* The conception of immortality that makes it consist simply in the continued life of the human race on earth in an endless succession of generations, but which denies any existence to the individual after death, is what Tennyson called it, "a faith as vague as all unsweet."

> That each, who seems a separate whole,
>   Should move his rounds, and fusing all
>   The skirts of self again, should fall
> Remerging in the general Soul,
>
> Is faith as vague as all unsweet:
>   Eternal form shall still divide
>   The eternal soul from all beside;
> And I shall know him when we meet;
>
> And we shall sit at endless feast,
>   Enjoying each the other's good:
>   What vaster dream can hit the mood
> Of Love on earth?[2]

[1]Originally prepared and delivered in response to an invitation from an Association of business men in New York City.
[2]Tennyson, "In Memoriam." Cf. *Op. cit.*, p. 299[1].

The heart of the normal man cannot reconcile itself to the sacrifice of its individual existence. Even when he thinks himself intellectually unable to believe in personal immortality, he feels that he *needs* to believe in it. Herbert Spencer felt himself unable to hold the theory of personal immortality, but his heart spoke out in indignant protest against the conclusion of his intellect. In the last chapter of the last book he published, he said,

After contemplating the inscrutable relation between brain and consciousness, and finding that we can get no evidence of the existence of the last without the activity of the first, we seem obliged to relinquish the thought that consciousness continues after physical organization has become inactive. But it seems a strange and repugnant conclusion that, with the cessation of consciousness at death, there ceases to be any knowledge of having existed. With his last breath it becomes to each the same thing as though he had never lived.[3]

Professor Huxley wrote to John Morley a letter whose jocose tone poorly disguised the terrible shrinking of his soul from the thought of personal extinction, expressed in these two significant sentences:

It is a curious thing that I find my dislike to the thought of extinction increasing as I get older and nearer the goal. It flashes across me at all sorts of times, with a sort of horror, that in 1900 I shall probably know no more of what is going on than I did in 1800.[4]

Certainly nothing less than personal immortality could satisfy the heart of the Heavenly Father. The Fatherhood of God, as Jesus expressed and taught it, means that God loves individual men. He would miss them if they ceased to be. If they were to

[3]*Facts and Comments*, p. 301. The quotation is closely paralleled by the following from the *Autobiography* (Vol. II, p. 549, Appleton 1904 ed.):

"Lastly come the insoluble questions concerning our own fate: the evidence seeming so strong that the relations of mind and nervous structure are such that cessation of the one accompanies dissolution of the other, while, simultaneously, comes the thought, so strange and so difficult to realize, that with death there lapses both the consciousness of existence and the consciousness of having existed.

"Thus religious creeds . . . I have come to regard with a sympathy based on community of need: feeling that dissent from them results from inability to accept the solutions offered, joined with the wish that solutions could be found."

This restatement by Spencer of the above paragraph appearing in *Facts and Comments*, strongly suggests that the relation of our brain cells to consciousness and the bearing of that relationship upon the continuance or discontinuance of life after physical death was a persistent problem in Spencer's mind. (Ed.)

[4]Cf. Huxley, Leonard, *Life and Letters of Thomas Henry Huxley*, 1900 ed., Vol. II, p. 67.

drop out of existence in death, one each moment, year after year, century after century, he would be perpetually and hopelessly mourning for his children "because they are not." A corollary of the Fatherhood of God is the personal immortality of the children of God.

I mean by immortality not merely the continuance of personal existence, but a *high grade of personal existence.* We may not know much about the details of the life after death, but we are not left without a clue. In the long evolution of life, that which is highest and best in one stage of development, though it occur only infrequently, is the prophecy of that which is to be commonplace and characteristic of the next higher stage. If we can, therefore, ascertain what is highest and best in life as we now know it, we shall have a clue as to that which is to characterize the life to come. Clearly, the best thing we ever see in the present life is invincible good will expressing itself in increasingly efficient action. Friendship and work suggest the highest and best things we know. In the future life, then, there will be highly developed friendships and vast enterprises, sufficient to tax the enlarging powers of ambitious, energetic men. It was a civilization of friendly workmen, doing "greater works" than his own earthly works, that Jesus saw as he looked forward to the coming Kingdom of God.

II

How Does the Daily Practice of Immortality Influence Character?

What constitutes character has already become sufficiently evident. Character is a growing good will expressing itself in increasingly efficient action. It reveals itself in friendliness and work. The daily practice of immortality makes a man a truer friend and a better workman.

It makes a man a truer friend because *it necessitates a higher estimate of personality in general.* Personality becomes more valuable when it is recognized as something that will last. Durability is an element of value. A soap bubble may be, for a moment, as beautiful as a diamond, but it is less valuable than a diamond partly because it is less lasting. A passing mood may, for a moment, be as satisfactory as character, but it has less value because it does not last.

Furthermore, when a person is recognized as immortal, his personality instantly assumes new dignity. He is seen to be doing a bigger thing, to be making a longer journey than was at first apparent. A man is seen walking along the street with many others. No especial attention is paid to him. He will probably soon turn into a yard and be at home. But when the word passes about that this man is a famous pedestrian,[5] taking the long walk from New York to San Francisco, all the people come out from their houses and clap their hands to cheer him on. He is doing a big thing. He is making a long journey. He will cross the level stretches of vast western prairies, and will pass through the ups and downs of mountain ranges to arrive at his far destination. In like fashion, when we make it real to ourselves that this common man we pass on the street is an immortal spirit, he assumes a new dignity. He is on a long journey. He will climb the ups and downs, and travel the level stretches of eternity.

The daily practice of immortality, which leads to a higher estimate of personality, necessarily *leads us to take more pains with our friendships*. The value of a relationship depends upon the significance of things related. Friendship is a personal relationship and its value depends upon the significance of the personalities related. A friendship between immortal personalities has a unique value. It at once becomes necessary for a man to take pains to fit himself for such a friendship. He will take time to cultivate such friendships. It is worth while to do so for he and the men about him have a long, long journey to make together. If he finds himself on a Pullman car going from New York to San Francisco, he looks about upon his fellow passengers with more interest because they have some distance to travel together. If he is on a steamer at the wharf in San Francisco bound for Hong Kong, he looks about upon his fellow passengers with still greater interest. He tries to establish friendly relations with them, for they have a long journey to make together. If he sees someone on board with whom he has had a misunderstanding, he finds an early opportunity to talk the matter over and come to an agreement, for he

[5]Edward P. Weston, cf. *The Nation,* Vol. 89, July 22, 1909, p. 71. (Ed.)

and the other man have a long way to go together. If between himself and any among them difference of opinion has led into strained relationships at some past time, he takes early opportunity to seek an understanding, for they have a long way to travel together. Thus the daily practice of immortality makes a man realize that he and the men whom he meets every day are travelling a long road together.

The daily practice of immortality makes a man *take more pains with his work*. It makes him a better business man. It makes him a more invincibly honest man. He sees greater reason for being honest. There is greater reason for being honest with a man than with a dog, because a man is a more valuable being than a dog. There is greater reason for being honest with an immortal man than with a mortal man,[6] for the personality of the immortal man is the more valuable. As the *Wall Street Journal* a few years ago said:

There is no one who would not prefer to do business with a person who really believes in a future life. . . . The question, therefore, of practical, immediate and tremendous importance to Wall Street, quite as much as any other part of the world, is, has there been a decline in the faith in the future life?[7]

But the daily practice of immortality improves the quality, not merely of business activity but of all the rest of life. It does so for a fundamental reason. The man engaged in the daily practice of immortality realizes that his chance for work in the future depends upon the way in which his work is done now. If he does a slovenly piece of work now he cannot leave its effects behind him. A slovenly piece of work registers itself in the personality of him who does it. He goes on, a more slovenly personality than he was before he did the slovenly piece of work. He will be less fit for the high occupations of the far future. On the other hand, work faithfully done registers itself in the personality of him who does it. He goes on, a more competent personality, capable of assuming larger responsibilities in the industries of eternity. One who knows the laws of life has said, "Thou hast been faithful over

---

[6] It will be noted that this is one of the few instances in which Doctor Bosworth employed relative mortality. In very large part, he held to absolute standards. (Ed.)
[7] *The Wall Street Journal.* Cf. *The Literary Digest,* Feb. 2, 1907, p. 169.

a few things. I will set thee over many things." The kind of job a man may anticipate in the future life, depends upon the way in which he does the job he has now.

The daily practice of immortality influences character not only by directly leading a man to take more pains with his friendships and his work, but it also *gives the peace and poise that are essential to the highest character*. It makes the frictions of life less irritating. Life is made up of many small things, some of them very annoying. If life is to be the peaceful experience it seems meant to be there must be steadily present in life something large enough to make small things always seem small. A man can endure the small discomforts of a poor ship and disagreeable weather, if he knows that every throb of the engines is bringing him nearer to wife and children. When a man has walked all day up the valley of the Visp and finally sees the Matterhorn rising in quiet majesty into the enfolding sky, he forgets the blister on his foot. The daily practice of immortality makes the small frictions of life seem to be the small things that they really are. The mountains of eternity cast the spell of their peace daily over his life.

The daily practice of immortality gives peace and poise by affording relief from the irritation incident to envying other men. It does this by making one feel sure that *he shall have plenty of chance finally*. When another man steps forward to take the position one would like for himself, it is not necessary to elbow him nervously to one side. Let the other man take the place. Bid him God-speed and wish him all success. Sometime and somewhere you will have your chance to do the biggest thing you are capable of doing. In a large organization there must always be first class men in secondary places. When an officer falls in battle there must be a subordinate officer already in possession of the needed capabilities, prepared to step instantly forward and take up the work of his superior without loss of efficiency in the army. If a leader in a great business enterprise suddenly drops out there must be a subordinate ready instantly to step forward and do the work of his superior. First class men will be ready, with entire good will, to occupy second class places for a time if they feel sure that sometime and somewhere every man shall have his chance to do the biggest thing of which he is capable. The daily practice of immortality gives a man this assurance. He can apply Charles Kingsley's aphorism to the work of eternity: "Have thy tools ready. God will find thee work."

The daily practice of immortality gives a man the peace and poise essential to character by relieving him in large measure of the *dread of death*. Death becomes simply an incident in eternal life. It ushers a man, who is ready, into an enlargement of opportunity. He can look upon death as a friendly phenomenon. It becomes to him what Professor Edward Rowland Sill has represented it to be:

> What if some morning, when the stars were paling,
> And the dawn whitened, and the East was clear,
> Strange peace and rest fell on me from the presence
> Of a benignant Spirit standing near:
>
> And I should tell him, as he stood beside me:—
> "This is our Earth,—most friendly Earth, and fair;
> Daily its sea and shore through sun and shadow
> Faithful it turns, robed in its azure air:
>
> "There is blest living here, loving and serving,
> And quest of truth, and serene friendships dear:
> But stay not, Spirit! Earth has one destroyer,—
> His name is Death: flee, lest he find thee here!"
>
> And what if then, while the still morning brightened,
> And freshened in the elm the Summer's breath,
> Should gravely smile on me the gentle angel,
> And take my hand and say, "My name is Death"?[8]

III

WHAT IS THE RELATION OF JESUS TO THE DEVELOPMENT OF THE GROWING SENSE AND DAILY PRACTICE OF IMMORTALITY?

First of all, immortality is demanded in order adequately to account for Jesus himself. But further, the theory of immortality is necessary in order to explain the death of Jesus. If a soul capable of Jesus' moral attainment, his vision of eternal life, his sure confidence in immortality for himself and his friends could be hopelessly extinguished in such death torture as he suffered, we should lose all confidence in the rationality of the universe. If one could live the life Jesus lived, with his perfect trust in the Heavenly

[8]Sill, *The Poetical Works Of,* Household Ed., 1906, p. 346.

Father, his unreserved devotion to men, sure sense of success beyond the grave, and then have such a life and such holy expectation end forever in the horrible death he died, men could be pardoned for desiring to put themselves out of existence on the slightest provocation. Richard Watson Gilder has given this thought characteristic expression:

> Thus, thus to aspire, and thus at last to fall!
> Such anguish! Such betrayal! Who could paint
> That tragedy! one human, piteous cry,—
> "Forsaken!"—and black death! If he was God,
> 'Twas for an instant only, his despair;
> Or was he man, and there is life beyond,
> And, soon or late, the good rewarded are,
> Then, too, is recompense.
> But was he man,
> And death ends all; then was that tortured death
> On Calvary a thing to make the pulse
> Of memory quail and stop.[9]

Jesus' love and present fellowship are daily guarantee of a share in his immortality. "Because I live, ye shall live also," is the constant message from him that incites to the daily practice of immortality. His love is a love that lays hold on a man, never again to let him go. Paul felt its power when he said that death could not destroy it, nor life outlast it; that no angel could woo it away, and no devil steal it away; that no height could rise above it, and no depth yawn beneath it,—"I am persuaded that neither death nor life, nor angels nor principalities, nor things present nor things to come, nor height nor depth, nor any other creation shall be able to separate us from the love of God which is in Christ Jesus."

In some such manner does the daily practice of immortality bring us under the spell of Eternity, an Eternity which is not a future expectation but a present fact, something that has already begun, and is for the present being measured out to us in the form of impressive human days. The daily practice of immortality, under the daily discipline of Jesus, in the midst of these human days, will steadily bring character into stable conformity with that of the Eternal Lord.

[9]"In Palestine." Cf. *Op. cit.,* pp. 241–242.

INDEX

INDEX

Ability, 210, 211, 227
Alexander, C. F., 263
Art, fine, of getting on, 211ff.
Atlantic Monthly, The, 125
Aware of God, 44, 48, 307

Barnabas, 102
Bergson, Henri, 7, 10
Bousset, Wilhelm, 63
Browning, Robert, 194, 210, 256, 301
Brotherhood, 246, 248, 274, 308
Buddha, 249
Bushnell, Horace, 235–236

Calvin, John, 11
Carpenter, Edward, 35
Character, 319, 322
Chesterton, G. K., 222, 226
Christian disposition, 56
Christian experience, 7, 11, 67, 135
Christian Religion, central idea in, 135ff.;
    continuity, 137; indestructibility, 139;
    of superior quality, 139; constructive-
    ness, 140; unity, 141; redemptive, 142;
    immortality, 144
Christian way of living, 43f., 56
Christianity, a world religion, 105
Church, The, x, 79, 192, 218, 243, 298
"Civilization of friendly workmen," 305
Conduct, 201ff.
"Corruption," 202f.
Creative career, 66
Creed, 265
Criticism, how disarm, 216, 218, 225

Damascus, 99, 110
Death, 26, 73
Death of Christ, 120, 261
Destiny, 201ff.
Determinism, 286, 287
Discovery of God, 231ff., 307
Dooley, Mr., 225
Doubt among friends of Jesus, 153ff.

Emerson, 222
Eternal life, 204
Eucken, Adolf, 137
Evolution, 20, 21, 38, 68

Faith, 120, 173ff., 233
"Flesh," meaning to Paul, 201

Ford, Henry, 47
Forgiveness, 253ff.
Foss, Sam Walter, 227
Friendship, 194, 205, 280f., 306, 312, 320
Fundamental religious ideas, x
Future life, 121, 300

Gentiles, 100, 104
Gilder, Richard Watson, 178, 233, 238, 250, 324
Giving, 193
God, x, 15, 231f., 256, 261f., 280; His purpose, 34
Golden Rule, 51
Good will, 33, 44, 174, 259
Gospel, 243ff., 253
Gossip, 218
Graham, Gorgon, 209, 225

Hadfield, J. A., 87
Hawthorne, Julian, 222
Herman, E., 33
Honesty, 211, 212, 215
Horton, R. F., 285
Huxley, Thomas J., 86, 318

Immortality, 73, 83f., 247, 310, 317ff.; personal, 90, 145
Inner Circle, 154, 163
Intelligent Good Will, 16, 17
"Invincible Good Will," 59

Jennings, H. S., 39
Jesus Christ, x, 63, 109, 127, 237, 248, 313, 323–324; *see* Death of Christ
John Baptist, 155, 157

Kelvin, Lord, 85

Leuba, James H., 83
Life, Meaning of, 293ff.
Life after death, x, 73f., 83f., 146
Life of God, 36, 44; *see* also under God
Lincoln, Abraham, 45
Love, 16
Love of enemy, 50, 255
Love: disapproving, 254; approving, 264; unchangeable, 270
Luke, 102
Luther, Martin, 11

327

Man (mankind), 8f.
Men, x, 220–221
Messiah, 73, 76, 99, 110, 153ff., 168, 177
Messianic Movement, 99, 116–117
Money, N. T. concerning, 189ff., 297
Money-giving, 191, 192
Moral liberation, 76; character, 126, 176, 193
Mosaic Law, function of, 121

Natural Law, 286
Nazarenes, 98, 100, 116
Nirvana, 249

Obedience to Mosaic Law, 116
Opportunity, 247, 322

Paul, 97ff., 109ff., 180f., 190f., 201
Paul's conception of Christ, 112, 118; of Jesus, 113–114
Personality, 63f., 88, 92, 118–119, 319; of Christ, 109, 146
Power, friendly use of, 295, 297, 299, 305ff.
Preaching, 214
Prayer, 33f., 237, 269ff., 279ff.; how answered, 270–271, 273, 383; objections, 271–272
Predestination, 286
Progress, ix, 2, 7, 10, 18, 28, 38, 55, 78, 91; is progress possible, 2
Psychic action, law of, 286
Purpose, 109

Race,—wise, powerful, sincere, friendly, 33, 89, 282, 309
Racial immortality, 89
Reconciliation, 77
Redemption, 76

Religion, meaning, 5, 127, 135
Religion of Jesus, 6, 11, 128, 129, 130
Religion, search for a satisfactory, 125ff.
Religious experience, 127, 128, 131, 245
Resistance vs. non-resistance, 58, 59
Resurrection, 178
Righteous, to be, 181, 183
Ruskin, 46

Schweitzer, Albert, 67–68
Selfishness, 78, 195, 196, 206f.
Silas, 102
Sill, Edward Rowland, 323
Sin, 297; may be forgiven, 253
Snowden, 27
Social result, 49, 89, 282
Spencer, Herbert, 86, 318
Spirit, 203f.
Suffering, 25f., 79, 295
Sympathy, respectful, 218, 220, 224

Talmud, 112
Tarsus, 97
Tennyson, 232, 235, 240, 259, 285, 300, 317
Timothy, 102

Unfinished universe, The, 85, 92, 146

Vast Force, 17
Vast Life, 17, 33

Watts, Isaac, 263
Weston, Edward P., 320
Whitehead, A. N., 5
Whittier, 203, 238, 257
Will, 16
Will of God, 20, 45–46, 65, 246
Work, 48, 84, 91, 205, 245, 306, 321
Wordsworth, 47